WEBER'S™
BARBECUE
ANYTIME

Over 190 inspirational recipes to help you get the most out of your barbecue

By Jamie Purviance
Photography by Tim Turner

D1332923

weber

An Hachette UK Company
www.hachette.co.uk

First published in Great Britain in 2012 by
Hamlyn, a division of Octopus Publishing
Group Ltd
Endeavour House
189 Shaftesbury Avenue
London
WC2H 8JG
www.octopusbooks.co.uk

This edition published in 2012

ISBN 978-0-600-62413-4

A CIP catalogue record for this book is
available from the British Library

Printed and bound in China

10 9 8 7 6 5 4 3 2 1

www.weber.com®

www.sunset.com

ABOUT THIS BOOK

Let's face it. Life is complicated and some days are crazier than others. We lead busy, action-packed lives and time is of the essence. Some days we travel at the speed of light and dinner needs to happen without delays and without hassles. Other days we roll along at a more relaxed pace, so spending a few extra minutes in the kitchen is no big deal.

Whatever your speed, this book is all about options. Some of the recipes are easy. They require only about fifteen minutes of active prep time and about ten ordinary supermarket ingredients. Other recipes are a bit more adventurous and involve a few more ingredients and a little more prep time so that you can try some interesting variations.

Throughout the book you'll find helpful tips for shaving off precious time, even with traditional barbecue classics. Now let's get to it. It's time to grill.

CONTENTS

STOCKING YOUR STORE CUPBOARD

Really, the hardest part of making dinner is shopping for dinner. If you have to shop for more than half the ingredients in a recipe you want to make today, you are in trouble. But if you have an inventory of wisely chosen items, most of the ingredients in any given recipe will already be at home and ready to go. Now you are starting from a position of strength. Now you just need to shop a couple of times a week to add fresh foods and replenish your stores. The key is that you always keep your shopping a few days ahead of your grilling schedule so you never have to buy more than a handful of ingredients at a time.

So what should be in your store cupboard? For seasonings, you will obviously need salt and pepper. These seem so ordinary that it is easy to skip over them and focus on more unusual ingredients, but don't underestimate the enormous value of good sea salt and ground black peppercorns, especially when you are making simple food. Grinding peppercorns seconds before you add them to a recipe would be ideal, though it takes quite a bit of time to grind more than a fraction of a teaspoon, so go ahead and grind a few tablespoons at a time in a spice mill or coffee grinder, and keep the grounds in a little bowl or glass jar. The flavours will remain strong for a few days.

You will also need some dried herbs and spices – not every type and species grown under the sun, but just a selection of the basics. The spices most useful for grilling are ground cumin, chilli powder, garlic granules, paprika and cayenne pepper. These create the basis of many barbecue spice rubs and they are featured prominently in the world's most exciting grilling cultures. Some of the most versatile dried herbs are oregano, thyme, rosemary and dill. You can work them into spice rubs and use them to flavour lots of marinades and sauces.

To make marinades, pastes, sauces, glazes, etc., you will need some other store cupboard items, especially oils (at least olive oil and rapeseed oil), vinegars (balsamic and white wine) and a few concentrated condiments (like Dijon mustard, soy sauce and Worcestershire sauce). If you want some simple, no-cook options for sauces, keep some bottled salsa and barbecue sauce in your cupboard. What could be easier on a busy night than pouring a good salsa or sauce over something simple like chicken breasts or steaks that you have quickly oiled, seasoned and grilled?

The key is that you always keep your shopping a few days ahead of your grilling schedule so you never have to buy more than a handful of ingredients at a time.

The items in the 'good to have' list may not be as important day after day as the essentials, but they are still really helpful for making quick meals more interesting. Imagine, for instance, that it's Tuesday night and you need something to jazz up grilled pork chops or prawns. If you toss a few roasted red peppers and a couple of sun-dried tomatoes in a food processor or blender with some oil and vinegar, and then season the purée with salt and pepper, there's your dipping sauce. To fill out the plate, add some vermicelli lightly coated with pesto or maybe some creamy white beans warmed in a bit of tomato sauce seasoned with crushed red chilli flakes. See how easy dinner can be with a well-stocked store cupboard?

Your freezer can be a treasure chest and a real time saver, too. Sausages, boneless chicken pieces and individually wrapped steaks take just a few hours to defrost. The quickest method is to submerge them (still tightly wrapped in plastic) in a bowl of cold water. Change the water every half hour for safety reasons. Plan on 1–2 hours per 500g/ 1 lb of meat to defrost most meats and poultry. They will thaw even faster if you use a thick stainless-steel frying pan instead of a mixing bowl, because the thick metal does a better job of conducting the heat of the room through the water and into the meat. No kidding. Nonstick and cast-iron pans don't work nearly as well as the heavy stainless-steel ones. As tempting as it is to use a microwave oven for defrosting meats, don't do it. The outer surfaces of the meat will actually begin to cook before the interior is soft.

A WELL-STOCKED STORE-CUPBOARD

ESSENTIALS

CONDIMENTS
- [ ] balsamic vinegar
- [ ] barbecue sauce
- [ ] Dijon mustard
- [ ] salsa in a jar
- [ ] soy sauce
- [ ] white wine vinegar
- [ ] Worcestershire sauce

OIL AND SPICES
- [ ] rapeseed oil
- [ ] dried herbs
- [ ] extra-virgin olive oil
- [ ] ground black pepper
- [ ] sea salt
- [ ] spices

GOOD TO HAVE

CONDIMENTS
- [ ] capers
- [ ] chicken stock
- [ ] chilli sauce
- [ ] hoisin sauce
- [ ] honey
- [ ] mayonnaise
- [ ] mustards
- [ ] peanut sauce
- [ ] pesto
- [ ] pickles
- [ ] pitted olives
- [ ] prepared horseradish
- [ ] tomato sauce
- [ ] vinegar

OIL AND SPICES
- [ ] flavoured oils
- [ ] spice rubs

GOOD TO HAVE (CONT.)

FRESH PRODUCE
- [ ] bags of pre-chopped vegetables and salads: peppers
    broccoli florets
    coleslaw
    mixed greens
    trimmed green beans
- [ ] fresh salsas

MEAT/POULTRY/SEAFOOD
- [ ] boneless chicken pieces
- [ ] chops
- [ ] sausages
- [ ] prawns (peeled and deveined)
- [ ] steaks

DAIRY
- [ ] ice cream
- [ ] grated cheeses

OTHER
- [ ] breadcrumbs
- [ ] canned beans
- [ ] canned chipotle chillies in adobo sauce
- [ ] cornmeal/polenta
- [ ] dried pasta
- [ ] hot fudge sauce
- [ ] peeled garlic cloves in plastic containers
- [ ] refrigerated pizza dough
- [ ] rice
- [ ] roasted red peppers in a jar
- [ ] salad dressing
- [ ] flaked almonds
- [ ] sugar, granulated and brown
- [ ] sun-dried tomatoes packed in oil

STOCKING YOUR STORE CUPBOARD

Another smart strategy for saving time and money is to buy meat in bulk or 'value packs'. You can grill what you want right away and freeze the rest for later. Meats freeze better than vegetables or fish because they are sturdier and don't hold as much water. Water expands in the freezer and can break the cell structure of food, which can leave tender vegetables and fish limp and unappealing when they are thawed and then cooked. Meats stand up relatively well, but don't leave them in the freezer for too long. After a few months, the quality deteriorates. Besides, if you are using this strategy properly, you should defrost meats every few weeks and replenish your freezer supply with fresh ones.

Buying chicken and other meats in bulk or 'value packs' saves more than money. It can also save you the time required to run to the shops on a busy day, if you have frozen servings waiting for you in the freezer. The key is to wrap each individual portion separately in clingfilm, and then store all the wrapped portions in a heavy-duty, resealable freezer bag. That way, you can defrost just the number of servings you need that day. Be sure to mark the bag with the date when the meat was first frozen, and try to use all the portions within a few weeks.

MUST-HAVE TOOLS

Tongs
Look for heavy-duty tongs that are about 40 cm/16 inches long, feel comfortable in your hand, have sturdy metal pincers and are dishwasher safe. A locking mechanism is nice for keeping them closed when not in use.

Spatula
The material should be solid, heavy-gauge metal with a thin yet rigid blade about 10 cm/4 inches wide. Look for a bent (offset) neck that puts the blade lower than the handle. The total length should be about 40 cm/16 inches.

Grill Brush
Spring for a solid, sturdy, long-handled brush with stiff stainless steel bristles.

Perforated Grill Pan
Get a thick metal pan that is big enough to accommodate the food in a single layer. The holes should be wide enough to allow heat and smoke to reach the food directly, and the rim of the pan should be low enough that you can slide a spatula under the food.

Timer
The best ones have extra large digits for easy reading, loud alarms, belt clips and the flexibility to count up from zero as well as down from whatever time you pick.

Instant-read Thermometer
You can buy an inexpensive thermometer with a dial face or a more expensive one with a digital face. Ideally the sensor will be very close to the tip so you can easily pinpoint the area of the food you want to measure.

Insulated Barbecue Mitts/Oven Gloves
Invest in a pair with good-quality materials and workmanship that will hold up well over time.

NICE TO HAVE

Roasting Trays
Portable surfaces for oiling and seasoning foods. Convenient landing pads for food coming hot off the grill.

Cast-iron Frying Pan
Once it gets hot on the grill, you can sauté, stew, pan-roast or bake just about anything in it without ever worrying that the pan will discolour or deteriorate. Get one that is at least 25 cm/10 inches in diameter.

Chimney Starter
The simple design lets you start charcoal quickly and evenly without using lighter fluid. Look for one with two handles – one heatproof side handle for lifting and a hinged top handle for support – and a capacity to hold about 80 to 100 briquettes.

Basting Brush
You can now find brushes with silicone bristles that are dishwasher safe. Much better than synthetic/natural bristles that you have to wash by hand.

Skewers
Bamboo skewers are always an option for kebabs, though flat metal skewers or double-pronged ones do a better job of holding the food in place.

KNIVES

Good grilling requires a good set of knives. How much you spend on each knife is not nearly as important as how comfortable it feels in *your* hand. Uncomfortable knives sit in a drawer or knife block doing no good at all, no matter how much they cost. A comfortable knife at any price is a pleasure to use often, especially when you are using the right knife for the right job.

1 Sharpening Steel
This special metal rod grinds and realigns the edges of a knife blade.

2 Serrated Knife
Its jagged edge is great at sawing through crusty bread, slicing through tender vegetables and carving meats.

3 Chef's Knife
This is your number one, most important tool for slicing, dicing and carving almost anything.

4 Santoku Knife
A good all-purpose knife for smaller hands. Oval cut-outs along the edge help to reduce friction, which prevents foods from sticking to the blade.

5 Boning Knife
The thin, somewhat flexible blade moves easily along the edges of bones and in between tight spaces.

6 Paring Knife
A short tool that is especially effective at peeling, trimming and chopping vegetables.

USING A SHARPENING STEEL – THE BUTCHER'S METHOD

All knives lose their sharp edges when you run them across chopping boards again and again. They turn dull just from cutting food. If your knives are dull, you'll need to work harder and longer to cut your food, raising the chances that you will slip while exerting too much force.

A steel doesn't sharpen a knife as much as it straightens the crooked edges. The safest way to do this is with the 'butcher's method', shown to the left.

PREP SCHOOL

If you intend to reduce the amount of time it takes you to make dinner, get some quick recipes but also get serious about speeding up your prep time. For each recipe in this book, the prep time refers to the number of minutes you're actively getting your food ready to grill. It includes hands-on prep work like slicing, dicing, seasoning and mixing, all of which can go faster or slower, depending on your level of organization and knife skills.

Before you pull any food out of the refrigerator or start chopping, read the whole recipe from start to finish. People typically skip this step and discover too late that they don't have a required ingredient or tool, or they realize that a certain step, like marinating or simmering, will take much more time than they expected. Suddenly dinner is in trouble, or at least delayed.

Also, begin with a clean kitchen. Cluttered work surfaces and dirty dishes in the sink are major obstacles to efficient prep work. Taking some time to clear your work spaces before you start will save you time later.

And continue to clean as you go. In the process of almost every recipe, there are idle minutes when you are waiting for something to happen – like the grill temperature to rise or an ingredient to reach room temperature. These are moments when you can wipe down your chopping boards, rinse your utensils, or just put away some unused ingredients so you have plenty of counter space and you are ready to go for the next step.

Give yourself as much room as possible to do your slicing and dicing. Your chopping boards should be at least 40 cm/16 inches in length and width, and ideally you will have at least two of them: one for raw meats, poultry and fish, and one for everything else. Finally, make sure you have a rubbish bin nearby for your scraps, or put a bowl near your chopping board to collect the scraps and discard them later.

Cut the onion in half through the stem and root ends. Peel off the skin and possibly one layer of each half with a paring knife. Trim about 1 cm/ ½ inch from the stem end of each half, but during the rest of the chopping, keep the root end on each half intact; otherwise the onion will fall apart. Lay each half, flat side down, on a chopping board. Hold the onion steady with the fingertips of one hand. With the other hand, make a series of horizontal cuts from the stem towards the root end but not through it. Then make a series of vertical cuts, with the tip of the knife cutting almost but not quite through the root end. Then cut each half crossways to create an evenly sized dice. The size of the dice depends on how far apart you make each horizontal, vertical and crossways cut.

PREP SCHOOL

PREPPING AN ONION FOR KEBABS

First trim the stem and root ends from the onion and cut it in half lengthways. Peel each half and then set the onion on one of the cut sides. Cut each half into four equal quarters. The innermost layers of each quarter are too small for kebabs – they would fall off the skewers. Use the outer two or three layers of each quarter as a section of onion to slide on to a skewer.

SLICING AN ONION

A round onion tends to move on a chopping board, which can be dangerous, so use one hand to hold it firmly in place. Use the other hand to cut straight down. You want thick, even slices. Slices thinner than 8 mm/ 1/3 inch often fall apart on the grill, and slices that are not the same thickness from edge to edge cook unevenly and fall apart.

PREP SCHOOL

PEELING AND CHOPPING GARLIC

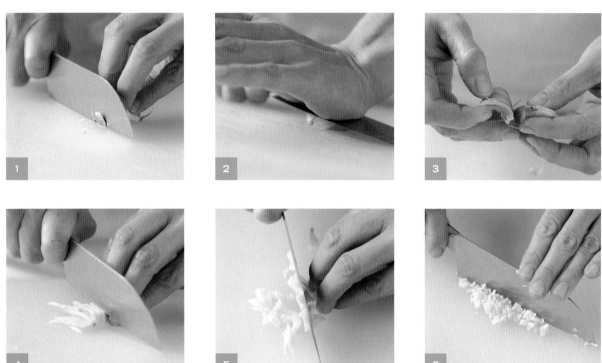

Trim the root end from each garlic clove and crush the clove with the side of a knife to loosen the skin. Be sure the edge of the knife is facing away from you. Peel off the skin. For a very even chop, cut the clove into thin slices first, and then line up the slices in a row so you can cut across the slices. Repeat with all the cloves and finally rock your knife over the chopped garlic until all of it is chopped as finely as you want.

DICING AN AVOCADO

Cut a ripe avocado lengthways around the stone and then twist the halves in opposite directions. Tap the exposed stone with the heel of a chef's knife. It will pull out from the avocado. Carefully push the stone off the blade of the knife. You can chop the avocado in its skin by cross-hatching it and then scooping the little pieces into a bowl with a spoon.

PREP SCHOOL

CHOPPING A JALAPEÑO CHILLI PEPPER

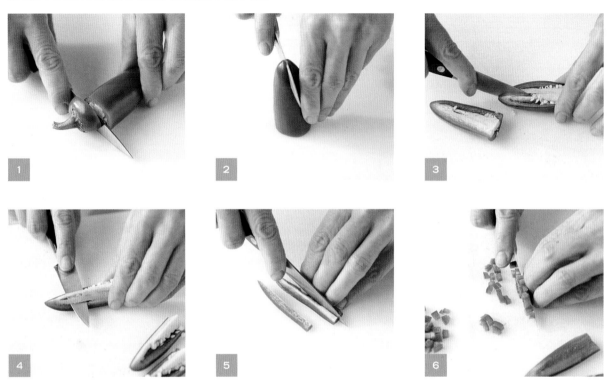

With a paring knife, trim off the stem end and cut the chilli in half lengthways. Most of the pepper's heat is in the whitish veins and seeds. Remove as much of those as you want by cutting each half in half and running your knife under the seeds and discarding them, always with the edge of the knife facing away from you. Then cut the chilli into thin strips. Line up the strips and cut across them to create finely chopped chillies. People with sensitive skin should do this wearing rubber gloves.

DICING A PLUM TOMATO

Quarter the tomato lengthways to expose the seeds and watery pulp. Using a paring knife, scoop just under the pulp in each quarter and discard it. Always face the edge of the knife blade away from you. Then, with the skin side facing down, cut each quarter into thin strips. Line up the thin strips and cut across them to dice the tomato, leaving behind any bits of the stalk.

PREP SCHOOL

PREPPING A PEPPER

The goal is to create a uniform piece of pepper that will lie flat on the grill. Begin by trimming off the stem and bottom ends. Stand the pepper up and cut an opening down one side. Put the pepper on its side, with the opening facing up. Position your knife inside so you can make a cut between the inner wall of the pepper and the undesirable core/seeds. Go back and trim any whitish areas off the inner wall of the pepper. Now you have lots of surface area you can lay flat on the hot cooking grate, where it will caramelize or char evenly.

CHOPPING GINGER

The skin of fresh ginger is quite fibrous, so scrape it off with the edge of a spoon. A spoon will create less waste than a vegetable peeler or paring knife. Then rub the peeled ginger along the tiny, sharp blades of a handheld grater, which is also an efficient tool for grating garlic cloves, the zest of citrus fruits and hard cheeses.

PREP SCHOOL

CUTTING MEAT FOR KEBABS

The primary goal is to cut chunks of meat that will cook evenly on skewers. Start by cutting slices at least 2.5 cm/1 inch thick, and then cut each slice into chunks at least 2.5 cm/1 inch in all directions. Smaller chunks tend to overcook and turn dry quickly. Also be careful not to cram the chunks together on skewers. They cook more evenly when you leave a bit of space between them.

BUTTERFLYING A PORK CHOP

Begin with a boneless centre-cut pork chop at least 2.5 cm/1 inch thick. Cut into the middle of the fat side to within about 1 cm/½ inch of the other side, so that the chop opens up like a butterfly. Flatten the meat with the palm of your hand and trim off any excess fat. Lay the chop between two large sheets of clingfilm. Use the flat side of a meat tenderizer (or the bottom of a small, heavy frying pan) to flatten the meat to an even thickness of about 5 mm/¼ inch. This creates a *paillard*.

REMOVING SKIN FROM A PORK FILLET

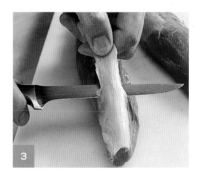

The thin layer of sinew on the surface of a pork fillet is called silver skin. Slip the tip of a sharp, thin boning knife under one end of the silver skin. Grab the loosened end with your fingertips. Then slide the knife away from you just underneath the skin, with the knife blade angled slightly upwards. The 'cleaned' fillets should have hardly any visible skin or surface fat.

PREP SCHOOL

SKINNING A FISH FILLET

Along one end of the fillet, cut a slit all the way through the skin large enough to get your finger though. Holding the skin steady with your finger in the slit, angle the blade of a large, sharp chef's knife inside the seam between the flesh and skin. Cut away from you and over the top of the skin, always with the knife angled slightly downwards so you don't cut into the fish fillet.

PEELING AND DEVEINING PRAWN

To peel each prawn, grab the shell just above the tail and break it loose. Peel off the shell together with all the little legs. With a sharp paring knife, make a shallow slit along the back of each prawn, being careful not to cut too deep. Lift any black vein out of the slit and discard it. Whether you leave the tail on or not is up to you. Some people like to use it as a handle.

PREP SCHOOL

BUTTERFLYING A WHOLE CHICKEN

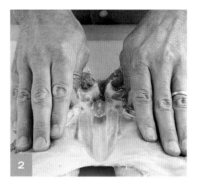

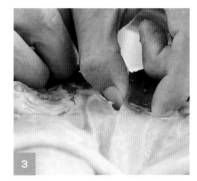

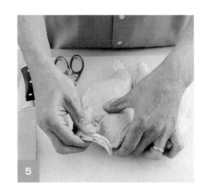

Pull out and discard the loose clumps of fat that are typically just inside the chicken. Turn the chicken over so that the back is facing up and the neck end is closest to you. Use poultry shears to cut along both sides of the backbone and then discard it. Open the chicken like a butterfly spreading its wings, and press down to flatten it. Run your fingertips along both sides of the breastbone to expose it. Dig your fingers along the breastbone until it comes loose from the meat. Then pull it out and discard it. Fold the wing tips behind the chicken's back to prevent them from burning. Now you have overcome one of the key cooking challenges of a whole chicken: an uneven shape. By butterflying (or spatchcocking) the bird, you have created a relatively even shape.

BUTTERFLYING A CHICKEN BREAST

Lay the breast lengthways on the board, with the narrow end farthest from you and the slightly thicker side to your right. Use one hand to hold the breast in place. With the blade of your knife running parallel to the board, make a shallow slit halfway up the thicker side of the breast, but do not cut into the narrow end. Using the tip of your knife, make the cut deeper and deeper until you are almost but not all the way to the other side of the breast. Now you have a pocket suitable for filling.

PREP SCHOOL

TRUSSING A CHICKEN

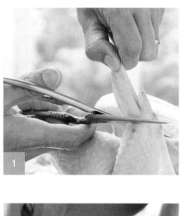

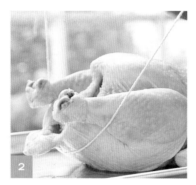

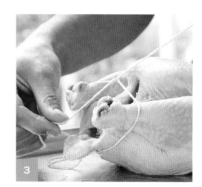

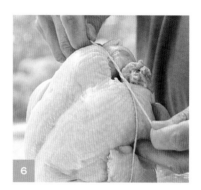

The wing tips have almost no meat and they tend to burn, so remove them at the joint with poultry shears. Slide a 120-cm/48-inch length of kitchen string under the legs and back. Lift both ends of the string and cross them between the legs. Then run one end under one drumstick. Run the other end under the other drumstick and pull both ends to draw the drumsticks together. Bring the string along both sides of the chicken so that it holds the legs and wings against the body. Tie a knot in the ends between the neck and the top of the breast. If necessary, push the breast down a little to expose more of the neck.

SETTING A CHICKEN ON A ROTISSERIE

Position one set of fork prongs on the far end of the centre rod (spit) and slide the spit into the opening between the neck and the knotted twine, through the chicken, and out the other side, just underneath the drumsticks. Slide the other set of fork prongs on the spit and drive the prongs into the back of the chicken. Make sure the chicken is centred on the spit before tightening the fork prongs into place.

GAS V. CHARCOAL

Gas

Let's settle one issue right up front. Gas is quicker than charcoal. Lighting a gas grill, in most cases, is as simple as lifting the lid, turning on the gas and igniting the burners. After you have opened the valve on your propane tank all the way (or turned on the gas at the source), wait a minute for the gas to travel through the gas line, and then turn each burner to high, making sure one burner has ignited before turning on the next.

Charcoal

Certainly, gas grills start up faster than charcoal grills, and turning a knob is easier than raking coals, but there are compelling reasons why some people will grill only with charcoal and other people will choose charcoal over gas whenever they have a little time available.

The amount of time required to fire up a charcoal grill can be as little as 15–20 minutes, if you are using certain equipment.

1 The easiest method involves a chimney starter, which is an upright metal cylinder with a handle on the outside and a wire rack inside. You simply fill the space under the wire rack with a few sheets of wadded-up newspaper or a few paraffin cubes, and then fill the space above the rack with briquettes.

2 Once you light the newspaper, some impressive thermodynamics channel the heat evenly throughout the briquettes.

3 When the briquettes are lightly covered with white ash, put on two insulated barbecue mitts or oven gloves and grab hold of the two handles on the chimney starter. The swinging handle is there to help you lift the chimney starter and safely aim the coals just where you want them.

WHAT SIZE WORKS BEST?

The size of your grill will also affect your timing. If you use a grill that is too small for the amount of food you want to cook, you will have to cook the food in batches, which of course takes more time and runs the risk of some of the food turning cold before all of it is cooked.

Remember that frequently you will want to grill two or three items at once. That might require having two or three zones of heat, and each zone needs to have enough room for the number of people you are feeding.

Here are recommendations based on the number of people eating.

GAS

👥 : A GRILL WITH ONE OR TWO BURNERS

👥👥 : A GRILL WITH THREE OR FOUR BURNERS

👥👥👥+ : A GRILL WITH SIX BURNERS

CHARCOAL

👥 : AN 45-CM/18-INCH–DIAMETER GRILL

👥👥 : A 55-CM/22-INCH–DIAMETER GRILL

👥👥👥+ : A 65-CM/26-INCH–DIAMETER GRILL

GRILLING TIME

DIRECT HEAT

Direct heat works well for small, tender pieces of food that cook quickly, such as hamburgers, steaks, chops, boneless chicken pieces, fish fillets, shellfish and sliced vegetables. It sears the surface of these foods, developing flavours, textures and caramelization while it cooks the food all the way to the centre.

INDIRECT HEAT

Indirect heat works better for larger, tougher foods that require longer cooking times, such as roasts, whole chickens and ribs. It is also the proper way to finish cooking thicker foods or bone-in cuts that have been seared or browned first over direct heat.

Heat Configurations

1 The most flexible charcoal configuration is a two-zone fire. That means the coals are spread out on one side of the charcoal grate and the other side has no coals at all. This allows you to cook with both direct and indirect heat.

You can set up a similar configuration on a gas grill by leaving some of the burners on and turning one or two of them off.

How hot your charcoal grill is depends on how much charcoal you use and how long it has been burning. The coals are at their hottest when they are newly lit. Over time they gradually lose heat. The heat of your gas grill depends of course on how you adjust the burners.

After the coals or gas burners are fully lit, close the lid and wait for about 10 minutes so the temperature rises to at least 260°C/500°F on the lid's thermometer. This makes the cooking grate much easier to clean and it improves the grill's ability to sear.

Wearing an insulated barbecue mitt or oven glove, use a long-handled grill brush to scrape off any bits and pieces that may be stuck to the grate.

There is no need to oil the grate before grilling. Oil would just drip into the grill and potentially cause flare-ups. You can avoid wasting oil and improve the chances of food releasing more easily by oiling the food, not the grate.

2 Once your grill is preheated and brushed clean, bring out all the food and other supplies you will need and organize them on a tray. If you have everything chopped and measured beforehand, the cooking will go faster and you won't have to run back into the kitchen. Don't forget clean plates and serving dishes for serving the food.

Keep the Lid Closed as Much as Possible

Whether using a charcoal grill or a gas grill, keeping the lid closed as much as possible is really important. The grill's lid limits the amount of air getting to the fire, thus preventing flare-ups, and it helps to cook food on the top and bottom simultaneously. While the bottom of the food is almost always exposed to more intense heat, the lid reflects some heat down and speeds up the overall cooking time. Without the lid, the fire would lose heat more quickly and many foods would take much longer to cook, possibly drying out.

A few flames flickering under your food for a few seconds are to be expected in grilling. Don't worry. But if the flames last longer and threaten to burn your food, move the food to a cooler part of the grill until the flames subside.

DONENESS

CHECKING STEAKS FOR DONENESS

Steaks get firmer as they grill, so one way to judge their doneness is by pressing the surface of a steak with your fingertip. When the meat is no longer soft, but is not yet firm, it has reached a doneness somewhere near medium rare (see below for more specifics with the 'hand test'). A more scientific approach is to use an instant-read meat thermometer. If you are sure to position the thermometer sensor right in the middle of the steak, you'll have a perfectly accurate reading of doneness (see page 285 for a doneness chart). Perhaps the most straightforward approach is to have a look at the colour of the meat inside the steak. On the under-side of the steak (the side that will face the plate), cut a little slit down to the centre of the meat and look inside. When it's cooked just the way you want it, turn the steak over and press the surface with your fingertip. Note how it feels so that next time you won't need to cut into your steak.

USING THE HAND TEST

Most raw steaks are as soft as the base of your thumb when your hand is relaxed. If you touch your first finger and thumb together, and then press the base of your thumb, that's how most steaks feel when they are rare. If you touch your middle finger and thumb together, and then press the base of your thumb, that's how most steaks feel when they are medium rare.

DONENESS

Pork Chops. The one on the left, with raw meat in the centre, is clearly under-cooked. The chop on the right, with a dry, grey appearance, is overcooked. The chop in the middle, with a little bit of pink in the centre, is cooked to 65°C/150°F, which is just right. The meat gives a little under the pressure of a fingertip.

Chicken. The meat near the bone usually takes the longest to cook. If the juices near the bone are clear and the meat there is no longer pink, the chicken is done.

Ribs. If you bend a rack of ribs backwards, with the bone side facing up, and the meat tears easily along the bone, the meat is done.

Fish Fillet. With almost every kind of fish, you should get it off the grill before it flakes from overcooking. You are looking for an internal temperature of 52–55°C/125–130°F, but that's sometimes difficult to measure with fillets or steaks, so look at the internal appearance. The whitish colour should be opaque (not translucent) all the way to the centre.

Prawns. As prawns cook, the meat tightens up and turns opaque. The prawn on the left is undercooked (still a little translucent). The prawn on the right is overcooked (shrunken and dry). The prawn in the middle is just right.

Scallops. After grilling, the interior of a scallop should be barely opaque, like the one in the centre. The scallop on the left is a little under cooked and the scallop on the right is overcooked.

RUBS

A rub is a mixture of spices, herbs and other seasonings (often including sugar) that can quickly give a boost of flavours to foods before grilling. This page and the next provide some mighty good examples, along with recommendations for which foods they complement, but dare to be different. One of the steps towards developing your own style at the grill is to concoct a signature rub recipe or two. Only you will know exactly what ingredients are blended in your special jar of 'magic dust'.

A word about freshness: Ground spices lose their aromas in a matter of months (8 to 10 months maximum). If you have been holding on to a little jar of coriander for years, waiting to blend the world's finest version of curry powder, forget about it. Dump the old, tired coriander and buy some freshly ground. Better yet, buy whole coriander seeds and grind them yourself. Whatever you do, store your spices and spice rubs in airtight containers away from light and heat, to best preserve their flavours and fragrances.

How Long?

If you leave a rub on for a long time, the seasonings intermix with the juices in the meat and produce more pronounced flavours, as well as a crust. This is good to a point, but a rub with a lot of salt and sugar will draw moisture out of the meat over time, making the meat tastier, yes, but also drier. So how long should you use a rub? Here are some guidelines.

CLASSIC BARBECUE SPICE RUB

Makes: about 75 ml/3 fl oz

4 teaspoons sea salt
2 teaspoons pure chilli powder
2 teaspoons soft light brown sugar
2 teaspoons garlic granules
2 teaspoons paprika
1 teaspoon celery seeds
1 teaspoon ground cumin
½ teaspoon ground black pepper

1 Mix the ingredients in a small bowl.

CAJUN RUB

Makes: about 75 ml/3 fl oz

2 teaspoons garlic granules
2 teaspoons onion flakes
2 teaspoons dried thyme
2 teaspoons dried oregano
2 teaspoons sea salt
2 teaspoons paprika
1½ teaspoons soft light brown sugar
1 teaspoon smoked paprika
1 teaspoon ground black pepper

1 Mix the ingredients in a small bowl.

TOASTED CUMIN RUB

Makes: about 4 tablespoons
SPECIAL EQUIPMENT: spice mill

2 teaspoons cumin seeds
1 teaspoon mustard seeds
1 teaspoon coriander seeds
2 teaspoons paprika
2 teaspoons sea salt
2 teaspoons soft brown sugar
½ teaspoon garlic granules
½ teaspoon ground cayenne pepper

1 Toast the cumin, mustard and coriander seeds for 2–3 minutes in a frying pan over medium-heat until fragrant, shaking the pan occasionally. Transfer the seeds to a spice mill. Add the remaining ingredients and pulse until finely ground.

CARIBBEAN RUB

Makes: about 4 tablespoons

1 tablespoon soft light brown sugar
1 tablespoon garlic granules
1 tablespoon dried thyme
2½ teaspoons sea salt
¾ teaspoon ground black pepper
¾ teaspoon ground allspice

1 Combine the ingredients in a small bowl.

RUB KEY

good on red meat
good on pork
good on poultry
good on seafood
good on vegetables

TIME	TYPES OF MEAT
Up to 15 minutes:	Small foods, such as shellfish, cubed meat for kebabs and vegetables
15–30 minutes:	Thin cuts of boneless meat, such as chicken breasts, fish fillets, pork fillet, chops and steaks
30 minutes–1½ hours:	Thicker cuts of boneless or bone-in meat, such as leg of lamb, whole chickens and beef joints
2–8 hours:	Big or tough cuts of meat, such as racks of ribs, whole hams, pork shoulders and turkeys

RUBS

FRENCH ROAST SPICE RUB

Makes: about 3½ tablespoons

2 tablespoons coarsely ground French
    roast coffee beans
2 teaspoons sea salt
1 teaspoon soft light brown sugar
¾ teaspoon ground black pepper
½ teaspoon garlic granules

1 Mix the ingredients in a small bowl.

STEAK HOUSE RUB

Makes: about 3 tablespoons
SPECIAL EQUIPMENT: spice mill

2 teaspoons black peppercorns
2 teaspoons mustard seeds
2 teaspoons paprika
1 teaspoon garlic granules
1 teaspoon sea salt
1 teaspoon soft light brown sugar
¼ teaspoon chilli powder

1 Using a spice mill crush the
peppercorns and mustard seeds. Pour
into a small bowl and add the remaining
ingredients. Mix thoroughly.

SANTA FE SPICE RUB

Makes: about 2 tablespoons

1½ teaspoons sea salt
1 teaspoon ground black pepper
1 teaspoon ground cumin
1 teaspoon soft light brown sugar
½ teaspoon ancho chilli powder
½ teaspoon dried oregano

1 Mix the ingredients in a small bowl.

NEW ORLEANS BARBECUE RUB

Makes: about 3 tablespoons

1 tablespoon smoked paprika
1 teaspoon garlic granules
1 teaspoon onion flakes
1 teaspoon dried oregano
1 teaspoon dried thyme
1 teaspoon sea salt
¼ teaspoon ground cayenne pepper

1 Mix the ingredients in a small bowl.

BEEF RUB

Makes: about 75 ml/3 fl oz

4 teaspoons sea salt
1 tablespoon chilli powder
1 tablespoon onion flakes
1½ teaspoons garlic granules
1 teaspoon paprika
1 teaspoon dried marjoram
½ teaspoon ground cumin
½ teaspoon ground black pepper
¼ teaspoon ground cinnamon

1 Mix the ingredients in a small bowl.

PORK RUB

Makes: about 4 tablespoons

2 teaspoons chilli powder
2 teaspoons ground black pepper
2 teaspoons sea salt
2 teaspoons ground cumin
2 teaspoons dried oregano
1 teaspoon garlic granules

1 Mix the ingredients in a small bowl.

CHICKEN AND SEAFOOD RUB

Makes: about 75 ml/3 fl oz

4 teaspoons onion flakes
4 teaspoons garlic granules
1 tablespoon sea salt
2 teaspoons chilli powder
2 teaspoons ground black pepper

1 Mix the ingredients in a small bowl.

MAGIC RUB

Makes: 2 tablespoons

1 teaspoon powder mustard
1 teaspoon onion flakes
1 teaspoon paprika
1 teaspoon sea salt
½ teaspoon garlic granules
½ teaspoon ground coriander
½ teaspoon ground cumin
½ teaspoon ground black pepper

1 Mix the ingredients in a small bowl.

ASIAN RUB

Makes: about 4 tablespoons

2 tablespoons paprika
2 teaspoons sea salt
2 teaspoons ground coriander
2 teaspoons Chinese five-spice powder
1 teaspoon ground ginger
½ teaspoon ground allspice
½ teaspoon ground cayenne pepper

1 Mix the ingredients in a small bowl.

MARINADES

Marinades work more slowly than rubs, but they can seep in a little deeper. Typically, a marinade is made with some acidic liquid, some oil and some combination of herbs and spices. These ingredients can 'fill in the gaps' when a particular meat, fish or vegetable (yes, vegetable) lacks enough taste or richness. They can also give food characteristics that reflect regional/ethnic cooking styles.

If indeed your marinade includes some acidic liquid, be sure to use a non-reactive container. This is a dish or bowl made of glass, plastic, stainless steel or ceramic. A container made of aluminium, or some other metals, will react with acids and add a metallic flavour to food.

How Long?

The right times vary depending on the strength of the marinade and the food you are marinating. If your marinade includes intense ingredients, such as soy sauce, alcohol or hot chillies and spices, don't overdo it. A fish fillet should still taste like fish, not a burning-hot, salt-soaked piece of protein. Also, if an acidic marinade is left too long on meat or fish, it can make the surface mushy or dry. Here are some general guidelines to get you going.

LEMON-MINT MARINADE

Makes: about 75 ml/3 fl oz

3 tablespoons extra-virgin olive oil
1 teaspoon finely grated lemon zest
2 tablespoons fresh lemon juice
1 tablespoon finely chopped mint leaves
1 teaspoon finely chopped garlic
1 teaspoon sea salt
½ teaspoon ground black pepper

1 Whisk the ingredients in a small bowl.

TANDOORI MARINADE

Makes: about 150 ml/ ¼ pint

250 ml/8 fl oz plain yogurt
¼ cup fresh lemon juice
1 tablespoon finely chopped fresh ginger
1 tablespoon finely chopped garlic
1 tablespoon paprika
2 teaspoons ground cumin
2 teaspoons sea salt
1 teaspoon ground turmeric
½ teaspoon ground cayenne pepper

1 Combine the ingredients in a small bowl.

CREOLE MUSTARD MARINADE

Makes: about 150 ml/ ¼ pint

3 tablespoons Creole mustard
3 tablespoons extra-virgin olive oil
3 tablespoons red wine vinegar
2 teaspoons Worcestershire sauce
2 teaspoons finely chopped garlic
1 teaspoon dried thyme
½ teaspoon sea salt
½ teaspoon ground black pepper

1 Whisk the ingredients in a small bowl.

SWEET BOURBON MARINADE

Makes: about 475 ml/16 fl oz

125 ml/4 fl oz bourbon
125 g/4 oz soft brown sugar
75 ml/3 fl oz soy sauce
75 ml/3 fl oz fresh lemon juice
2 tablespoons Worcestershire sauce
2 teaspoons finely chopped garlic
2 teaspoons finely chopped thyme leaves

1 Whisk the ingredients in a medium bowl.

MARINADE KEY

good on red meat
good on pork
good on poultry
good on seafood
good on vegetables

TIME	TYPES OF MEAT
15–30 minutes:	Small foods, such as shellfish, fish fillets, cubed meat for kebabs and tender vegetables
1–3 hours:	Thin cuts of boneless meat, such as chicken breasts, pork fillet, chops and steaks, as well as sturdy vegetables
2–6 hours:	Thicker cuts of boneless or bone-in meat, such as leg of lamb, whole chickens and beef joints
6–12 hours:	Big or tough cuts of meat, such as racks of ribs, whole hams, pork shoulders and turkeys

MARINADES

PROVENÇAL MARINADE

Makes: about 350 ml/12 fl oz

1 small onion, roughly chopped
25 g/1 oz flat-leaf parsley, leaves and
    tender stems
4 tablespoons fresh rosemary leaves
4 large garlic cloves
2 tablespoons Dijon mustard
2 tablespoons tomato purée
2 teaspoons sea salt
½ teaspoon ground black pepper
125 ml/4 fl oz dry white wine
4 tablespoons extra-virgin olive oil

1 Process the ingredients, except the
wine and oil, in a food processor or
blender until finely chopped. Add the
wine and oil and process until fairly
smooth.

GREEK ISLAND MARINADE

Makes: about 150 ml/ ¼ pint

15 g/ ½ oz flat-leaf parsley, roughly
    chopped
4 tablespoons dry white wine
4 tablespoons extra-virgin olive oil
 Grated zest and juice of ½ lemon
1 teaspoon garlic granules
1 teaspoon dried oregano
1 teaspoon paprika
¾ teaspoon sea salt
¼ teaspoon ground black pepper

1 Whisk the ingredients in a small bowl.

WORCESTERSHIRE PASTE

Makes: about 4 tablespoons

2 tablespoons extra-virgin olive oil
2 tablespoons Worcestershire sauce
2 teaspoons cracked black pepper
2 teaspoons garlic granules
1½ teaspoons sea salt
1 teaspoon smoked paprika
1 teaspoon ground cumin
½ teaspoon ground cinnamon

1 Whisk the ingredients in a small bowl.

TERIYAKI MARINADE

Makes: about 300 ml/ ½ pint

4 tablespoons extra-virgin olive oil
¼ cup soy sauce
¼ cup soft brown sugar
2 tablespoons rice wine (mirin)
1 large shallot, grated
1 tablespoon sesame seeds
1 tablespoon grated fresh ginger
2 garlic cloves, grated or finely chopped
1 teaspoon toasted sesame oil
1 teaspoon ground black pepper

1 In a medium bowl whisk the
ingredients.

BEER MARINADE

Makes: about 300 ml/ ½ pint

250 ml/8 fl oz dark beer
2 tablespoons toasted sesame oil
1 tablespoon finely chopped garlic
1 teaspoon dried oregano
1 teaspoon sea salt
½ teaspoon ground black pepper
¼ teaspoon ground cayenne pepper

1 Whisk the ingredients in a medium
bowl.

MOJO MARINADE

Makes: about 250 ml/8 fl oz

125 ml/4 fl oz fresh orange juice
2 tablespoons fresh lime juice
2 tablespoons soy sauce
2 tablespoons extra-virgin olive oil
1 tablespoon finely chopped garlic
½ teaspoon hot pepper sauce
½ teaspoon ground cumin
¼ teaspoon sea salt
¼ teaspoon ground black pepper

1 Whisk the ingredients in a small bowl.

COCONUT-GINGER MARINADE

Makes: about 600 ml/1 pint cups

25 g/1 oz fresh coriander, leaves and
    tender stems
10 garlic cloves
10-cm/4-inch piece fresh ginger, cut
    into thin slices
425-g/14-oz can unsweetened coconut
    milk, stirred
175 ml/6 fl oz low-salt soy sauce
4 tablespoons honey

1 Combine the coriander, garlic and
ginger in a food processor or blender.
Process until the ingredients are finely
chopped. Transfer to a large bowl and
add the remaining ingredients. Mix well.

SAUCES

Sauces open up a world of flavours for grillers. They offer us almost limitless ways for distinguishing our food and making it more interesting. Once you have learned some of the fundamentals about balancing flavours and some of the techniques for holding sauces together, you are ready to develop your own. A little more of this. A little less of that. Maybe a few more minutes simmering over the fire. Sauces are playgrounds for discovery. Learn the basics and build from there.

SMOKED PAPRIKA BUTTER

Makes: about 125 ml/4 fl oz
SPECIAL EQUIPMENT: spice mill

2 teaspoons coriander seeds *or* 1 table-
    spoon ground coriander
125 g/4 oz stick butter, softened
2 teaspoons smoked paprika
¼ teaspoon ground cayenne pepper

1 Toast the coriander seeds for about 2 minutes in a small frying pan over a medium heat, stirring occasionally, until aromatic and slightly darker in colour. Transfer to a spice mill and pulse until ground. Pour into a small bowl and mix thoroughly with the butter, paprika and cayenne pepper.

TEN-MINUTE BARBECUE SAUCE

Makes: about 175 ml/6 fl oz

125 ml/4 fl oz ketchup
4 tablespoons water
1 tablespoon Worcestershire sauce
1 tablespoon red wine vinegar
1 teaspoon soft light brown sugar
1 teaspoon chilli powder
1 teaspoon onion flakes
¼ teaspoon ground black pepper

1 Whisk the ingredients in a small saucepan. Simmer over a low heat for about 10 minutes to allow the sugar to fully dissolve and all of the flavours to blend, stirring occasionally.

RED WINE SAUCE

Makes: about 175 ml/6 fl oz

2 tablespoons finely chopped shallot
350 ml/12 fl oz dry red wine
1 tablespoon tomato purée
2 teaspoons balsamic vinegar
½ teaspoon Worcestershire sauce
40 g/1½ oz unsalted butter, cut into 3
    pieces
Sea salt
Ground black pepper

1 Bring the shallot and wine to the boil in a small saucepan over a high heat. Then immediately reduce the heat to medium and simmer for 15–20 minutes until the wine has reduced to about 125 ml/4 fl oz. Add the tomato purée, vinegar and Worcestershire sauce. Remove from the heat and add the butter piece by piece, whisking to incorporate the butter into the sauce. Season with salt and pepper.

BOURBON-BACON SAUCE

Makes: about 475 ml/16 fl oz

4 bacon rashers, cut into 1-cm/½-inch
    dice
2 cup small onions, finely chopped
1 tablespoon finely chopped garlic
125 ml/4 fl oz ketchup
4 tablespoons black treacle
4 tablespoons mustard
4 tablespoons bourbon
2 tablespoons soft brown sugar
2 tablespoons Worcestershire sauce
⅛ teaspoon hot pepper sauce

1 Cook the bacon for about 10 minutes in a medium saucepan over a medium heat, stirring occasionally, until crisp. Reduce the heat to low, add the onion and garlic, and cook for about 5 minutes until soft. Add the remaining ingredients and simmer for 5 minutes. Remove from the heat and let cool.

AVOCADO SAUCE

Makes: about 350 ml/12 fl oz

1 avocado, diced
75 g/3 oz finely diced cucumber
4 tablespoons soured cream
50 g/2 oz spring onions, thinly sliced
    (white and light green parts only)
4 tablespoons roughly chopped dill
    weed
2 tablespoons fresh lime juice
¼ teaspoon Tabasco sauce
 Sea salt

1 Purée all the ingredients, except the salt, in a food processor or blender until smooth. Season with salt. Pour the sauce into a medium bowl, cover, and refrigerate until ready to use.

SAUCE KEY

good on red meat
good on pork
good on poultry
good on seafood
good on vegetables

SAUCES

ROOT BEER BARBECUE SAUCE

Makes: about 750 ml/1¼ pints

1 tablespoon extra-virgin olive oil
2 small onions, finely chopped
1 teaspoon finely chopped garlic
½ teaspoon grated fresh ginger
250 ml/8 fl oz root beer
250 ml/8 fl oz ketchup
125 ml/4 fl oz fresh orange juice
2 tablespoons Worcestershire sauce
2 tablespoons soft light brown sugar
½ teaspoon grated lemon zest
Sea salt
Ground black pepper

1 Warm the oil in a medium saucepan over a medium heat. Add the onion and cook for 3–4 minutes until tender but not browned, stirring occasionally. Add the garlic and ginger and cook for about 1 minute until fragrant. Add the root beer, ketchup, orange juice, Worcestershire sauce and brown sugar, whisking until smooth. Simmer over a medium-low heat for 20–30 minutes, stirring occasionally until the sauce is thick and coats the back of a wooden spoon. Remove the saucepan from the heat and stir in the lemon zest. Season with salt and pepper.

ORANGE-GINGER SAUCE

Makes: about 175 ml/6 fl oz

150 g/5 oz orange marmalade
2 tablespoons cider vinegar
1 tablespoon soy sauce
2 teaspoons grated fresh ginger
⅛ teaspoon ground black pepper

1 Mix the ingredients in a small saucepan over a medium heat. Cook the sauce for 3–4 minutes until liquefied and bubbling, stirring occasionally. Remove from the heat and allow to cool to room temperature before serving.

TOMATO-CHIMICHURRI SAUCE

Makes: about 250 ml/8 fl oz

25 g/1 oz flat-leaf parsley
125 ml/4 fl oz extra-virgin olive oil
15 g/½ oz fresh coriander
4 tablespoons oil-packed sun-dried tomatoes, drained
3 garlic cloves
¾ teaspoon crushed red chilli flakes
Sea salt
Ground black pepper

1 Combine all the ingredients except the salt and pepper in a food processor or blender. Pulse until you get a semi-smooth consistency. Season with salt and pepper. Transfer to a small bowl and set aside until ready to use.

CREAMY MUSTARD SAUCE

Makes: about 175 ml/6 fl oz

15 g/½ oz unsalted butter
2 tablespoons finely chopped shallot
2 tablespoons cognac or brandy (optional)
125 ml/4 fl oz beef stock
175 g/6 fl oz whipping cream
3 tablespoons wholegrain mustard
Sea salt

1 Melt the butter in a medium frying pan over a medium heat, . Add the shallot and cook for 1–2 minutes until softened, , stirring often. Add the cognac, if using, and cook for about 30 seconds until reduced to a glaze. Add the stock and bring to the boil over a high heat. Cook for 2–3 minutes until the stock reduces by half. Add the cream and bring to a simmer (not a boil). Whisk in the mustard and simmer for 3–5 minutes until the sauce is reduced to 175 ml/6 fl oz and is thick enough to coat the back of a spoon. Season with salt.

HORSERADISH-LEMON CREAM SAUCE

Makes: about 350 ml/12 fl oz

250 ml/8 fl oz sour cream
2 tablespoons plus 1 teaspoon prepared horseradish
¼ teaspoon finely grated lemon zest
2 tablespoons fresh lemon juice
2 tablespoons finely chopped shallot
1 tablespoon finely chopped flat-leaf parsley
2 teaspoons Worcestershire sauce
½ teaspoon sea salt
½ teaspoon ground black pepper

1 Combine the ingredients in a medium bowl and stir until well blended. The sauce should have the consistency of thick cream.

BASIL-ROCKET PESTO

Makes: about 125 ml/4 fl oz

65 g/2½ oz baby rocket
40 g/1½ oz basil leaves
2 tablespoons roughly chopped toasted walnuts
1 garlic clove
½ teaspoon finely grated lemon zest
4 tablespoons extra-virgin olive oil
Sea salt
Ground black pepper

1 Combine the rocket, basil, walnuts, garlic and lemon zest in a food processor or blender and pulse until coarsely chopped. With the machine running, gradually add the oil and process until well blended. Season with salt and pepper.

DRESSINGS

Dressings serve many of the same purposes as sauces. Essentially they coat grilled and non-grilled ingredients in layers of moist, delicious flavours. But dressings tend to be simpler than sauces, because usually the ingredients require no cooking at all. You just mix them in a bowl or blender. Any of these can be made a few hours before you plan to serve them.

CUMIN VINAIGRETTE

Makes: about 175 ml/6 fl oz

2 tablespoons red wine vinegar
1 teaspoon Dijon mustard
1 teaspoon honey
1 teaspoon ground cumin
¼ teaspoon crushed red chilli flakes
125 ml/4 fl oz extra-virgin olive oil
½ teaspoon sea salt
¼ teaspoon ground black pepper

1 Whisk or pulse the vinegar, mustard, honey, cumin and red chilli flakes in a small bowl or in a blender. Slowly drizzle in the oil while whisking until the dressing has emulsified. Season with the salt and pepper.

RED WINE VINAIGRETTE

Makes: about 125 ml/4 fl oz

4 tablespoons extra-virgin olive oil
2 tablespoons red wine vinegar
1 teaspoon finely chopped garlic
½ teaspoon sea salt
¼ teaspoon ground black pepper

1 Whisk the ingredients in a small bowl.

ORANGE-FENNEL DRESSING

Makes: about 125 ml/4 fl oz
SPECIAL EQUIPMENT: spice mills

¾ teaspoon fennel seeds
¼ teaspoon sea salt
75 ml/3 fl oz extra-virgin olive oil
1 teaspoon finely grated orange zest
2 tablespoons fresh orange juice
1 tablespoon white wine vinegar
1 tablespoon finely chopped shallot

1 Put the fennel seeds and salt in a spice mill and process until finely ground. Pour into a small bowl and add the remaining ingredients. Whisk until emulsified.

BLUE CHEESE DRESSING

Makes: about 125 ml/4 fl oz

4 tablespoons crumbled blue cheese
2 tablespoons soured cream
2 tablespoons mayonnaise
1 tablespoon buttermilk
½ teaspoon cider vinegar

1 Combine the ingredients in a small bowl. Cover and refrigerate until ready to serve.

BASIL VINAIGRETTE

Makes: about 150 ml/ ¼ pint

40 g/1½ oz basil leaves
15 g/½ oz flat-leaf parsley, leaves and tender stems
1 tablespoon fresh lemon juice
1 tablespoon red wine vinegar
1 small garlic clove, finely chopped
75 ml/3 fl oz extra-virgin olive oil
½ teaspoon sea salt
¼ teaspoon ground black pepper

1 Pulse the basil, parsley, lemon juice, vinegar and garlic in a food processor or blender until coarsely chopped. With the machine running, slowly add the oil. Transfer to a small bowl and season with the salt and pepper.

HONEY-LIME DRESSING

Makes: about 250 ml/8 fl oz

4 tablespoons fresh lime juice
3 tablespoons honey
2 tablespoons finely chopped shallot
1 tablespoon Dijon mustard
1 tablespoon finely chopped fresh rosemary leaves
1 teaspoon sea salt
½ teaspoon ground black pepper
75 ml/3 fl oz extra-virgin olive oil

1 Whisk the lime juice, honey, shallot, mustard, rosemary, salt and pepper in a small bowl. Slowly whisk in the oil to make a smooth dressing.

DRESSING KEY
good on red meat
good on pork
good on poultry
good on seafood
good on vegetables

DRESSINGS

HERB AND SHALLOT VINAIGRETTE

Makes: about 150 ml/ ¼ pint

4 tablespoons extra-virgin olive oil
3 tablespoons white wine vinegar
3 tablespoons finely chopped fresh
    herbs, such as basil, chives,
    flat-leaf parsley, or your favourite
    combination
1 teaspoon finely chopped shallot
½ teaspoon Dijon mustard
¼ teaspoon sea salt
⅛ teaspoon ground black pepper

1 Whisk the ingredients in a small bowl.

CREAMY DILL DRESSING

Makes: about 150 ml/ ¼ pint

125 ml/4 fl oz mayonnaise
2 tablespoons finely chopped dill weed
2 teaspoons fresh lemon juice
½ teaspoon sea salt
¼ teaspoon ground black pepper

1 Whisk the ingredients in a small bowl.

SESAME-SOY DRESSING

Makes: about 125 ml/4 fl oz

4 tablespoons rapeseed oil
2 tablespoons fresh lime juice
1 tablespoon soy sauce
2 teaspoons soft light brown sugar
2 teaspoons toasted sesame oil
½ teaspoon grated fresh ginger
¼ teaspoon crushed red chilli flakes

1 Whisk the ingredients in a small bowl.

LEMON-OREGANO DRESSING

Makes: about 250 ml/8 fl oz

125 ml/4 fl oz extra-virgin olive oil
4 tablespoons fresh lemon juice
4 tablespoons finely chopped oregano
1 tablespoon finely chopped garlic
2 teaspoons coarsely ground black
    pepper
½ teaspoon sea salt

1 Whisk the ingredients in a small bowl.

BUTTERMILK DRESSING

Makes: about 175 ml/6 fl oz

75 ml/3 fl oz buttermilk
75 ml/3 fl oz mayonnaise
2 tablespoons finely chopped dill weed
½ teaspoon finely grated lemon zest
2 tablespoons fresh lemon juice
2 teaspoons granulated sugar
2 teaspoons Dijon mustard

1 Whisk the ingredients in a small bowl.

SHERRY VINAIGRETTE

Makes: about 300 ml/½ pint

175 ml/6 fl oz extra-virgin olive oil
4 tablespoons sherry vinegar
2 tablespoons finely chopped shallot
1½ tablespoons finely chopped
    marjoram
1 tablespoon Dijon mustard
½ teaspoon sea salt
¼ teaspoon ground black pepper

1 Whisk the ingredients in a medium
bowl.

MINTY FETA DRESSING

Makes: about 125 ml/4 fl oz

75 g/3 oz feta cheese
4 tablespoons mint leaves
2 tablespoons extra-virgin olive oil
2 tablespoons water
1 tablespoon white wine vinegar
1 small garlic clove, roughly chopped
Sea salt
Ground black pepper

1 Combine all the ingredients except the salt
and pepper in a food processor or blender.
Blend until thick and smooth, scraping down
the sides as needed. Season with salt and
pepper.

LEMON-MUSTARD DRESSING

Makes: about 250 ml/8 fl oz

3 tablespoons red wine vinegar
1½ tablespoons finely chopped shallot
2 teaspoons fresh lemon juice
1 tablespoon Dijon mustard
150 ml/ ¼ pint extra-virgin olive oil
Sea salt
Ground black pepper

1 Whisk the vinegar, shallot, lemon juice and
mustard in a small bowl. Slowly whisk in the
oil until it is emulsified. Season with salt and
pepper.

WHAT'S THE DEAL WITH
PROPANE?

Propane, sometimes called liquefied petroleum gas, is one of the cleanest burning of all fossil fuels. One particularly interesting propane trait is that it's a gas that condenses into a liquid when compressed. This outstanding property makes it very easy to store in tanks and the perfect fuel source for firing up your gas grill.

GAS PLANT

GAS WELL

C₃H₈

DID YOU KNOW?
The propane industry was born in 1910 when Dr Walter O. Snelling, a chemistry and explosives expert for the US Bureau of Mines, began experimenting with volatile fumes that formed in a container of petrol.

SO HOW CAN YOU TELL HOW MUCH PROPANE IS LEFT IN YOUR TANK?

1 Use a built-in tank scale, which is available on certain grill makes and models.

2 Make sure your valve is closed and carefully pour hot water down the side of your tank. Then run your hand slowly along the tank where the hot water touched. The tank will feel noticeably cold up to the level where the propane stops.

3 Buy a liquid crystal sticker at a DIY store. The sticker will change colour to signal the fullness of your tank.

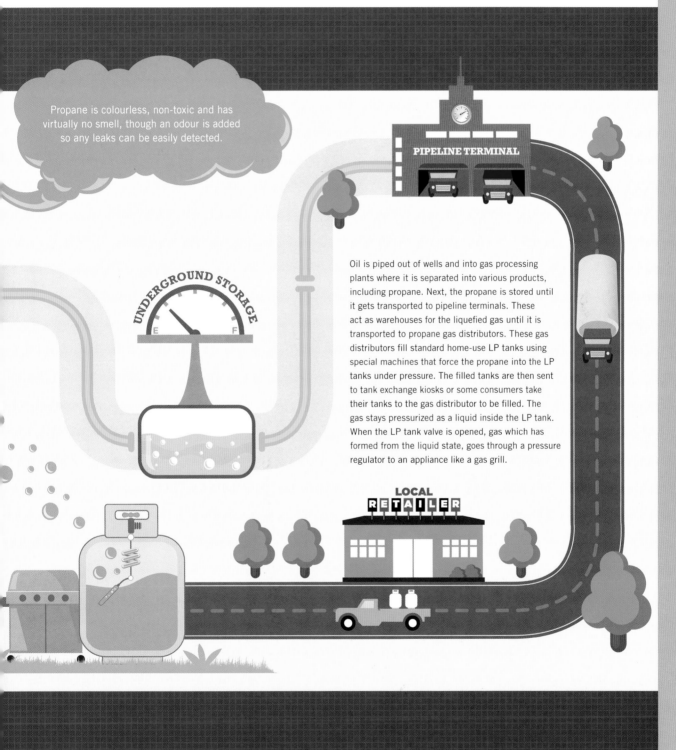

Propane is colourless, non-toxic and has virtually no smell, though an odour is added so any leaks can be easily detected.

PIPELINE TERMINAL

UNDERGROUND STORAGE

Oil is piped out of wells and into gas processing plants where it is separated into various products, including propane. Next, the propane is stored until it gets transported to pipeline terminals. These act as warehouses for the liquefied gas until it is transported to propane gas distributors. These gas distributors fill standard home-use LP tanks using special machines that force the propane into the LP tanks under pressure. The filled tanks are then sent to tank exchange kiosks or some consumers take their tanks to the gas distributor to be filled. The gas stays pressurized as a liquid inside the LP tank. When the LP tank valve is opened, gas which has formed from the liquid state, goes through a pressure regulator to an appliance like a gas grill.

LOCAL RETAILER

HOW DOES SMOKE
FLAVOUR FOOD?

Long before the days of refrigeration, smoking was a matter of life and death. It was how our ancestors preserved meat, fish and game birds to have on hand when fresh food was scarce. While other means of preservation eventually made smoking obsolete in the sense of survival, there was no way to replace the wonderfully layered taste of smoked foods. Cooks all over the world have sustained the art of smoking and refined how we can use it today primarily for flavour.

Inside a grill or smoker, smouldering wood fills the air with aromatic smoke, and food inherits the unique flavours of the wood, be it hickory, apple, mesquite or any other type. Hardwoods are most commonly used for smoking because their molecules burn and caramelize to create a milder, more palatable taste than softwoods. Smokers are easy to find these days, and many of them do a great job of slow-cooking big hunks of meat like beef brisket and pork shoulder, but you can also smoke just about anything in a charcoal grill or a gas grill equipped with a smoker box.

DOES SMOKE REALLY FOLLOW YOU?

Yes, actually. As all the minuscule particles that make up a smoke cloud float through the air, they react to changes in the airflow around them. To explain, a campfire or smoking grill will be taking in air from every direction. Your body's presence in the line of airflow creates a vacuum, thus drawing smoke towards you. So no matter what side of the fire you move to, the vacuum effect will come with you, making the smoke come with you too.

DID YOU KNOW?
When the Chinese were constructing the Great Wall, they used smoke signals to communicate with each other from tower to tower.

THE FUNDAMENTALS OF FIRE

Fire is a side effect of a rapid chemical reaction (oxidation) that produces energy in the form of heat and light. It is created from the interplay of three basic elements: fuel, heat and oxygen. When combined together in the right amounts, they form an essential combination for combustion.

CHAIN REACTION

FUEL

Solid fuels (like wood and charcoal) and liquid fuels (like oil and propane) do not burn. It's the vapours or gases that are produced when these materials are heated that burn. Some fuels burn completely, leaving nothing behind. Other fuels such as wood don't burn completely and leave carbon (or char) and non-combustible minerals (ash) behind.

OXYGEN O_2

Oxygen is an invisible gas in the air. Its role in fire is to sustain combustion. A fire can't burn or sustain itself without oxygen, and it has to be mixed with the right amount of fuel to ignite. Oxygen makes up about 21 per cent of the atmosphere.

A CASE OF THE VAPOURS

Gas molecules break apart and rearrange themselves, combining with oxygen to form water and carbon dioxide in a process called oxidation. This 'burning' releases energy creating heat, light and sound.

A burning fire creates a sustaining chemical reaction that feeds a fire more heat so that it can continue until oxygen or fuel is depleted. Without this chain reaction, the fire goes out.

heat + fuel

$$\frac{heat + fuel}{vapor}$$

vapor

vapor [vey-per] noun: visible particles of moisture floating or suspended in the air, as smoke, fog, steam

DID YOU KNOW?

A crackling fire is often considered a thing of beauty. But oddly enough, Hephaestus, the Greek god of fire and metalworking, is considered the only 'ugly' god in ancient mythology.

HEAT

The minimum temperature it takes to reach the point at which a material produces enough vapours to burn is called the flash point. The ignition point is the temperature at which the vapour will ignite when exposed to a spark, flame or ignition source.

Wood Ignition Point: 260°C/500°F

Charcoal Ignition Point: 349°C/660°F

EVERYDAY MEALS IN UNDER 30 MINUTES

EVERYDAY MEALS IN UNDER 30 MINUTES

KIDS WILL LOVE THEM

42 PORTOBELLO MUSHROOM CHEESEBURGERS

48 HOT DOGS WITH BACON AND CHIPOTLE CHILLI

QUICK-FIX SNACKS

58 LEMON CHICKEN CAESAR SALAD

66 GINGER-HONEY GLAZED PRAWNS

HEALTHY MIDWEEK MEALS

53 MISO-GINGER PORK CHOPS WITH
   SESAME GREEN BEANS

59 CHICKEN AND PEACH SALAD WITH
   SWEET-HOT DRESSING

56 HERBED CHICKEN WITH GRILLED CORN ON THE COB 80 GRILLED CHOCOLATE SANDWICHES

74 GRILLED POTATO WEDGES WITH FRESH HERBS
   AND BUTTER

77 ASPARAGUS WITH GREEN GODDESS DIP

63 GARLIC-SAGE TURKEY STEAKS WITH
   CRANBERRY SAUCE

73 TUNA STEAKS WITH LEMON VINAIGRETTE

PORTOBELLO MUSHROOM CHEESEBURGERS

SERVES: 4
PREP TIME: 10 MINUTES
GRILLING TIME: 8–10 MINUTES

BURGERS
750 g/1½ lb minced beef (80% lean)
50 g/2 oz Portobello mushrooms, finely chopped
4 tablespoons roasted red pepper (from a jar), finely chopped
1 teaspoon dried Italian herb seasoning
1 teaspoon garlic salt
½ teaspoon ground black pepper

4 thin slices provolone cheese
4 ciabatta rolls *or* burger buns
4 tablespoons sun-dried tomato paste
4 red or green lettuce leaves

1 Prepare the grill for direct cooking over high heat (230–290°C/450–550°F).

2 Gently combine the burger ingredients in a large bowl and shape into four burgers of equal size and thickness, each about 1.5 cm/¾ inch thick. Make a shallow indentation about 2.5 cm/1 inch wide with your thumb or the back of a spoon in the centre of each burger. This will help the burgers cook evenly and prevent them from puffing on the grill.

3 Brush the cooking grates clean. Grill the burgers over **direct high heat** for 8–10 minutes, with the lid closed as much as possible and turning the burgers once when they will release easily from the grate without sticking, until cooked to medium doneness. During the last minute of grilling time, place a slice of cheese on each burger to melt, and toast the rolls cut side down. Build each burger with sun-dried tomato paste and lettuce leaves.

Ordinary mushroom cheeseburgers put the mushroom on top, but this one has you finely chopping the portobello mushrooms and blending the pieces into the meat along with chopped roasted peppers and seasoning. The flavoursome moisture of the vegetables makes for wonderfully juicy burgers. They taste even better with sun-dried tomato spread.

In place of lettuce, try baby rocket that's been drizzled with a little olive oil and balsamic vinegar. The rocket gives the burgers an extra peppery bite. If you prefer to forgo the bun altogether, use the bowled shape of portobello mushrooms to hold a filling that looks and tastes a lot like meat loaf draped in melted cheese.

RIB-EYE STEAKS WITH ANCHO CHILLI SAUCE

SERVES: 4

PREP TIME: 15 MINUTES, PLUS ABOUT 30 MINUTES FOR
THE SAUCE

GRILLING TIME: 6–8 MINUTES

SAUCE

1 dried ancho chilli, about 5 g/¼ oz
350 ml/12 fl oz dry red wine
2 garlic cloves
125 ml/4 fl oz tomato ketchup
2 teaspoons Worcestershire sauce
½ teaspoon ground cumin

PASTE

2 tablespoons extra-virgin olive oil
1 tablespoon Dijon mustard
1 tablespoon finely chopped oregano
2 teaspoons sea salt
1 teaspoon ground black pepper

4 boneless rib-eye steaks, each 250–300 g/8–10 oz and about
2.5 cm/1 inch thick, trimmed of excess fat

1 Cut off and discard the stem of the chilli, then cut the chilli
open and remove and discard the seeds. Combine the chilli,
wine and garlic in a small saucepan. Bring the mixture to the
boil over a medium-high heat. Cook for 5–10 minutes, until
about 175 ml/6 fl oz wine remains. Set aside for 20 minutes,
keeping the chilli submerged so that it softens completely.

2 Pour the contents of the saucepan into a food processor.
Process for 1 full minute to purée the chilli. Pour the mixture
into a small saucepan along with the remaining sauce
ingredients. Mix well and then heat the sauce over a medium
heat for about a minute. Set aside.

3 Prepare the grill for direct cooking over high heat
(230–290°C/450–550°F).

4 Mix the paste ingredients in a small bowl. Smear the steaks
evenly on both sides with the paste. Allow the steaks to stand at
room temperature for 15–30 minutes before grilling.

5 Brush the cooking grates clean. Grill the steaks over *direct
high heat*, with the lid closed as much as possible and turning
once or twice (if flare-ups occur, move the steaks temporarily
over indirect heat), until cooked to your desired doneness, 6–8
minutes for medium rare. Remove from the grill and leave to
rest for 3–5 minutes. While the steaks rest, warm the sauce
over a low heat. Serve the steaks warm with the sauce.

STEAK AND EGGS

SERVES: 4
PREP TIME: 10 MINUTES
GRILLING TIME: 10–14 MINUTES
SPECIAL EQUIPMENT: 30-CM/12-INCH CAST-IRON
 FRYING PAN

2 sirloin steaks, each 300–375 g/10–12 oz and about
 2.5 cm/1 inch thick, trimmed of excess fat
Extra-virgin olive oil
Sea salt
Ground black pepper
¾ teaspoon smoked paprika
25 g/1 oz unsalted butter
8 large eggs

1 Prepare the grill for direct cooking over high heat
(230–290°C/450–550°F).

2 Lightly brush the steaks on both sides with oil and season
evenly with salt, pepper and the paprika. Allow the steaks to
stand at room temperature for 15–30 minutes before grilling.

3 Brush the cooking grates clean. Grill the steaks over **direct
high heat**, with the lid closed as much as possible and turning
once or twice (if flare-ups occur, move the steaks temporarily
over indirect heat), until cooked to your desired doneness,
6–8 minutes for medium rare. When you turn the steaks, place
a 30-cm/12-inch cast-iron frying pan on the cooking grate to
preheat. Remove the steaks from the grill and leave to rest for
3–5 minutes. Lower the temperature of the grill to medium heat
(180–230°C/350–450°F).

4 Coat the frying pan with the butter. Crack the eggs into the
pan and season them with salt and pepper. Cook over **direct
medium heat**, with the lid closed as much as possible, until
cooked as desired, 4–6 minutes for partially runny yolks. Cut
each steak in half and place on individual plates. Transfer the
eggs to the plates and serve immediately.

SIRLOIN STEAKS WITH TOMATO AND BLUE CHEESE VINAIGRETTE

SERVES: 4
PREP TIME: 15 MINUTES
GRILLING TIME: 6–8 MINUTES

4 sirloin steaks, each 250–300 g/8–10 oz and about
    2.5 cm/1 inch thick, trimmed of excess fat
Extra-virgin olive oil
Sea salt
Ground black pepper

VINAIGRETTE
1 tablespoon finely chopped shallot
2 teaspoons red wine vinegar
1 teaspoon Dijon mustard
20 cherry tomatoes, quartered
4 tablespoons finely chopped basil
50 g/2 oz Gorgonzola cheese, crumbled

1 Prepare the grill for direct cooking over high heat
(230–290°C/450–550°F).

2 Lightly brush the steaks on both sides with oil and season
evenly with salt and pepper. Allow the steaks to stand at room
temperature for 15–30 minutes before grilling.

3 Whisk the shallot, vinegar, mustard, ¼ teaspoon salt and
¼ teaspoon pepper in a bowl. Slowly whisk in 2 tablespoons
of oil, forming a smooth vinaigrette. Add the tomatoes and basil.
Mix well.

4 Brush the cooking grates clean. Grill the steaks over **direct
high heat**, with the lid closed as much as possible and turning
once or twice (if flare-ups occur, move the steaks temporarily
over indirect heat), until cooked to your desired doneness,
6–8 minutes for medium rare. Remove from the grill and leave
to rest for 3–5 minutes. Add the cheese to the vinaigrette. Mix
gently. Serve the steaks warm with the vinaigrette spooned over
the top.

HOT DOGS WITH BACON AND CHIPOTLE CHILLI

SERVES: 8

PREP TIME: 15 MINUTES, PLUS ABOUT 20 MINUTES FOR THE CHILLI

GRILLING TIME: 5–7 MINUTES

CHILLI

2 bacon rashers, finely chopped

1 onion, finely chopped

1 tablespoon finely chopped jalapeño chilli

2 teaspoons finely chopped garlic

500 g/1 lb minced steak (85% lean)

1 canned chipotle chilli in adobo sauce, chopped
   or 1 teaspoon chipotle chilli powder

1 teaspoon smoked paprika

½ teaspoon ground cumin

½ teaspoon sea salt

250 ml/8 fl oz ready-made tomato sauce

125 ml/4 fl oz lager *or* beef stock *or* water

8 all-beef hot dogs, each about 125 g/4 oz

8 hot dog rolls

125 g/4 oz mature Cheddar cheese, grated

1 Heat the bacon and half the onion in a large frying pan over a medium heat for about 5 minutes, stirring occasionally, until the bacon is crisp and browned. Add the jalapeño chilli and garlic and cook for about 1 minute until fragrant. Add the minced steak and cook for about 5 minutes, stirring and breaking up the meat with the side of a spoon, until the meat loses its raw look. Add the chipotle chilli, paprika, cumin and salt and mix well. Stir in the tomato sauce and beer and bring to a simmer. Reduce the heat to medium-low and simmer for about 10 minutes, stirring occasionally, until the liquid thickens. Keep the chilli warm.

2 While the chilli simmers, prepare the grill for direct and indirect cooking over medium heat (180–230°C/350–450°F).

3 Cut a few shallow slashes in each hot dog. Wrap the hot dog rolls in a foil parcel.

4 Brush the cooking grates clean. Grill the hot dogs over **direct medium heat** for 5–7 minutes, with the lid closed as much as possible and turning occasionally, until lightly marked on the outside and hot all the way to the centre. During the last 3 minutes of grilling time, warm the parcel with the rolls over **indirect medium heat**.

5 Place the hot dogs in the rolls. Top each with chilli, cheese and the remaining chopped onion. Serve warm.

CHORIZO AND BEEF SKEWERS WITH CHIMICHURRI

SERVES: 4
PREP TIME: 10 MINUTES
GRILLING TIME: 4–6 MINUTES
SPECIAL EQUIPMENT: METAL OR BAMBOO SKEWERS
(IF USING BAMBOO, SOAK IN WATER FOR AT LEAST
30 MINUTES)

CHIMICHURRI
50 g/2 oz flat-leaf parsley, leaves and tender stalks
2 garlic cloves
4 tablespoons extra-virgin olive oil
2 tablespoons white wine vinegar
½ teaspoon crushed red chilli flakes
Sea salt
Ground black pepper

500 g/1 lb sirloin steak, about 2.5 cm/1 inch thick, trimmed of
excess fat, cut into 2.5-cm/1-inch cubes
375 g/12 oz fully cooked chorizo sausages, cut crossways into
2.5-cm/1-inch pieces

1 Whizz the parsley and garlic in a food processor until finely chopped. With the machine running, add the oil, vinegar and 1 tablespoon water in a steady stream. Season with the chilli flakes, ½ teaspoon salt and ½ teaspoon pepper. Pour about half of the chimichurri into a small bowl.

2 Prepare the grill for direct cooking over high heat (230–290°C/450–550°F).

3 Season the cubed steak with ¼ teaspoon salt and ⅛ teaspoon pepper. Thread the steak and chorizo pieces alternately on to skewers. Brush the meat with the chimichurri sauce left in the food processor.

4 Brush the cooking grates clean. Grill the skewers over **direct high heat**, with the lid closed as much as possible and turning 2 to 3 times (watch for flare-ups), until the steak is cooked to your desired doneness, 4–6 minutes for medium rare. Serve warm with the reserved chimichurri spooned over the top.

SIMPLE PORK CHOPS WITH GRILLED PINEAPPLE

SERVES: 4
PREP TIME: 10 MINUTES
GRILLING TIME: 8–10 MINUTES

RUB
1½ teaspoons sea salt
1 teaspoon dried oregano
¼ teaspoon garlic granules
¼ teaspoon onion flakes
¼ teaspoon ground black pepper

4 bone-in pork loin chops, each about 250 g/8 oz and
    2.5 cm/1 inch thick, trimmed of excess fat
Extra-virgin olive oil

4 slices fresh pineapple, each about 1 cm/½ inch thick

1 Prepare the grill for direct cooking over medium heat (180–230°C/350–450°F).

2 Combine the rub ingredients in a small bowl. Lightly coat the chops on both sides with oil and season evenly with the rub. Allow the chops to stand at room temperature for 15–30 minutes before grilling.

3 Brush the cooking grates clean. Grill the chops over **direct medium heat** for 8–10 minutes, with the lid closed as much as possible and turning once or twice, until they are still slightly pink in the centre. At the same time, grill the pineapple over **direct medium heat** for 4–6 minutes, turning once, until well marked on both sides. Remove the chops and the pineapple from the grill and leave the chops to rest for 3–5 minutes. Cut the pineapple slices into quarters and serve with the chops.

VIETNAMESE PORK FILLET SALAD WITH SPICY PEANUT VINAIGRETTE

SERVES: 4
PREP TIME: 15 MINUTES
GRILLING TIME: 4–6 MINUTES

VINAIGRETTE

125 ml/4 fl oz rapeseed oil
4 tablespoons unsalted crunchy peanut butter
3 tablespoons rice vinegar
3 tablespoons finely chopped fresh coriander
2 teaspoons soy sauce
1 teaspoon hot chilli-garlic sauce

2 pork fillets, each 375–500 g/12 oz–1 lb, trimmed of excess fat and skin, cut crossways into medallions about 3.5 cm/1½ inches thick

SALAD

1 green leaf lettuce, torn into bite-sized pieces
2 carrots, cut into very thin julienne strips
½ cucumber, very thinly sliced

Sliced spring onions (optional)

1 Whisk the vinaigrette ingredients in a bowl. Set aside 5 tablespoons of the vinaigrette for basting the pork and 5 tablespoons for serving. Brush the medallions all over with the remaining vinaigrette and allow to stand at room temperature for 15–30 minutes before grilling.

2 Prepare the grill for direct cooking over medium heat (180–230°C/350–450°F).

3 Brush the cooking grates clean. Grill the medallions over **direct medium heat** for 4–6 minutes, with the lid closed as much as possible and turning and brushing with the reserved vinaigrette once, until the outsides are evenly seared and the centres are barely pink. Remove from the grill and leave to rest for 3–5 minutes.

4 Evenly divide the salad ingredients and the pork medallions between four plates. Drizzle some of the vinaigrette over the top. Serve with any remaining vinaigrette and sliced spring onions, if liked.

MISO-GINGER PORK CHOPS WITH SESAME GREEN BEANS

SERVES: 4
PREP TIME: 15 MINUTES
GRILLING TIME: 8–10 MINUTES
SPECIAL EQUIPMENT: PERFORATED GRILL PAN

4 tablespoons white miso paste (sometimes labelled *shiro* miso)
2 tablespoons grated fresh ginger
2 tablespoons soy sauce
2 tablespoons toasted sesame oil

4 boneless pork loin chops, each about 175 g/6 oz and
    2.5 cm/1 inch thick, trimmed of excess fat

½ teaspoon wasabi paste
500 g/1 lb fresh green beans, trimmed
1 tablespoon sesame seeds (black or white, or a combination)

Vegetable oil

1 Combine the miso, ginger, half the soy sauce and half the sesame oil in a small bowl. Spread the chops on both sides with the paste and marinate at room temperature for 15–30 minutes.

2 Prepare the grill for direct cooking over medium heat (180–230°C/350–450°F) and preheat the grill pan.

3 Combine the remaining soy sauce, sesame oil and the wasabi paste in a large bowl. Add the green beans and turn to coat them thoroughly. Sprinkle the sesame seeds over the beans and toss gently to distribute the seeds evenly.

4 Brush the cooking grates clean. Wipe almost all the paste from the chops and lightly brush with vegetable oil. Grill the chops over **direct medium heat** for 8–10 minutes, with the lid closed as much as possible and turning once or twice, until they are still slightly pink in the centre. At the same time, spread the green beans in a single layer on the grill pan, reserving any dressing that remains in the bowl, and grill over **direct medium heat** for 5–7 minutes, turning occasionally, until they are browned in spots and crisp-tender. Remove the chops and beans from the grill and leave the chops to rest for 3–5 minutes.

5 Drizzle the beans with the reserved dressing and serve with the pork chops.

BUTTERFLIED PORK CHOPS WITH PLUM, MINT AND JALAPEÑO SALSA

SERVES: 4–6
PREP TIME: 15 MINUTES
GRILLING TIME: 8–10 MINUTES

4 centre-cut butterflied pork loin chops, each about 300 g/10 oz
    and 1.5–2.5 cm/¾ to 1 inch thick, trimmed of excess fat
1¼ teaspoons sea salt
4 ripe plums, cut into bite-sized pieces
½ jalapeño chilli, deseeded and finely chopped
5 tablespoons finely chopped mint
1½ teaspoons granulated sugar
¼ teaspoon ground coriander
¼ teaspoon ground black pepper
2 teaspoons extra-virgin olive oil

1 Season the pork chops on both sides with 1 teaspoon of the salt. Allow the chops to stand at room temperature for 15–30 minutes.

2 Prepare the grill for direct cooking over medium heat (180–230°C/350–450°F).

3 Gently combine the plums, jalapeño, mint, sugar, coriander, pepper and the remaining ¼ teaspoon salt in a medium bowl. Set aside.

4 Lightly brush the pork chops on both sides with the oil. Brush the cooking grates clean. Grill the chops over **direct medium heat** for 8–10 minutes, with the lid closed as much as possible and turning once or twice, until they are stilll slightly pink in the centre. Remove from the grill and leave to rest for 3–5 minutes. Serve warm topped with the salsa.

GAMMON STEAKS WITH GRILLED PEARS AND VINEGAR GLAZE

SERVES: 4
PREP TIME: 15 MINUTES
GRILLING TIME: 8–12 MINUTES

2 gammon steaks, each about 1 pound and ½ inch thick
2 ripe pears, peeled, quartered and cored
1 tablespoon vegetable oil

GLAZE
175 g/6 oz soft brown sugar
6 tablespoons cider vinegar
3 tablespoons Dijon mustard
⅛ teaspoon crushed red chilli flakes

1 Prepare the grill for direct cooking over medium heat (180–230°C/350–450°F).

2 Pat the gammon steaks dry and then brush the gammon and pears with the oil.

3 Combine the glaze ingredients in a small saucepan over a medium heat. Bring the mixture to the boil, and then reduce the heat to maintain a steady simmer. Cook for 8–9 minutes until a syrupy glaze forms.

4 Brush the cooking grates clean. Grill the gammon and pears over **direct medium heat** for 8–12 minutes, with the lid closed as much as possible and turning once, until the gammon is hot and the pears are tender and nicely marked. Remove from the grill as they are done. Cut the steaks into individual serving pieces. Arrange the pear quarters beside the meat and serve hot, drizzled with the vinegar glaze.

HERBED CHICKEN WITH GRILLED CORN ON THE COB

SERVES: 4
PREP TIME: 15 MINUTES
GRILLING TIME: 10–15 MINUTES

50 g/2 oz unsalted butter, softened
2 large garlic cloves, finely chopped
4 boneless, skinless chicken breasts, each about 175 g/6 oz
2 tablespoons extra-virgin olive oil
2 tablespoons finely chopped mixed herbs, such as rosemary and thyme
½ teaspoon sea salt
¼ teaspoon ground black pepper
4 fresh corn cobs, outer leaves and silk removed

1 Prepare the grill for direct cooking over medium heat (180–230°C/350–450°F).

2 Mash the butter and garlic with a fork in a small bowl.

3 Lightly coat the chicken on both sides with the oil and season evenly with the herbs, salt and pepper.

4 Brush the cooking grates clean. Grill the chicken, smooth (skin) side down first, over **direct medium heat** for 8–12 minutes, with the lid closed as much as possible and turning once or twice, until the meat is firm to the touch and opaque all the way to the centre. At the same time, grill the corn over **direct medium heat** for 10–15 minutes, turning occasionally, until browned in spots and tender. Remove the chicken and corn from the grill and leave the chicken to rest for 3–5 minutes.

5 Spread the garlic butter on the grilled corn and serve with the chicken.

On stressful nights when it seems like all the demands in your life are colliding and you're not sure how you will possibly get dinner on the table in time, stop right there and make a quick and easy meal based on chicken and sweetcorn. Fresh herbs bring just enough flavour to make it interesting. For a variation, try substituting herbs like oregano, marjoram, tarragon or sage for the thyme and rosemary.

LEMON CHICKEN CAESAR SALAD

SERVES: 4
PREP TIME: 15 MINUTES
GRILLING TIME: 8–12 MINUTES
SPECIAL EQUIPMENT: PERFORATED GRILL PAN

DRESSING
5 tablespoons fresh lemon juice
3 large garlic cloves, crushed
1 tablespoon Dijon mustard
1 tablespoon Worcestershire sauce
¾ teaspoon sea salt
½ teaspoon ground black pepper
175 ml/6 fl oz extra-virgin olive oil

250 g/8 oz small cherry tomatoes
3 slices rustic bread, cut into 1-cm/½-inch cubes
4 boneless, skinless chicken breasts, each about 175 g/6 oz

1 large romaine lettuce or 3 hearts of romaine, chopped
100 g/3½ oz Parmesan cheese, freshly grated

1 Prepare the grill for direct cooking over medium heat (180–230°C/350–450°F) and preheat the grill pan.

2 Whizz the lemon juice, garlic, mustard, Worcestershire sauce, salt and pepper in a blender until smooth. With the machine running, add the oil in a slow, steady stream, blending until emulsified.

3 Toss the tomatoes and bread cubes with 2 tablespoons of the dressing in a bowl. Pour 2 tablespoons of the dressing over the chicken breasts and turn to coat them evenly.

4 Brush the cooking grates clean. Grill the chicken, smooth (skin) side down first, over **direct medium heat** for 8–12 minutes, with the lid closed as much as possible and turning once or twice, until the meat is firm to the touch and opaque all the way to the centre. During the last 2–3 minutes of grilling time, spread the tomatoes and bread cubes in a single layer on the grill pan and cook, turning occasionally, until the tomatoes start to blister and the bread is toasted. Remove everything from the grill and leave the chicken to rest for 3–5 minutes. Cut the chicken crossways into 1-cm/½-inch slices.

5 Toss the lettuce with the dressing and the cheese in a large bowl. Divide the salad, chicken, tomatoes and croutons evenly between four plates. Serve immediately.

CHICKEN AND PEACH SALAD WITH SWEET-HOT DRESSING

SERVES: 4
PREP TIME: 15 MINUTES
GRILLING TIME: 16–22 MINUTES

DRESSING
150 ml/¼ pint Dijon mustard with honey
2 teaspoons finely chopped garlic
2 teaspoons hot pepper sauce
2 teaspoons fresh lemon juice
Extra-virgin olive oil
Sea salt
Ground black pepper

4 ripe peaches, halved
1 onion, cut crossways into 8-mm/⅓-inch slices
4 boneless, skinless chicken breasts, each about 175 g/6 oz
150 g/5 oz lamb's lettuce *or* rocket

1 Combine the mustard, garlic, hot sauce and lemon juice in a medium bowl. Gradually whisk in 125 ml/4 fl oz oil. Season with salt and pepper. Reserve 125 ml/4 fl oz of the dressing to use for basting; save the rest for serving.

2 Prepare the grill for direct cooking over medium heat (180–230°C/350–450°F).

3 Lightly brush both sides of the peach halves and onion slices with oil, then brush the chicken on both sides with more oil. Season the peaches, onion slices and chicken evenly with salt and pepper.

4 Brush the cooking grates clean. Grill the peaches and onion over **direct medium heat** for 8–10 minutes, with the lid closed as much as possible, turning once or twice and basting with the dressing during the last minute of grilling time, until the peaches are slightly charred and the onion is tender. Remove from the grill. Cut the peach halves into wedges and chop the onion slices.

5 Grill the chicken, smooth (skin) side down first, over **direct medium heat** for 8–12 minutes, with the lid closed as much as possible and turning and basting with the dressing once or twice, until the meat is firm to the touch and opaque all the way to the centre. Remove from the grill and leave to rest for 3–5 minutes. Discard any remaining dressing used for basting. Cut the chicken into thin slices on the diagonal.

6 Divide the lamb's lettuce between four bowls and add equal amounts of the chicken, peaches and onion to each. Season with salt and pepper and serve with the reserved dressing to drizzle over the top.

CURRY CHICKEN BREASTS WITH AUBERGINE AND TOMATO

SERVES: 4
PREP TIME: 15 MINUTES
GRILLING TIME: 8–12 MINUTES

4 boneless, skinless chicken breasts, each about 175 g/6 oz
4 tablespoons rapeseed oil
4½ teaspoons curry powder
1¼ teaspoons sea salt
2 Japanese aubergines, 375–500 g/12–16 oz in total, cut into
  1-cm/½-inch pieces
2 shallots, finely chopped
1 tablespoon finely chopped serrano chilli (with seeds)
500 g/1 lb cherry tomatoes, quartered
1 tablespoon runny honey
1 teaspoon red wine vinegar
¼ teaspoon ground black pepper
2 tablespoons finely chopped fresh coriander

1 Prepare the grill for direct cooking over medium heat (180–230°C/350–450°F).

2 Lightly coat the chicken on both sides with 1 tablespoon of the oil and season evenly with 4 teaspoons of the curry powder and ¾ teaspoon of the salt.

3 Heat the remaining 3 tablespoons oil in a large frying pan over a medium-high heat. Add the aubergine, shallots, chilli and the remaining curry powder. Sauté for 4–6 minutes, stirring often, until the aubergine begins to brown. Add the tomatoes, 125 ml/4 fl oz water, honey, vinegar, pepper and the remaining salt and cook for about 4 minutes, stirring occasionally, until the aubergine is soft and the liquid has evaporated. Add the coriander and mix well. Set aside.

4 Brush the cooking grates clean. Grill the chicken, smooth (skin) side down first, over **direct medium heat** for 8–12 minutes, with the lid closed as much as possible and turning once or twice, until the meat is firm to the touch and opaque all the way to the centre. Remove from the grill and leave to rest for 3–5 minutes. Serve warm with the aubergine and tomatoes.

DUCK AND SPINACH SALAD

SERVES: 4
PREP TIME: 15 MINUTES
GRILLING TIME: 8–10 MINUTES

150 g/5 oz baby spinach
475-g/15-oz can chickpeas, rinsed
75 g/3 oz red onion, thinly sliced
8 tablespoons coarsely chopped mint
65 g/2½ oz feta cheese, crumbled

Extra-virgin olive oil
1 tablespoon red wine vinegar

2 duck breasts, each 150–175 g/5–6 oz, skin removed,
    patted dry
1 teaspoon ground cumin
Sea salt
Ground black pepper

1 Combine the spinach, chickpeas, onion, mint and half the feta in a large bowl; cover and refrigerate.

2 Whisk 3 tablespoons oil and the vinegar in a small bowl. Set aside.

3 Prepare the grill for direct cooking over medium-low heat (about 180°C/350°F).

4 Lightly brush the duck breasts on both sides with oil and season evenly with the cumin and salt and pepper. Brush the cooking grates clean. Grill the duck breasts, smooth (skin) side down first, over **direct medium-low heat**, with the lid closed as much as possible and turning once, until cooked to your desired doneness, 8–10 minutes for medium rare. Transfer to a carving board and leave to rest for 3–5 minutes. Cut crossways into 8-mm/⅓-inch slices.

5 Add the duck slices to the salad. Whisk the oil and vinegar again and add enough of it to coat the ingredients lightly. Season with salt and pepper. Sprinkle the remaining feta over the salad and serve.

GARLIC-SAGE TURKEY STEAKS WITH CRANBERRY SAUCE

SERVES: 4–6
PREP TIME: 15 MINUTES
GRILLING TIME: 4–6 MINUTES

3 tablespoons extra-virgin olive oil
1 tablespoon finely chopped sage
2 teaspoons finely chopped garlic
1½ teaspoons sea salt
½ teaspoon ground black pepper

8 turkey breast fillets, each 75–125 g/3–4 oz and about
   1 cm/½ inch thick

SAUCE
1 Granny Smith apple, peeled, cored and cut into
   1-cm/½-inch pieces
375 g/12 oz cranberries, rinsed and drained
125 ml/4 fl oz apple juice
125 g/4 oz granulated sugar
¼ teaspoon ground cloves
¼ teaspoon sea salt

1 Prepare the grill for direct cooking over medium heat (180–230°C/350–450°F).

2 Combine the oil, sage, garlic, salt and pepper in a shallow baking dish. Put the turkey fillets in the dish and turn to coat them evenly. Set aside at room temperature for as long as 20 minutes while you make the sauce.

3 Combine the sauce ingredients in a saucepan. Bring to the boil and then reduce to a simmer. Cover and cook for 6–10 minutes until all the cranberries have popped. Set aside to cool.

4 Brush the cooking grates clean. Grill the turkey fillets over **direct medium heat** for 4–6 minutes, with the lid closed as much as possible and turning once or twice, until the meat is firm to the touch and no longer pink in the centre. Remove from the grill and serve warm with the sauce spooned over the top.

SCALLOP SALAD WITH CITRUS VINAIGRETTE

SERVES: 4
PREP TIME: 15 MINUTES
GRILLING TIME: 4–6 MINUTES

6 tablespoons extra-virgin olive oil
Finely grated zest of 1 lime
3 tablespoons fresh lime juice
2 tablespoons runny honey
1 shallot, finely chopped
1 tablespoon finely chopped flat-leaf parsley
Sea salt
Ground black pepper

16 large scallops, each about 50 g/2 oz

125 g/4 oz mixed salad leaves

1 Prepare the grill for direct cooking over high heat (230–290°C/450–550°F).

2 Whisk 4 tablespoons of the oil, the lime zest and juice, honey, shallot and parsley in a small bowl. Season with salt and pepper.

3 Remove and discard the small, tough side muscle that might be left on each scallop. Lightly brush the scallops with the remaining oil and season evenly with salt and pepper.

4 Brush the cooking grates clean. Grill the scallops over **direct high heat** for 4–6 minutes, with the lid closed as much as possible and turning once or twice, until lightly browned and just opaque in the centre. Remove from the grill.

5 Whisk the vinaigrette again. Toss the salad leaves in a bowl with just enough of the vinaigrette to coat lightly. Arrange equal amounts of the salad and scallops on individual plates. Serve with the remaining vinaigrette.

SALMON WITH CHIPOTLE BUTTER

SERVES: 4
PREP TIME: 10 MINUTES
GRILLING TIME: 8–11 MINUTES

BUTTER
75 g/3 oz unsalted butter, softened
2–3 canned chipotle chillies in adobo sauce, with excess
    sauce wiped off, deseeded and finely chopped
1 teaspoon finely chopped garlic
Sea salt

4 salmon fillets (with skin), each 175–250 g/6–8 oz and about
    2.5 cm/1 inch thick, pin bones removed
2 tablespoons vegetable oil
Ground black pepper
1 lime, cut into wedges

1 Combine the butter ingredients, including ½ teaspoon salt, in a bowl.

2 Prepare the grill for direct cooking over high heat (230–290°C/450–550°F).

3 Generously brush the salmon fillets on both sides with the oil and season evenly with salt and pepper. Brush the cooking grates clean. Grill the salmon over **direct high heat** for 6–8 minutes, with the lid closed as much as possible, until you can lift the fillets off the cooking grate with tongs without sticking. Turn the fillets over and continue cooking to your desired doneness, 2–3 minutes for medium rare. Slip a spatula between the skin and the flesh, and lift the salmon from the grill. Smear some chipotle butter on top of each fillet and serve warm with lime wedges.

GINGER-HONEY GLAZED PRAWNS

SERVES: 4; 6 AS A STARTER
PREP TIME: 15 MINUTES
GRILLING TIME: 2–4 MINUTES

SAUCE
4 tablespoons soy sauce
1 spring onion (white and light green parts only), thinly sliced
1 tablespoon rice vinegar
1 teaspoon chilli oil

GLAZE
3 tablespoons runny honey
1 tablespoon rice vinegar
1 teaspoon grated fresh ginger

1 kg/2 lb large prawns, peeled and deveined, tails left on
2 tablespoons vegetable oil
Sea salt
Ground black pepper

1 Prepare the grill for direct cooking over high heat (230–290°C/450–550°F).

2 Combine the sauce ingredients in a small serving bowl.

3 Whisk the glaze ingredients in a large bowl until smooth.

4 Coat the prawns with the vegetable oil in another large bowl and season evenly with salt and pepper.

5 Brush the cooking grates clean. Grill the prawns over **direct high heat** for 2–4 minutes, with the lid closed as much as possible and turning once or twice, until they are firm to the touch and just turning opaque in the centre. Transfer the prawns to the large bowl with the glaze and toss to coat.

6 Arrange the prawns on a serving dish and serve warm with the sauce.

SEARED TUNA WITH CUCUMBER-RADISH SALAD

SERVES: 4
PREP TIME: 15 MINUTES
GRILLING TIME: 2–4 MINUTES

SALAD
1 shallot, thinly sliced into rings
1 cucumber, cut crossways into 3-mm/⅛-inch slices
6 radishes, thinly sliced
1 tablespoon wholegrain mustard
Sea salt

SAUCE
1 tablespoon balsamic vinegar
1 tablespoon runny honey

4 tuna fillets, each 175–250 g/6–8 oz and 2.5–3.5 cm/1–1½
   inches thick
Vegetable oil
Ground black pepper

1 Combine the salad ingredients in a large bowl then season with salt. Set aside at room temperature until ready to serve, stirring occasionally.

2 Prepare the grill for direct cooking over high heat (230–290°C/450–550°F).

3 Combine the sauce ingredients in a small bowl.

4 Lightly brush the tuna fillets with oil and season evenly with salt and pepper.

5 Brush the cooking grates clean. Grill the tuna over **direct high heat** for 2–4 minutes, with the lid open and turning once, just until seared on both sides but still raw inside. Remove from the grill and cut the tuna crossways into 5-mm/¼-inch slices. Divide the salad evenly between serving plates and top with sliced tuna. Drizzle the sauce over.

PRAWN AND SAUSAGE SKEWERS WITH ROMESCO SAUCE

SERVES: 4-6
PREP TIME: 15 MINUTES
GRILLING TIME: 2–4 MINUTES
SPECIAL EQUIPMENT: 8 METAL OR BAMBOO SKEWERS
   (IF USING BAMBOO, SOAK IN WATER FOR AT LEAST
   30 MINUTES)

SAUCE
2 garlic cloves
3 roasted red peppers (from a jar), drained
1–2 slices rustic bread, crusts removed, cubed, about
   40 g/1½ oz in total
25 g/1 oz flaked almonds, toasted
1 tablespoon sherry vinegar
1 teaspoon smoked paprika
½ teaspoon sea salt
Extra-virgin olive oil

500 g/1 lb large prawns, peeled and deveined, tails left on
500 g/1 lb fully cooked smoked spicy sausages, cut crossways
   into 1-cm/½-inch pieces

1 lemon, cut into wedges

1 Whizz the garlic in a food processor or blender until finely chopped. Add the peppers, bread and almonds and process to combine. Add the vinegar, paprika and salt and, with the motor running, slowly add 4 tablespoons oil. Blend until almost smooth. If the sauce is too thick, add about 1 tablespoon of water and blend.

2 Prepare the grill for direct cooking over high heat (230–290°C/450–550°F).

3 Thread the prawns and sausage pieces alternately on to eight skewers. Lightly brush with oil.

4 Brush the cooking grates clean. Grill the skewers over **direct high heat** for 2–4 minutes, with the lid closed as much as possible and turning once or twice, until the prawns are firm to the touch and just turning opaque in the centre. Remove from the grill and serve warm with the sauce and lemon wedges.

RED SNAPPER WITH CAPER-PARSLEY BUTTER

SERVES: 4
PREP TIME: 10 MINUTES
GRILLING TIME: 4–5 MINUTES

125 g/4 oz unsalted butter
2 tablespoons finely chopped flat-leaf parsley
1 tablespoon fresh lemon juice
1 tablespoon small capers, rinsed

4 red snapper fillets or sea bass fillets (with skin), each
    125–150 g/4–5 oz and about 1 cm/½ inch thick
Extra-virgin olive oil
Sea salt
Ground black pepper

1 Prepare the grill for direct cooking over high heat (230–290°C/450–550°F).

2 Melt the butter in a small saucepan over a medium heat. Add the parsley, lemon juice and capers and stir to combine. Remove from the heat and keep warm while you grill the fish.

3 Lightly brush both sides of the fillets with oil and season evenly with salt and pepper. Brush the cooking grates clean. Grill the fillets, flesh side down first, over **direct high heat** for 4–5 minutes, with the lid closed as much as possible and carefully turning with a spatula after 3 minutes, until the fish just barely begins to flake when you poke it with the tip of a knife.

4 Remove from the grill and serve warm over a bed of sautéed spinach, if liked, with the butter sauce spooned over the top.

SALMON STEAKS WITH SUN-DRIED TOMATO DRESSING

SERVES: 4
PREP TIME: 10 MINUTES
GRILLING TIME: 8–11 MINUTES

1 tablespoon red wine vinegar
2 teaspoons chopped oregano
½ teaspoon crushed red chilli flakes
Sea salt
Extra-virgin olive oil
6 tablespoons sun-dried tomatoes in olive oil, drained, patted
    dry and roughly chopped

4 salmon steaks, each 175–250 g/6–8 oz and about 2.5 cm/
    1 inch thick, pin bones removed
Ground black pepper

1 Prepare the grill for direct cooking over high heat (230–290°C/450–550°F).

2 Whisk the vinegar, oregano, chilli flakes and ¼ teaspoon salt in a bowl. Gradually whisk in 4 tablespoons of oil. Stir in the sun-dried tomatoes. Set the dressing aside until ready to use.

3 Brush the salmon on both sides with oil and season evenly with salt and pepper.

4 Brush the cooking grates clean. Grill the salmon over **direct high heat** for 6–8 minutes, with the lid closed as much as possible, until you can lift the steaks off the cooking grate without sticking. Turn the steaks over and cook to your desired doneness, 2–3 minutes for medium rare.

5 Transfer each salmon steak to a plate. Spoon the dressing evenly over the top and serve immediately.

TUNA STEAKS WITH LEMON VINAIGRETTE

SERVES: 4
PREP TIME: 15 MINUTES
GRILLING TIME: ABOUT 8 MINUTES

VINAIGRETTE
2 tablespoons extra-virgin olive oil
Finely grated zest and juice of 1 lemon
1 small shallot, finely diced

4 tuna steaks, each about 250 g/8 oz and 2.5 cm/1 inch thick
½ teaspoon sea salt
¼ teaspoon ground black pepper
Lemon wedges
4 tablespoons small basil leaves *or* roughly chopped basil

1 Prepare the grill for direct cooking over high heat (230–290°C/450–550°F).

2 Whisk the vinaigrette ingredients in a small bowl until well blended. Coat the tuna steaks on both sides with the vinaigrette and season evenly with the salt and pepper.

3 Brush the cooking grates clean. Grill the tuna over **direct high heat** for about 8 minutes, with the lid closed as much as possible and turning once, until just turning opaque throughout. Remove from the grill.

4 Serve warm with lemon wedges and fresh basil sprinkled on top.

GRILLED POTATO WEDGES WITH FRESH HERBS AND BUTTER

SERVES: 4
PREP TIME: 10 MINUTES
GRILLING TIME: 8–10 MINUTES

2 tablespoons extra-virgin olive oil
½ teaspoon sea salt
½ teaspoon ground black pepper
2 large King Edward potatoes, each cut into 8 wedges

25 g/1 oz unsalted butter, melted
1 teaspoon Dijon mustard

4 tablespoons finely chopped herbs, such as rosemary, thyme, chives, dill and flat-leaf parsley

1 Prepare the grill for direct cooking over medium heat (180–230°C/350–450°F).

2 Combine the oil, salt and pepper in a bowl. Add the potato wedges to the bowl and toss to coat evenly.

3 Brush the cooking grates clean. Grill the potatoes over **direct medium heat** for 8–10 minutes, with the lid closed as much as possible and turning occasionally, until they are golden brown and quite tender. Transfer the potatoes back to the bowl.

4 Mix the butter and mustard in a small bowl. Drizzle over the potatoes. Add the herbs and stir to coat the potatoes evenly. Serve warm.

AUBERGINE AND TOMATO SALAD

SERVES: 4
PREP TIME: 10 MINUTES
GRILLING TIME: ABOUT 8 MINUTES

2 large rounded aubergines, cut crossways into 1-cm/½-inch slices
2 beefsteak tomatoes, cut crossways into 1-cm/½-inch slices
Extra-virgin olive oil
Sea salt
Ground black pepper

500 g/1 lb mozzarella cheese, cut into 8-mm/⅓-inch slices
10 basil leaves

1 Prepare the grill for direct cooking over medium heat (180–230°C/350–450°F).

2 Brush the aubergine and tomato slices with oil and season evenly with salt and pepper. Brush the cooking grates clean. Grill over **direct medium heat**, with the lid closed as much as possible and turning once, until the vegetables are tender and nicely marked. The aubergines will take about 8 minutes and the tomatoes will take 2–4 minutes. Remove from the grill as they are done.

3 Divide the aubergines, tomatoes, cheese and basil between four plates. Drizzle with a little more olive oil or your favourite salad dressing, if liked.

ASPARAGUS WITH GREEN GODDESS DIP

SERVES: 6
PREP TIME: 10 MINUTES
GRILLING TIME: 6-8 MINUTES

DIP
4 tablespoons flat-leaf parsley
2 spring onions (white and light green parts only), coarsely chopped
2 tablespoons roughly chopped tarragon
150 ml/¼ pint soured cream
75 ml/3 fl oz mayonnaise
2 tablespoons fresh lemon juice
2 tablespoons small capers, rinsed

1 kg/2 lb asparagus
2 tablespoons extra-virgin olive oil
1 teaspoon sea salt

1 Prepare the grill for direct cooking over medium heat (180–230°C/350–450°F).

2 Pulse the parsley, spring onions and tarragon in a food processor until finely chopped. Add the soured cream, mayonnaise and lemon juice and process until smooth. Add the capers and pulse until combined. Transfer to a serving bowl and refrigerate until ready to serve.

3 Remove and discard the tough bottom of each asparagus spear by grasping at each end and bending it gently until it snaps at its natural point of tenderness, usually about two-thirds of the way down the spear.

4 Spread the asparagus on a large plate. Drizzle with the oil and season with the salt. Roll the spears in the oil until they are evenly coated.

5 Brush the cooking grates clean. Grill the asparagus (laid at right-angles to the bars of the grate) over **direct medium heat** for 6–8 minutes, with the lid closed as much as possible and turning occasionally, until browned in spots but not charred. Remove from the grill and serve warm with the dip.

APRICOT PIE À LA MODE SUNDAES

SERVES: 6
PREP TIME: 15 MINUTES
GRILLING TIME: 6–8 MINUTES

275 ml/9 fl oz caramel sauce
2 tablespoons Scotch whisky *or* rum
6 firm but ripe apricots, halved lengthways
25 g/1 oz unsalted butter, melted

Vanilla ice cream
75 g/3 oz shortbread biscuits, coarsely crushed
25 g/1 oz sliced almonds, toasted and chopped

1 Prepare the grill for direct cooking over medium heat (180–230°C/350–450°F).

2 Mix the caramel sauce and whisky in a bowl. Set aside. Toss the apricots with the melted butter in another bowl.

3 Brush the cooking grates clean. Grill the apricots, cut side down first, over **direct medium heat** for 6–8 minutes, with the lid closed as much as possible and turning once, until heated through.

4 Arrange two apricot halves over two scoops of ice cream in six sundae dishes. Drizzle each with 2–3 tablespoons of caramel-whisky sauce and top with about 2 tablespoons of biscuit crumbs. Decorate with a sprinkle of almonds and serve immediately.

Warm fruit pie à la mode is a quintessential summertime pleasure, and this recipe delivers all the taste without all the work. Sweet, tart apricots and crunchy biscuit crumbs stand in for the pie, while ice cream and caramel sauce add the delicious finishing touches.

GRILLED CHOCOLATE SANDWICHES

8 slices rustic white bread, each about 1 cm/½ inch thick
(from a large loaf, slices should be roughly 16 × 10 cm/
6½ × 4 inches)
8 teaspoons orange marmalade
250 g/8 oz good-quality plain chocolate
75 g/3 oz unsalted butter, melted
2 tablespoons icing sugar

1 Prepare the grill for direct cooking over medium-low heat
(about 180°C/350°F).

2 Lay four of the bread slices on a work surface.
Spread 2 teaspoons of marmalade on each. Place a
quarter of the chocolate on each of the four slices,
breaking the chocolate into pieces to fit the shape of
the bread. Top each slice with one of the remaining
slices of bread and brush melted butter on to both
sides of each sandwich.

3 Brush the cooking grates clean. Grill the
sandwiches over *direct medium-low heat* for 4–5
minutes, with the lid closed as much as possible
and turning once, until the bread is golden brown
and crispy and the chocolate is melted. Remove the
sandwiches from the grill and let them rest for about
1 minute. Using a large serrated knife, cut each
sandwich in half on the diagonal or into three pieces.
Lightly dust the sandwiches with icing sugar and
serve.

CARAMELIZED PEACHES WITH BRIE AND ALMONDS

SERVES: 4
PREP TIME: 10 MINUTES
GRILLING TIME: 8–10 MINUTES

50 g/2 oz soft brown sugar
25 g/1 oz unsalted butter, melted
4 ripe peaches, halved
2 tablespoons vegetable oil
150 g/5 oz Brie cheese, cut into 8 slices, each about 5 mm/
    ¼ inch thick
2 tablespoons chopped toasted almonds

1 Prepare the grill for direct cooking over medium heat (180–230°C/350–450°F).

2 Combine the brown sugar and butter in a small bowl.

3 Lightly brush the peaches with the oil. Brush the cooking grates clean. Grill the peaches, cut side down, over **direct medium heat** for 5–6 minutes, with the lid closed as much as possible, until the peaches are lightly charred and beginning to soften. Turn the peaches over and top evenly with the brown sugar-butter mixture. Continue to grill for 3–4 more minutes until the peaches are tender.

4 Remove the peaches from the grill and top each with a slice of cheese. Leave for about 5 minutes to let the cheese melt as the peaches cool. Serve with almonds sprinkled on top.

WEEKEND TREATS

WEEKEND TREATS

PUB-STYLE LUNCHES

90 WARM FOCACCIA SANDWICHES WITH
   BURRATA CHEESE

91 PORTOBELLO, SPINACH AND EMMENTAL QUESADILLAS

SPORTS AFTERNOON/MOVIE NIGHT

102 SOUTHERN STEAK WITH ROASTED TOMATOES

122 SODA CAN CHICKEN

UTTERLY INDULGENT

98 PROVENÇAL STEAKS WITH CARAMELIZED SHALLOTS

113 FOIL-WRAPPED SPARERIBS

130 **SALMON SLIDERS WITH SPICY GINGER SAUCE AND PICKLED VEGETABLES**

123 **TOASTED CHICKEN PANINI WITH TOMATO AND ROCKET**

125 **TURKEY WRAPS WITH MINT CHUTNEY**

126 **BEER MARINATED-MAHI-MAHI WITH GUACAMOLE**

97 **BLUE CHEESE BURGERS WITH RED ONIONS**

137 **WARM BANANA CHOCOLATE SUNDAES**

FARMHOUSE BREAKFAST

SERVES: 4
PREP TIME: 15 MINUTES
GRILLING TIME: 19–26 MINUTES
SPECIAL EQUIPMENT: 30-CM/12-INCH CAST-IRON
    FRYING PAN

8 large eggs
Butter
4 slices crusty bread, each about 2.5 cm/1 inch thick
8 thick bacon rashers
¼ teaspoon sea salt
¼ teaspoon ground black pepper
1 garlic clove, halved, *or* jam

1 Prepare the grill for direct cooking over medium heat (180–230°C/350–450°F).

2 Crack all the eggs gently into a large bowl, keeping the yolks intact. Butter the bread slices on both sides.

3 Brush the cooking grates clean. Arrange the bacon in a single layer in a 30-cm/12-inch cast-iron frying pan, with pieces on the bottom and around the sides. Grill over **direct medium heat**, for 15–20 minutes, with the lid closed as much as possible and turning and rearranging the bacon as it cooks and shrinks, until crisp. Drain the bacon on kitchen paper then wrap in foil and keep warm on the grill's warming rack or in a low oven.

4 Use a large serving spoon to scoop out about half the bacon grease from the pan, leaving a 3-mm/⅛-inch layer on the bottom. Gently pour all the eggs into the pan at once and season with the salt and pepper. Place the bread directly on the grill and cook both the eggs and the bread over **direct medium heat**, with the lid closed as much as possible, until the eggs begin to cloud over on top (the yolks will be partially runny) and the bread is toasted. The eggs will take 4–6 minutes and the toast will take 3–4 minutes. Turn the bread once during grilling. Transfer the toast to the warming rack or oven with the bacon.

5 Using a serving spoon or spatula, cut the eggs apart and scoop them out of the pan one at a time. If savoury toast is liked, rub each side with the cut side of the garlic clove while the toast is still warm. Serve the eggs and toast immediately with the bacon.

BREAKFAST TOMATOES

SERVES: 4–6
PREP TIME: 15 MINUTES
GRILLING TIME: 5–8 MINUTES

3 tablespoons extra-virgin olive oil
1 tablespoon finely chopped thyme
1 teaspoon finely chopped oregano
½ teaspoon sea salt
¼ teaspoon ground black pepper
6 plum tomatoes, about 750 g/1½ lb in total, cut into 1-cm/
   ½-inch slices
1 baguette, cut crossways on the diagonal into 1-cm/½-inch
   slices
4 tablespoons freshly grated Parmesan cheese
1 teaspoon balsamic vinegar
4 tablespoons finely chopped basil

1 Prepare the grill for direct cooking over medium heat
(180–230°C/350–450°F).

2 Combine 1 tablespoon of the oil, the thyme, oregano, salt
and pepper in a large bowl. Add the tomato slices to the bowl
and turn them gently to coat each slice thoroughly.

3 Lightly brush the baguette slices with the remaining 2
tablespoons of oil. Brush the cooking grates clean. Grill the
baguette slices over ***direct medium heat*** for 1–2 minutes, with
the lid closed as much as possible and turning once, until
toasted. Transfer to a roasting tray and arrange in a single layer.

4 Grill the tomatoes over ***direct medium heat*** for 3–4 minutes,
with the lid closed as much as possible, until they are nicely
marked on the first side. Turn the slices over and sprinkle each
with cheese. Close the lid and grill the second side for 1–2
minutes until the tomatoes are soft but not falling apart and
the cheese has begun to melt. Remove from the grill and place
each tomato on a piece of grilled bread. Drizzle each tomato
slice with a few drops of the vinegar. Sprinkle with the basil and
serve immediately.

RED FLANNEL HASH

SERVES: 4–6
PREP TIME: 30 MINUTES
GRILLING TIME: 50–57 MINUTES
SPECIAL EQUIPMENT: 30-CM/12-INCH CAST-IRON
    FRYING PAN

8 thick bacon rashers, coarsely chopped
½ onion, thinly sliced
2 red beetroots, about 500 g/1 lb in total, cut into
    1-cm/½-inch pieces
1 teaspoon sea salt
½ teaspoon ground black pepper
2 tablespoons chopped thyme
1 large garlic clove, finely chopped
2 King Edward potatoes, about 750 g/1½ lb in total,
    cut into 1-cm/½-inch pieces
3 tablespoons champagne vinegar *or* white wine vinegar
125 g/4 oz goats' cheese, crumbled

8 large eggs, scrambled or fried (optional)
Fresh fruit such as orange slices (optional)

1 Prepare the grill for direct cooking over medium heat (180–230°C/350–450°F).

2 Brush the cooking grates clean. Spread the bacon out in a 30-cm/12-inch cast-iron frying pan. Grill over **direct medium heat** for 15–17 minutes, with the lid closed as much as possible and stirring the bacon pieces occasionally, until crisp. Using a slotted spoon, transfer the bacon to kitchen paper to drain. Carefully remove about 2 tablespoons of the bacon fat from the pan and discard.

3 Combine the onion, beetroot, salt, pepper and thyme in the pan and cook over **direct medium heat** for 10 minutes, with the lid closed as much as possible and stirring once. Add the garlic and potatoes and cook for 25–30 minutes, with the lid closed and stirring and scraping the bottom of the pan occasionally, until the beetroot and potatoes are tender and there are browned bits sticking to the pan.

4 Stir in the vinegar and all but 4 tablespoons of the bacon pieces. Top the hash with the cheese and the remaining bacon. Serve immediately with scrambled or fried eggs and fresh fruit, if liked.

WARM FOCACCIA SANDWICHES WITH BURRATA CHEESE

SERVES: 6
PREP TIME: 30 MINUTES
GRILLING TIME: 9–10 MINUTES

PESTO

75 g/3 oz basil
75 g/3 oz Parmesan cheese, freshly grated
4 tablespoons pine nuts, lightly toasted and cooled
1 large garlic clove
Extra-virgin olive oil
3 tablespoons white balsamic vinegar
Sea salt
Ground black pepper

SANDWICH

2 large peppers, 1 red and 1 yellow, each cut into 4 pieces
1 large red onion, cut crossways into 8-mm/⅓-inch slices
6 ciabatta rolls, halved horizontally
3 ripe tomatoes, cut into 8-mm/⅓-inch slices
250 g/8 oz *burrata* cheese *or* fresh mozzarella cheese, cut into irregular 8-mm/⅓-inch slices
50 g/2 oz baby rocket

1 Combine the basil, Parmesan cheese, pine nuts and garlic in a food processor and process to a coarse purée. With the motor running, gradually add 125 ml/4 fl oz oil through the feed tube and process until almost smooth. Transfer the pesto to a small bowl. Stir in the vinegar and season with salt and pepper.

2 Prepare the grill for direct cooking over medium heat (180–230°C/350–450°F).

3 Lightly brush both sides of the peppers and onion and the cut side of the rolls with oil.

4 Brush the cooking grates clean. Grill the peppers and onion over **direct medium heat** for about 8 minutes, with the lid closed as much as possible and turning once or twice, until browned in spots and tender. During the last minute of grilling time, toast the rolls over direct heat, cut side down, until lightly browned and grill marks appear.

5 Place the bottom half of the rolls, grilled side up, on a roasting tray. Spread a layer of pesto on the rolls. Top with the grilled peppers and onion slices, then the tomato slices, slightly overlapping. Dollop the burrata cheese over the tomatoes. Place the sandwiches on the roasting tray back on the grill, topping side up. Grill over **direct medium heat** for 1–2 minutes, with the lid closed, until the cheese softens and begins to melt slightly. Remove the sandwiches from the grill. Put the rocket on top of the cheese. Spread some of the remaining pesto (you may not need all of it) on the cut side of the top half of the rolls. Serve immediately.

PORTOBELLO, SPINACH AND EMMENTAL QUESADILLAS

SERVES: 4
PREP TIME: 15 MINUTES
GRILLING TIME: 16–21 MINUTES

AÏOLI
125 ml/4 fl oz mayonnaise
2 tablespoons fresh lime juice
1 tablespoon minced chipotle chillies in adobo sauce
1 tablespoon runny honey
1 teaspoon finely chopped garlic

QUESADILLAS
4 large portobello mushrooms, stalks and gills removed
Extra-virgin olive oil
400 g/13 oz Emmental cheese, grated
8 flour tortillas (20 cm/8 inches)
150 g/5 oz baby spinach

1 Whisk the aïoli ingredients in a serving bowl until smooth. Cover and refrigerate until ready to serve.

2 Prepare the grill for direct cooking over medium heat (180–230°C/350–450°F).

3 Generously brush the mushroom caps with oil. Brush the cooking grates clean. Grill the mushrooms over **direct medium heat** for 12–15 minutes, with the lid closed as much as possible, turning occasionally and, if necessary to prevent them from drying out, brushing with a bit more oil, until tender. Remove from the grill and cut into thin slices.

4 Decrease the temperature of the grill to low heat (130–180°C/250–350°F).

5 Assemble each quesadilla by spreading 4 tablespoons cheese on one half of each tortilla. Top the cheese with a quarter of the spinach, a quarter of the sliced mushrooms and another 4 tablespoons cheese. Fold the empty side of the tortillas over the fillings.

6 Brush the outside of the tortillas lightly with oil and grill over **direct low heat** for 4–6 minutes, with the lid closed as much as possible and turning once, until golden on both sides. Cut the quesadillas into wedges and serve warm with the aïoli.

STEAK WITH BLACK BEANS, CORN SALSA AND COTIJA CHEESE

SERVES: 4–6
PREP TIME: 30 MINUTES
GRILLING TIME: 33–45 MINUTES

SALSA
2 fresh corn cobs, outer leaves and silk removed
250 g/8 oz cherry tomatoes, quartered
1 small red onion, finely chopped
2 tablespoons finely chopped fresh basil or coriander
2–3 teaspoons finely chopped serrano chilli
2 teaspoons fresh lime juice
Extra-virgin olive oil
Sea salt
Ground black pepper

1 teaspoon ancho chilli powder
1 teaspoon ground cumin
750 g–1-kg/1½–2-lb beef rump joint, excess fat and skin removed
475-g/15-oz can black beans, rinsed
2 romaine lettuce hearts, thinly sliced
50 g/2 oz cotija or Parmesan cheese, crumbled

1 Prepare the grill for direct and indirect cooking over medium heat (180–230°C/350–450°F).

2 Brush the cooking grates clean. Grill the corn over **direct medium heat** for 10–15 minutes, with the lid closed as much as possible and turning occasionally until tender. Remove from the grill, allow to cool and cut the kernels off over a bowl. Stir in the remaining salsa ingredients, including 2 tablespoons oil, ½ teaspoon salt and ¼ teaspoon pepper. Set aside. Mix 2 tablespoons oil with the chilli powder, cumin, 1 teaspoon salt and ½ teaspoon pepper in a bowl, and smear all over the meat. Let stand at room temperature for 15–30 minutes before grilling.

3 Grill the meat over **direct medium heat** for 8–10 minutes, with the lid closed as much as possible and turning once, until well marked on both sides. Move over **indirect medium heat**, close the lid, and cook to your desired doneness, 15–20 minutes for medium rare. Remove from the grill and rest for about 5 minutes. Cut the meat across the grain into thin slices.

4 Cook the beans with 1 tablespoon oil for about 5 minutes in a saucepan over a low heat, stirring once or twice. Remove from the heat. Serve the steak with beans, lettuce, cheese and salsa.

RIB-EYE STEAKS WITH DRY ANCHO RUB

SERVES: 4
PREP TIME: 5 MINUTES
GRILLING TIME: 6–8 MINUTES

RUB
1 tablespoon ancho chilli powder
2 teaspoons soft brown sugar
2 teaspoons sea salt
1 teaspoon ground cumin
1 teaspoon dried oregano
1 teaspoon ground black pepper

4 boneless rib-eye steaks, each 250–300 g/8–10 oz and about
    2.5 cm/1 inch thick, trimmed of excess fat
Extra-virgin olive oil

1 Prepare the grill for direct cooking over high heat
(230–290°C/450–550°F).

2 Mix the rub ingredients in a small bowl.

3 Lightly coat the steaks on both sides with oil and season
evenly with the rub. Allow the steaks to stand at room
temperature for 15–30 minutes before grilling.

4 Brush the cooking grates clean. Grill the steaks over
direct high heat, with the lid closed as much as possible and
turning once (if flare-ups occur, move the steaks temporarily
over indirect heat), until cooked to your desired doneness,
6–8 minutes for medium rare. Remove from the grill and
leave to rest for 3–5 minutes. Serve warm.

STEAK SANDWICHES WITH ONION MARMALADE

SERVES: 4
PREP TIME: 30 MINUTES
GRILLING TIME: 10–12 MINUTES

CREAM
125 ml/4 fl oz mayonnaise
2 tablespoons prepared horseradish
½ teaspoon mustard powder

Extra-virgin olive oil
500 g/1 lb red onions, thinly sliced
2 teaspoons finely chopped garlic
1 teaspoon soft dark brown sugar
4 tablespoons balsamic vinegar
Sea salt
Ground black pepper

625 g/1¼ lb sirloin steak, about 2.5 cm/1 inch thick

2 tablespoons white wine vinegar
250 g/8 oz green cabbage, shredded
1 raw golden beetroot, about 5 cm/2 inches in diameter, peeled
    and coarsely grated

8 slices sourdough bread, each about 15 × 7 cm/6 × 3 inches
    and 1 cm/½ inch thick
4 thin slices Gruyère cheese

1 Combine the cream ingredients in a small bowl. Cover and chill.

2 Warm 2 tablespoons oil in a large heavy non-stick frying pan over a medium-high heat. Add the onions, 1 teaspoon of the garlic and the brown sugar. Cover the pan and cook for about 12 minutes, stirring occasionally, until the onions are deep golden brown. Add the vinegar and stir for 2–3 minutes, uncovered, until it is absorbed. Remove from the heat and season with salt and pepper.

3 Prepare the grill for direct cooking over medium-high heat (200–260°C/400–500°F).

4 Brush the steak on both sides with oil and season evenly with salt and pepper. Allow the steak to stand at room temperature for 15–30 minutes before grilling.

5 Whisk 3 tablespoons oil, the vinegar and the remaining garlic in a bowl. Add the cabbage and the beetroot. Toss to coat well. Season with salt and pepper. Leave to stand at room temperature for 15–20 minutes.

6 Brush the cooking grates clean. Grill the steak over **direct medium-high heat**, with the lid closed as much as possible and turning once or twice (if flare-ups occur, transfer the steak temporarily to indirect heat), until cooked to your desired doneness, 8–10 minutes for medium rare. Remove from the grill and leave to rest for 3–5 minutes.

7 While the steak rests, grill the bread slices over **direct medium-high** heat for about 1 minute until the bottoms are crispy and golden. Turn them over and arrange the cheese on top of four slices. Close the lid and grill for about 1 minute until the cheese has melted and the bottoms are crispy and golden. Transfer to a work surface.

8 Cut the steaks into thin slices. Build the sandwiches with equal amounts of the cream, steak and onion marmalade. Serve with the cabbage and beetroot slaw.

BEEF AND SUN-DRIED TOMATO STUFFED MUSHROOMS

SERVES: 4
PREP TIME: 30 MINUTES
GRILLING TIME: 19–26 MINUTES
SPECIAL EQUIPMENT: INSTANT-READ MEAT
    THERMOMETER

MARINADE
6 tablespoons extra-virgin olive oil
1 tablespoon balsamic vinegar
¾ teaspoon garlic salt
¼ teaspoon ground black pepper

4 large portobello mushrooms, each 10–12 cm/4–5 inches
    in diameter

FILLING
500 g/1 lb minced beef (80% lean)
25 g/1 oz panko breadcrumbs
½ mild onion, finely chopped
3 tablespoons finely chopped parsley
3 tablespoons finely chopped sun-dried tomatoes in olive oil
1 large egg
1 teaspoon Worcestershire sauce
½ teaspoon garlic salt
¼ teaspoon ground black pepper

50 g/2 oz fontina cheese, grated

1 Whisk all the marinade ingredients in a bowl.

2 Wipe the mushrooms clean with a damp cloth or kitchen paper. Remove and discard the stalks. Using a teaspoon, carefully scrape out and discard the gills from the mushroom caps. Place the mushrooms, gill side up, on a roasting tray and brush them on both sides with the marinade. Set aside at room temperature while you make the filling and prepare the grill for direct and indirect cooking over medium heat (180–230°C/350–450°F).

3 Gently combine the filling ingredients in a bowl until evenly incorporated.

4 Brush the cooking grates clean. Grill the mushrooms, gill side down, over **direct medium heat** for 4–6 minutes, with the lid closed, until the mushrooms begin to soften. Turn the mushrooms over and move them over **indirect medium heat**. Spoon equal amounts of the filling on top of each mushroom and continue grilling for 15–20 minutes until a thermometer inserted horizontally through the top of each registers 70°C/160°F. During the last minute of grilling time, top each mushroom with an equal amount of the cheese. Remove from the grill and serve with grilled bread, if liked.

BLUE CHEESE BURGERS WITH RED ONIONS

SERVES: 4
PREP TIME: 15 MINUTES
GRILLING TIME: 6–8 MINUTES

750 g/1½ lb minced beef (80% lean)
175 g/6 oz blue cheese, coarsely crumbled
Sea salt
Ground black pepper

8 pieces red onion, each about 5 mm/¼ inch thick and
    7.5 cm/3 inches across
Extra-virgin olive oil
8 small soft rolls, halved
40 g/1½ oz baby rocket

1 Prepare the grill for direct cooking over medium heat
(180-230°C/350–450°F).

2 Divide the mince into eight equal portions. Split each portion in half and shape into two burgers, each 7.5 cm/3 inches in diameter. Arrange eight burgers on a work surface and place a tablespoon of the cheese in the centre of each. Top with a second burger and squeeze the edges together, sealing the cheese inside. Season evenly with salt and pepper.

3 Keeping the onion slices intact, brush them with oil and season with salt and pepper.

4 Brush the cooking grates clean. Grill the burgers and onion slices over *direct medium heat* for 6–8 minutes, with the lid closed as much as possible and turning once, until the meat is cooked to medium and the onions are slightly charred. During the last minute of grilling time, toast the cut side of the rolls over direct heat.

5 Build the hamburgers with some rocket, a burger, more blue cheese and an onion slice. Serve warm.

PROVENÇAL STEAKS WITH CARAMELIZED SHALLOTS

SERVES: 4
PREP TIME: 15 MINUTES
GRILLING TIME: 28–35 MINUTES

1 tablespoon herbes de Provence
Sea salt
Ground black pepper
4 sirloin steaks, each 300–375 g/10–12 oz and about 2.5 cm/
    1 inch thick, trimmed of excess fat
Extra-virgin olive oil
250–300 g/8–10 oz shallots, cut into 5-mm/¼-inch rings
4 small courgettes, halved lengthways
1 tablespoon finely chopped flat-leaf parsley
¼ teaspoon sherry vinegar

1 Prepare the grill for direct cooking over medium heat (180–230°C/350–450°F).

2 Mix the herbes de Provence with 2 teaspoons salt and ½ teaspoon pepper in a small bowl. Lightly coat the steaks on both sides with oil and season evenly with the herb mixture. Allow the steaks to stand at room temperature for 15–30 minutes before grilling.

3 Mix the shallots with 2 tablespoons oil in a bowl. Spread the shallots in a single layer on one end of a sheet of aluminium foil, about 30 × 60 cm/12 × 24 inches. Fold the foil over the shallots and bring the ends together to secure them, folding them down tightly. Fold and tightly secure the two remaining sides to create a foil parcel. Brush the courgettes with oil.

4 Brush the cooking grates clean. Grill the shallot parcel over **direct medium heat** for 12–15 minutes, with the lid closed as much as possible and turning the parcel once or twice, until the shallots are tender. Carefully open the foil with tongs and continue to cook the shallots for 10–12 minutes more, stirring them once or twice, until golden brown. During the last 4–6 minutes of grilling time, grill the courgettes over **direct medium heat**, turning once, until crisp-tender. Remove from the grill and set aside. Increase the temperature of the grill to high heat (230–290°C/450–550°F).

5 Grill the steaks over **direct high heat**, with the lid closed as much as possible and turning once or twice (if flare-ups occur, move the steaks temporarily over indirect heat), until cooked to your desired doneness, 6–8 minutes for medium rare. Remove from the grill and leave to rest for 3–5 minutes.

6 Transfer the shallots to a small bowl. Add the parsley and vinegar and season with salt and pepper. Mix well. Cut the courgettes on the diagonal into bite-sized pieces. Serve the shallots and courgettes warm with the steaks.

PERUVIAN BEEF KEBABS AND SWEETCORN

SERVES: 6
PREP TIME: 30 MINUTES
GRILLING TIME: 22–30 MINUTES
SPECIAL EQUIPMENT: METAL OR BAMBOO SKEWERS
(IF USING BAMBOO, SOAK IN WATER FOR AT LEAST
30 MINUTES)

PASTE
2 red peppers
6 garlic cloves, coarsely chopped
2 tablespoons red wine vinegar
2 teaspoons ground cumin
1 teaspoon smoked paprika
1 teaspoon sea salt
½ teaspoon ground black pepper
125 ml/4 fl oz extra-virgin olive oil

1 kg/2 lb sirloin steak, about 3 cm/1¼ inches thick, cut into
    3-cm/1¼-inch cubes
3 fresh corn cobs, outer leaves and silk removed, each cut
    crossways into 6 pieces
1 large red pepper, cut into 3-cm/1¼-inch squares

1 Prepare the grill for direct cooking over medium heat
(180–230°C/350–450°F).

2 Brush the cooking grates clean. Grill the red peppers over
direct medium heat for 12–15 minutes, with the lid closed as
much as possible and turning occasionally, until the skins are
blackened and blistered all over. Place the peppers in a bowl
and cover with clingfilm to trap the steam. Leave to stand for
10–15 minutes. Remove the peppers from the bowl and peel
away and discard the charred skins, stalks and seeds.

3 Combine the roasted peppers, garlic, vinegar, cumin,
paprika, salt and pepper in a food processor. Pulse until the
peppers are chopped. With the machine running, gradually add
the oil through the feed tube to make a thick paste.

4 Place the meat in a large bowl and pour in one-third of the
paste. Turn to coat the meat evenly. Reserve the remaining
paste to brush on the corn and serve as a sauce. Thread the
meat and peppers alternately on to skewers. Allow the kebabs
to stand at room temperature for 15–30 minutes before grilling.

5 Lightly brush the corn with some of the remaining paste.
Grill the corn over **direct medium heat** for 10–15 minutes, with
the lid closed as much as possible and turning several times,
until browned in spots and tender. At the same time, grill the
kebabs over **direct medium heat**, turning occasionally, until
the peppers are crisp-tender and the meat is cooked to your
desired doneness, 6–8 minutes for medium rare. Remove from
the grill as they are done. Serve the kebabs and corn warm with
the remaining paste.

LEG OF LAMB WITH DECONSTRUCTED PESTO

SERVES: 6–8
PREP TIME: 30 MINUTES
GRILLING TIME: 30–45 MINUTES

3 tablespoons extra-virgin olive oil
8 garlic cloves, finely chopped
1 boneless leg of lamb, about 1.5 kg/3 lb, butterflied and
    trimmed of excess fat
1 tablespoon sea salt
1½ teaspoons ground black pepper

3 plum tomatoes, thinly sliced
40 g/1½ oz basil leaves, torn into small pieces
175 g/6 oz pitted kalamata olives, halved
50 g/2 oz Parmesan cheese
50 g/2 oz toasted pine nuts

1 Mix the oil and garlic in a small bowl. Coat the lamb all over with the oil mixture and season evenly with the salt and pepper. Allow the lamb to stand at room temperature for 15–30 minutes before grilling.

2 Prepare the grill for direct and indirect cooking over medium heat (180–230°C/350–450°F).

3 Brush the cooking grates clean. Sear the lamb over **direct medium heat** for 10–15 minutes, with the lid closed as much as possible and turning once, until nicely browned on both sides. Slide the lamb over **indirect medium heat**, close the lid and cook to your desired doneness, 20–30 minutes for medium rare. Remove from the grill and leave to rest for 5–10 minutes.

4 Cut the lamb crossways into 5-mm/¼-inch slices and divide evenly between plates. Top with tomato slices, basil and olives. Using a vegetable peeler, shave wide ribbons of cheese over each serving and garnish with the pine nuts. Serve immediately.

SOUTHERN STEAK WITH ROASTED TOMATOES

SERVES: 4
PREP TIME: 15 MINUTES
GRILLING TIME: 16–21 MINUTES

PASTE
4 tablespoons extra-virgin olive oil
1 tablespoon cider vinegar
1 tablespoon chilli powder
1 tablespoon smoked paprika
2 teaspoons garlic powder
1 teaspoon ground cumin
½ teaspoon ground black pepper
Sea salt

1 kg/2 lb skirt steak, about 1.5 cm/¾ inch thick, trimmed of
    excess fat, cut into 30-cm/12-inch long pieces

4 plum tomatoes, cored and halved lengthways
2 tablespoons finely chopped flat-leaf parsley or basil (optional)

1 Prepare the grill for direct and indirect cooking over medium heat (180–230°C/350–450°F).

2 Whisk the paste ingredients, including 1½ teaspoons salt, in a small bowl. Put 2 tablespoons of the paste in a bowl and set aside.

3 Spread the remaining paste on both sides of the steaks. Allow them to stand at room temperature for 15–30 minutes.

4 Add the tomatoes to the bowl with the paste and toss to coat them lightly. Brush the cooking grates clean. Grill the tomatoes over **indirect medium heat** for 12–15 minutes, with the lid closed as much as possible and turning once, until they turn very soft and begin to darken in spots. Remove from the grill and season with salt.

5 Grill the steaks over **direct medium heat**, with the lid closed as much as possible and turning once or twice (if flare-ups occur, move the steaks temporarily over indirect heat), until cooked to your desired doneness, 4–6 minutes for medium rare. Remove from the grill and leave to rest for 3–5 minutes.

6 Cut the steaks across the grain into 8-mm/⅓-inch slices. Serve warm with the roasted tomatoes, and fresh herbs if liked.

What skirt steak lacks in tenderness, it certainly overcomes with rich beefy flavour, particularly if you smear it with a quick spice paste. While the steaks sizzle on one side of the grill, roast some plum tomatoes brushed with the same paste on the other side. Then slice the steaks nice and thin so no one notices its 'chewiness'.

Another good approach is to sear it first and then simmer it for about an hour or so in a dark, tomato-based chilli made with ale.

GREEN CHILLI LAMB BURGERS

SERVES: 4
PREP TIME: 10 MINUTES
GRILLING TIME: 8–10 MINUTES

BURGERS
500 g/1 lb minced lamb
4 tablespoons canned diced green chillies, drained
1 tablespoon paprika
1 teaspoon crushed red chilli flakes
1 teaspoon sea salt
½ teaspoon ground black pepper

4 onion burger buns
4 soft lettuce leaves
1 beefsteak tomato, cut into 4 slices
Mayonnaise (optional)

1 Prepare the grill for direct cooking over medium heat (180–230°C/350–450°F).

2 Gently mix the burger ingredients in a large bowl. Shape the mixture into four burgers of equal size and thickness, each about 1.5 cm/¾ inch thick. Using your thumb or the back of a spoon, make a shallow indentation about 2.5 cm/1 inch wide in the centre of each burger. This will help the burgers cook evenly and prevent them from puffing on the grill.

3 Brush the cooking grates clean. Grill the burgers over **direct medium heat** for 8–10 minutes, with the lid closed as much as possible and turning once, until cooked to medium doneness. During the last minute of grilling time, toast the burger buns over direct heat.

4 Build the burgers with a lettuce leaf, a tomato slice, and mayonnaise if liked. Serve warm.

ITALIAN SAUSAGES WITH PEPPERS AND ONIONS

SERVES: 4
PREP TIME: 10 MINUTES
GRILLING TIME: 28–33 MINUTES

2 tablespoons extra-virgin olive oil
1 tablespoon finely chopped garlic
1 teaspoon sea salt
½ teaspoon dried oregano
¼ teaspoon crushed red chilli flakes
3 peppers, 1 red, 1 yellow and 1 orange, cut into large pieces
1 onion, cut crossways into 5-mm/¼-inch slices

5 uncooked Italian sausages, each about 125 g/4 oz, pierced a few times with a fork

1 Prepare the grill for direct and indirect cooking over medium heat (180–230°C/350–450°F).

2 Whisk the oil, garlic, salt, oregano and chilli flakes in a bowl. Add the peppers and onion slices and turn to coat them evenly.

3 Brush the cooking grates clean. Grill the peppers and onion over **direct medium heat** for about 8 minutes, with the lid closed as much as possible and turning once or twice, until tender. Remove from the heat, cut the peppers into thin strips and cut the onions in half or separate into rings.

4 Grill the sausages over **indirect medium heat** for 20–25 minutes, with the lid closed as much as possible and turning occasionally, until thoroughly cooked. If you'd like to brown the sausages, cook them over **direct medium heat** during the last 3–5 minutes of grilling time, turning once. Remove from the grill and cut each sausage into three pieces. Put the peppers and onions on a serving plate and pile the sausage pieces on top. Serve warm.

LAMB SAUSAGE PIZZAS

SERVES: 4
PREP TIME: 30 MINUTES
GRILLING TIME: 12–20 MINUTES

SAUSAGE
250 g/8 oz minced lamb
1 teaspoon fennel seeds
1 teaspoon paprika
½ teaspoon ground cumin
½ teaspoon sea salt
¼ teaspoon ground cayenne pepper

625 g/1¼ lb ready-made pizza dough
Vegetable oil

375 g/12 oz cherry tomatoes
1 small rounded aubergine, cut crossways into 5-mm/
    ¼-inch slices
250 g/8 oz mozzarella cheese, grated
24 kalamata olives

1 Combine the sausage ingredients in a small frying pan and sauté the mixture for about 10 minutes until the lamb is cooked through. Remove with a slotted spoon and set aside until ready to use.

2 Prepare the grill for direct cooking over medium heat (180–230°C/350–450°F).

3 Divide the dough into four equal pieces. Lightly brush four 23-cm/9-inch squares of baking paper on one side with oil. Using your fingers, flatten each piece of dough on a sheet of baking paper to create four rounds. Each round should be about 20 cm/8 inches in diameter and 5 mm/¼ inch thick. Lightly brush the tops with oil. Let the rounds stand at room temperature for 5–10 minutes.

4 Brush the cooking grates clean. Grill the tomatoes and aubergine over **direct medium heat**, with the lid closed as much as possible and turning once or twice, until the tomato skins burst and the flesh becomes very soft and the aubergine is tender. The tomatoes will take about 5 minutes and the aubergine will take 8–10 minutes. Remove from the grill as they are done. Put the tomatoes in a bowl and crush with a spoon. When the aubergine is cool enough to handle, cut into 1-cm/½-inch pieces.

5 Place the dough on the cooking grate with the paper sides facing up. Grill over **direct medium heat** for 2–5 minutes, with the lid closed as much as possible and rotating as needed for even cooking, until the dough is well marked and firm on the underside. Peel off and discard the baking paper. Transfer the bases to a work surface with the grilled sides facing up.

6 Evenly divide the sausage, tomatoes, aubergine, cheese and olives over the bases. Return the pizzas to the grill and cook over **direct medium heat** for 2–5 minutes, with the lid closed as much as possible and rotating the pizzas occasionally for even cooking, until the cheese has melted and the bottoms of the bases are crisp. Transfer to a chopping board and cut into slices. Serve warm.

RACK OF LAMB WITH AUBERGINE-PEPPER SALAD

SERVES: 4
PREP TIME: 30 MINUTES
MARINATING TIME: 4–6 HOURS
GRILLING TIME: 21–28 MINUTES

MARINADE
250 ml/8 fl oz low-sodium soy sauce
125 g/4 oz soft light brown sugar
75 ml/3 fl oz rice vinegar
2 tablespoons toasted sesame oil
2 tablespoons finely chopped garlic
2 tablespoons grated fresh ginger

2 racks of lamb, each 8 bones and about 750 g/1½ lb,
    frenched and trimmed of excess fat

3 long, slender aubergines, about 375 g/12 oz in total
2 peppers, 1 red and 1 yellow
1 tablespoon rice vinegar
2 spring onions, thinly sliced (white and light green parts only)
4 tablespoons finely chopped fresh coriander
2 teaspoons toasted sesame seeds

1 Whisk the marinade ingredients in a small bowl until the
sugar is dissolved. Place the lamb racks in a large, resealable
plastic bag and pour in 300 ml/½ pint of the marinade,
reserving the remainder. Press the air out of the bag and seal
tightly. Turn the bag to distribute the marinade and refrigerate
for 4–6 hours, turning the bag once or twice. Remove the bag
from the refrigerator 15–30 minutes before grilling the lamb.

2 Cut the aubergines lengthways into quarters. If the wedges
are thicker than 1.5 cm/¾ inch, cut into eighths. Destalk and
deseed the peppers and cut into 1.5-cm/¾-inch strips. Place
the vegetables in a large bowl and add 4 tablespoons of the
reserved marinade; toss to coat.

3 Prepare the grill for direct cooking over medium heat
(180–230°C/350–450°F).

4 Brush the cooking grates clean. Grill the aubergines and
peppers over **direct medium heat** for 6–8 minutes, with the
lid closed as much as possible and turning once or twice, until
tender and lightly charred. Transfer to a shallow dish and cover
with foil to keep warm.

5 Remove the lamb from the bag and discard the marinade.
Grill the lamb, bone side down first, over **direct medium heat**,
with the lid closed as much as possible and turning once
or twice (if flare-ups occur, move the racks temporarily over
indirect heat), until cooked to your desired doneness,
15–20 minutes for medium rare. Transfer to a serving plate,
tent loosely with foil and leave to rest for 5–10 minutes.

6 When the vegetables are cool enough to handle, peel away
and discard any blackened skin and then coarsely chop.

7 Whisk the remaining reserved marinade in a large bowl with
the rice vinegar. Add the aubergine, peppers, spring onions,
coriander and sesame seeds; toss to combine. Serve the lamb
warm with the salad.

MOROCCAN SPICED PORK CHOPS

SERVES: 4
PREP TIME: 15 MINUTES
GRILLING TIME: 16–18 MINUTES

RUB
Finely grated zest of 1 large lemon
1 tablespoon soft brown sugar
1 teaspoon sea salt
1 teaspoon ground turmeric
1 teaspoon ground cumin
¾ teaspoon ground black pepper
½ teaspoon ground cinnamon
½ teaspoon ground ginger

4 boneless pork loin chops, each about 175 g/6 oz and
    2.5 cm/1 inch thick, trimmed of excess fat
Extra-virgin olive oil

4 fresh apricots, halved
4 tablespoons sultanas

1 Prepare the grill for direct cooking over low heat
(130–180°C/250–350°F).

2 Mix the rub ingredients in a small bowl. Lightly brush the
chops on both sides with oil and season evenly with the rub.
Marinate the chops at room temperature for 15–30 minutes
while the grill preheats.

3 Brush the cooking grates clean. Grill the apricots, cut
side down, over **direct low heat** for 6–8 minutes, with the lid
closed as much as possible and turning once, until heated
through. Cooking times will vary depending on the ripeness of
the apricots. Remove from the grill and, when cool enough to
handle, cut into bite-sized pieces. Place in a bowl and add the
sultanas; stir to combine. Set aside while you grill the chops.

4 Grill the chops over **direct low heat** for about 10 minutes,
with the lid closed as much as possible and turning once or
twice, until they are still slightly pink in the centre. Remove from
the grill and leave to rest for 3–5 minutes. Serve warm with the
apricot-sultana mixture.

MARINATED PORK CHOPS WITH FRESH FRUIT SALSA

SERVES: 4
PREP TIME: 30 MINUTES
MARINATING TIME: 1 HOUR
GRILLING TIME: 14–18 MINUTES

MARINADE
250 ml/8 fl oz refrigerated pomegranate juice
Grated zest and juice of 1 orange
1 teaspoon chilli powder
1 teaspoon sea salt
½ teaspoon ground black pepper

4 bone-in pork loin chops, each about 250 g/8 oz and 2.5 cm/
    1 inch thick, trimmed of excess fat

SALSA
4 slices fresh pineapple, each about 1 cm/½ inch thick
4 fresh apricots, halved
1 teaspoon chilli powder
½ teaspoon crushed red chilli flakes
½ teaspoon sea salt

1 Combine the marinade ingredients in a large bowl. Place the chops in the bowl, turn to coat them in the marinade, cover and refrigerate for 1 hour. Allow the chops to stand at room temperature for 15–30 minutes before grilling.

2 Prepare the grill for direct cooking over medium heat (180–230°C/350–450°F).

3 Brush the cooking grates clean. Grill the pineapple and apricots over **direct medium heat** for 6–8 minutes, with the lid closed as much as possible and turning once, until warm throughout. Remove from the grill and coarsely chop. Put the fruit in a food processor and add the remaining salsa ingredients. Pulse until you have a chunky salsa.

4 Remove the chops from the bowl and discard the marinade. Grill the chops over **direct medium heat** for 8–10 minutes, with the lid closed as much as possible and turning once or twice, until they are still slightly pink in the centre. Remove from the grill and leave to rest for 3–5 minutes. Serve warm with the salsa.

BANH MI PORK FILLET SANDWICHES

SERVES: 4
PREP TIME: 20 MINUTES
GRILLING TIME: 16–22 MINUTES
SPECIAL EQUIPMENT: INSTANT-READ MEAT
THERMOMETER

1 pork fillet, about 500 g/1 lb, trimmed of excess fat and skin
6 tablespoons rapeseed oil
½ teaspoon sea salt
¼ teaspoon ground black pepper

125 g/4 oz unsalted, creamy peanut butter
4 tablespoons rice vinegar
2 teaspoons soy sauce
2 teaspoons hot chilli-garlic sauce
4 tablespoons mayonnaise
4 long sandwich rolls *or* baguette pieces 20 cm/8 inches long
4 lettuce leaves
2 carrots, peeled and coarsely grated
½ cucumber, very thinly sliced
15 g/½ oz fresh coriander

1 Lightly coat the pork fillet with 2 teaspoons of the oil and season evenly with the salt and pepper. Allow the meat to stand at room temperature for 15–30 minutes before grilling.

2 Prepare the grill for direct cooking over medium heat (180–230°C/350–450°F).

3 Brush the cooking grates clean. Grill the pork over **direct medium heat** for 15–20 minutes, with the lid closed as much as possible and turning about every 5 minutes, until the outside is evenly seared and the internal temperature registers 65°C/150°F on an instant-read meat thermometer. Remove from the grill and leave to rest for 3–5 minutes. Cut the pork into 5-mm/¼-inch slices.

4 Whisk the remaining 4 tablespoons oil, the peanut butter, vinegar, soy sauce and 1 teaspoon of the chilli-garlic sauce in a small bowl until smooth. In another small bowl combine the remaining chilli-garlic sauce and the mayonnaise.

5 Cut the rolls lengthways almost in half, keeping one long side intact, so they open like a book. Toast the rolls, cut side down, over **direct medium heat** for 1–2 minutes. Remove from the grill and spread one cut side of each roll with a generous amount of the peanut sauce. Spread about 1 tablespoon of the mayonnaise mixture on the other side. Arrange equal amounts of lettuce, carrot, cucumber, coriander and sliced pork on each sandwich. Serve with any extra peanut sauce.

QUICK AND EASY PULLED PORK FILLET

SERVES: 4-6
PREP TIME: 15 MINUTES
GRILLING TIME: 15–20 MINUTES
SPECIAL EQUIPMENT: INSTANT-READ MEAT
    THERMOMETER

SAUCE
250 ml/8 fl oz tomato ketchup
125 ml/4 fl oz water
25 g/1 oz unsalted butter
2 tablespoons cider vinegar
1 tablespoon black treacle
1 tablespoon Worcestershire sauce
1 teaspoon garlic granules
½ teaspoon ground black pepper

RUB
1 teaspoon sea salt
1 teaspoon chilli powder
¼ teaspoon garlic granules
½ teaspoon ground black pepper

2 pork fillets, each 375–500 g/12 oz–1 lb, trimmed of excess fat
    and skin
2 tablespoons extra-virgin olive oil

Cooked soft polenta (optional)

1 Whisk the sauce ingredients in a small saucepan. Bring the sauce to a simmer over a medium heat and simmer gently for about 5 minutes, whisking occasionally. Set aside to cool at room temperature.

2 Mix the rub ingredients in a small bowl.

3 Lightly coat all sides of the pork fillets with the oil and season evenly with the rub, pressing the spices into the meat. Allow the meat to stand at room temperature for 15–30 minutes before grilling.

4 Prepare the grill for direct cooking over medium heat (180–230°C/350–450°F).

5 Brush the cooking grates clean. Grill the pork over **direct medium heat** for 15–20 minutes, with the lid closed as much as possible and turning about every 5 minutes, until the outsides are evenly seared and the internal temperature registers 65°C/150°F on an instant-read meat thermometer. Remove from the grill and wrap with aluminium foil. Leave to rest for about 15 minutes or until cool enough to handle.

6 Cut the fillets crossways into quarters. Pull the warm meat apart with your fingers or use two forks to shred the meat. Moisten the pork with as much of the sauce as you like in a large bowl. Serve on a bed of soft polenta, if liked.

JERK PORK FILLET AND CUCUMBER-DILL SALAD

SERVES: 4
PREP TIME: 15 MINUTES
GRILLING TIME: 15–20 MINUTES
SPECIAL EQUIPMENT: INSTANT-READ MEAT
　　THERMOMETER

2 pork fillets, each 375–500 g/12 oz–1 lb, trimmed of excess
　　fat and skin
4 tablespoons extra-virgin olive oil
4 tablespoons jerk seasoning

2 tablespoons white wine vinegar
1 teaspoon granulated sugar
1 teaspoon Dijon mustard
2 tablespoons finely chopped dill
1 cucumber, 425–500 g/14–16 oz, halved lengthways and
　　thinly sliced
½ small red pepper, finely diced
1¼ teaspoons sea salt

Cooked white rice (optional)

1 Brush the pork fillets all over with 2 tablespoons of the oil and season evenly with the jerk seasoning. Allow the meat to stand at room temperature for 15–30 minutes before grilling.

2 Prepare the grill for direct cooking over medium heat (180–230°C/350–450°F).

3 Whisk the vinegar, sugar, mustard, dill and the remaining 2 tablespoons of oil in a bowl until the sugar dissolves. Add the cucumber and red pepper, toss to coat and keep refrigerated until ready to serve.

4 Brush the cooking grates clean. Grill the pork fillets over **direct medium heat** for 15–20 minutes, with the lid closed as much as possible and turning every 5 minutes, until the outsides are evenly seared and the internal temperature registers 65°C/150°F on an instant-read meat thermometer. Remove from the grill and leave to rest for 3–5 minutes. Cut the fillets crossways into 1-cm/½-inch slices.

5 Season the cucumber salad with the salt and divide the salad and pork slices evenly between individual plates. Serve with rice, if liked.

FOIL-WRAPPED SPARERIBS

SERVES: 4
PREP TIME: 30 MINUTES
GRILLING TIME: ABOUT 1½ HOURS
SPECIAL EQUIPMENT: 45-CM/18-INCH-WIDE HEAVY-DUTY
    ALUMINIUM FOIL

PASTE

4 tablespoons dry white wine
2 tablespoons finely chopped garlic
2 tablespoons finely chopped oregano
1 tablespoon finely chopped rosemary
1 tablespoon finely chopped thyme
1 tablespoon fennel seeds
1 tablespoon sea salt
2 teaspoons crushed red chilli flakes
1 teaspoon ground black pepper
75 ml/3 fl oz extra-virgin olive oil

2 racks pork spareribs, each 1.5–1.75 kg/3–3½ lb, trimmed
    into a square shape

Steamed tenderstem broccoli (optional)

1 Prepare the grill for direct cooking over medium heat
(180–230°C/350–450°F).

2 Mix the paste ingredients in a small bowl.

3 Remove the thin membrane from the back of each rack
of ribs. Cut each rack crossways in the middle to create two
smaller racks.

4 Season each half-rack evenly with the paste. Using eight
45 × 60 cm/18 × 24 inch sheets of heavy-duty aluminium foil,
double wrap each half-rack in its own package and seal tightly.

5 Brush the cooking grates clean. Place the foil-wrapped ribs
on the grill over **direct medium heat**, close the lid and cook
for 1¼ hours, turning the packages over once or twice for even
cooking, making sure not to pierce the foil.

6 Remove the packages from the grill and leave to rest for
about 10 minutes. Carefully open the packages, remove the
ribs and discard the rendered fat and foil. Return the ribs to the
grill over **direct medium heat**, close the lid and cook for 8–10
minutes, turning once or twice, until they are sizzling and lightly
charred. Remove from the grill and leave to rest for about 5
minutes. Cut the racks between the bones into individual ribs
and serve warm with tenderstem broccoli, if liked.

The possibility of tender spareribs off the grill in under 2 hours
might seem unthinkable, unless you know this wonderfully easy
and effective method of grilling them in foil. Sealed tightly in
pouches with wine, garlic and herbs, they steam in their own
aromatic juices and turn tender in about 1 hour 15 minutes.
Then take them out of their pouch and cook them on a sizzling
cooking grate until crispy on the edges.

TOMATO RED CHICKEN BREASTS

SERVES: 4
PREP TIME: 15 MINUTES
MARINATING TIME: 20–30 MINUTES
GRILLING TIME: 8–12 MINUTES

MARINADE
3 tablespoons extra-virgin olive oil
1 shallot, finely chopped
1 tablespoon red wine vinegar
2 teaspoons tomato purée
1 teaspoon crushed red chilli flakes
1 teaspoon sea salt
½ teaspoon dried oregano *or* basil
¼ teaspoon ground black pepper

4 boneless, skinless chicken breasts, each about 175 g/6 oz

Grilled aubergine (optional)

1 Whisk the marinade ingredients in a large bowl. Add the chicken breasts to the bowl and turn to coat them evenly. Allow the chicken to marinate at room temperature for 20–30 minutes before grilling.

2 Prepare the grill for direct cooking over medium heat (180–230°C/350–450°F).

3 Brush the cooking grates clean. Remove the chicken from the bowl and discard the marinade. Grill the chicken, smooth (skin) side down first, over ***direct medium heat*** for 8–12 minutes, with the lid closed as much as possible and turning once or twice, until the chicken is firm to the touch and opaque all the way to the centre. Remove from the grill and leave to rest for 3–5 minutes. Serve warm with grilled aubergine, if liked.

BARBADOS CHICKEN BREASTS

SERVES: 4
PREP TIME: 15 MINUTES
GRILLING TIME: 23–35 MINUTES

PASTE
2 tablespoons extra-virgin olive oil
2 tablespoons finely chopped onion
2 small jalapeño chillies, stems and seeds removed,
    finely chopped
2 teaspoons dried thyme
2 teaspoons ground allspice
2 teaspoons ground black pepper
½ teaspoon ground cayenne pepper
½ teaspoon ground cinnamon
½ teaspoon sea salt
Juice of 1 lime

4 chicken breasts (with bone and skin), each
    300–375 g/10–12 oz

Rice and beans (optional)

1 Prepare the grill for direct and indirect cooking over medium heat (180–230°C/350–450°F).

2 Mix the paste ingredients in a bowl. Using your fingertips, carefully lift the skin from the chicken breasts, leaving the skin closest to the breastbone attached. Run 1 teaspoon of the paste under the skin all over the exposed meat. Lay the skin back in place and spread the remaining paste evenly all over the chicken.

3 Brush the cooking grates clean. Grill the chicken, skin side down, over **direct medium heat** for 3–5 minutes, with the lid closed, until the skin is browned. Turn the chicken over and continue to grill over **indirect medium heat** for 20–30 minutes, with the lid closed, until the meat is opaque all the way to the bone. Remove from the grill and leave to rest for 3–5 minutes. Serve warm with rice and beans, if liked.

CHICKEN SALAD WRAPS WITH HERBED AÏOLI AND WATERCRESS

SERVES: 4–6
PREP TIME: 30 MINUTES
GRILLING TIME: 8–12 MINUTES

3 boneless, skinless chicken breasts, each about 175 g/6 oz
Extra-virgin olive oil
1 teaspoon chopped thyme
¼ teaspoon sea salt
Ground black pepper

12 flour tortillas, about 15 cm/6 inches in diameter

AÏOLI
75 ml/3 fl oz mayonnaise
1 teaspoon Dijon mustard
1 small garlic clove, finely chopped
1 tablespoon chopped basil
1 tablespoon chopped parsley

100 g/3½ oz small red grapes, halved
75 g/3 oz walnuts, chopped
2 spring onions (white and light green parts only), thinly sliced
1 small bunch watercress, leaves and tender stems

1 Prepare the grill for direct cooking over medium heat (180–230°C/350–450°F). Preheat the oven to 110°C/225°F/Gas Mark ¼.

2 Lightly coat the chicken on both sides with oil and season evenly with the thyme, salt and ⅛ teaspoon pepper.

3 Wrap the tortillas in barely moist kitchen paper and then tightly in aluminium foil. Place the package of tortillas in the oven to warm while grilling the chicken and preparing the aïoli.

4 Brush the cooking grates clean. Grill the chicken, smooth (skin) side down first, over *direct medium heat* for 8–12 minutes, with the lid closed as much as possible and turning once, until the meat is firm to the touch and opaque all the way to the centre. Remove from the grill and set aside to cool. Cut into 5-mm/¼-inch cubes.

5 Whisk the mayonnaise, mustard, garlic, basil, parsley, 2 tablespoons oil and ⅛ teaspoon pepper in a bowl.

6 Combine the chicken with the grapes, walnuts and spring onions in a large bowl then add as much of the aïoli as you like. Remove the tortillas from the oven. Divide the watercress and chicken salad between the tortillas. Wrap and serve.

SHREDDED BARBECUE CHICKEN SANDWICHES WITH QUICK COLESLAW

SERVES: 4–6
PREP TIME: 15 MINUTES
GRILLING TIME: 8–12 MINUTES

RUB
1 teaspoon paprika
1 teaspoon garlic granules
Sea salt
Ground black pepper

4 boneless, skinless chicken breasts, each about 175 g/6 oz
Vegetable oil

SLAW
4 tablespoons mayonnaise
1 tablespoon cider vinegar
½ teaspoon granulated sugar
250 g/8 oz prepared coleslaw blend of shredded green
    cabbage, red cabbage and carrots

4–6 burger buns
125 ml/4 fl oz ready-made barbecue sauce, at room
    temperature

1 Prepare the grill for direct cooking over medium heat (180–230°C/350–450°F).

2 Combine the paprika, garlic granules, 1 teaspoon salt and ½ teaspoon pepper in a small bowl. Lightly brush the chicken on both sides with oil and season evenly with the rub.

3 Whisk the mayonnaise, vinegar, sugar, ¼ teaspoon salt and ⅛ teaspoon pepper in a large bowl to make a smooth dressing. Add the coleslaw blend and mix well.

4 Brush the cooking grates clean. Grill the chicken, smooth (skin) side down first, over *direct medium heat* for 8–12 minutes, with the lid closed as much as possible and turning once or twice, until the meat is firm to the touch and opaque all the way to the centre. During the last 30 seconds–1 minute of grilling time, toast the burger buns, cut side down, over direct heat. Remove the chicken and the buns from the grill and leave the chicken to rest for 3–5 minutes. Shred or finely chop the chicken and put it in a large bowl. Add the barbecue sauce and mix well. Pile the chicken on to the buns and top with the slaw.

CHOPPED CHICKEN SALAD WITH HONEY-MUSTARD DRESSING

SERVES: 6
PREP TIME: 35 MINUTES
MARINATING TIME: ABOUT 1 HOUR
GRILLING TIME: 8–10 MINUTES

MARINADE
2 tablespoons extra-virgin olive oil
2 tablespoons finely chopped rosemary
1 tablespoon fresh lemon juice
1 tablespoon finely chopped garlic
1½ teaspoons sea salt
¼ teaspoon ground black pepper

6 boneless, skinless chicken thighs, about 75 g/3 oz each

DRESSING
250 ml/8 fl oz mayonnaise
6 tablespoons Dijon mustard
4 tablespoons runny honey
2 tablespoons fresh lemon juice

Sea salt
Ground black pepper

3 romaine lettuce hearts, chopped
500 g/1 lb cherry tomatoes, quartered
2 large avocados, chopped

½ small red onion, finely chopped
8 bacon rashers, cooked and crumbled
3 hard-boiled eggs, cut into wedges

1 Whisk the marinade ingredients in a small bowl. Place the chicken in a large, resealable plastic bag and pour in the marinade. Press the air out of the bag and seal tightly. Turn the bag several times to distribute the marinade and refrigerate for about 1 hour.

2 Prepare the grill for direct cooking over medium heat (180–230°C/350–450°F).

3 Combine the dressing ingredients in a small bowl. Season with salt and pepper.

4 Brush the cooking grates clean. Remove the chicken thighs from the bag and discard the marinade. Grill the chicken, smooth (skin) side down first, over **direct medium heat** for 8–10 minutes, with the lid closed as much as possible and turning once or twice, until the meat is firm and the juices run clear. Remove from the grill and leave to rest for 3–5 minutes. Cut the meat into bite-sized pieces.

5 Divide the chicken, lettuce, tomatoes, avocados, onion, bacon and eggs evenly between six plates. Drizzle the salad with the dressing and serve immediately.

SODA CAN CHICKEN

SERVES: 4

PREP TIME: 10 MINUTES

GRILLING TIME: 1¼–1½ HOURS

SPECIAL EQUIPMENT: INSTANT-READ MEAT
THERMOMETER

PASTE

Grated zest of 2 lemons

2 tablespoons fresh lemon juice

2 tablespoons finely chopped oregano

2 tablespoons finely chopped sage

1½ teaspoons sea salt

1 tablespoon soft brown sugar

½ teaspoon ground cayenne pepper

1 teaspoon ground black pepper

4 tablespoons extra-virgin olive oil

1 chicken, about 2 kg/4 lb, giblets and any excess fat removed

350-ml/12-fl oz can sparkling lemon-lime drink (not diet), at
room temperature

2 handfuls hickory wood chips, soaked in water for at least
30 minutes

1 Combine all the paste ingredients in a small bowl. Using your fingers, gently separate the skin from the meat, starting at the neck and moving along the breasts. Repeat with the thighs and legs, starting at the tail end. Spread most of the paste evenly on the meat under the skin and the rest on the outside of the chicken. Fold the wing tips behind the chicken's back.

2 Prepare the grill for indirect cooking over medium heat (180–230°C/350–450°F).

4 Open the drinks can and pour out about half of the liquid. Using a can opener, make four more holes in the top of the can. Put the can on a solid surface. Place the chicken cavity over the can.

5 Brush the cooking grates clean. Drain and scatter the wood chips directly over lit charcoal or put them in the smoker box of a gas grill, following manufacturer's instructions. When the wood chips begin to smoke, transfer the chicken-on-a-can to the grill, balancing it like a tripod. Grill over **indirect medium heat** for 1¼ to 1½ hours with the lid closed, until the juices run clear and an instant-read meat thermometer inserted in the thickest part of the thigh (not touching the bone) registers 70–74°C/160–165°F. Carefully remove the chicken-on-a-can from the grill (do not spill the contents of the can, as it will be very hot). Leave the chicken to rest for 10–15 minutes (the internal temperature will rise 5–10 degrees during this time). Carefully lift the chicken from the can and cut into serving pieces. Serve warm.

TOASTED CHICKEN PANINI WITH TOMATO AND ROCKET

SERVES: 4
PREP TIME: 15 MINUTES
GRILLING TIME: 10–13 MINUTES
SPECIAL EQUIPMENT: ROASTING TRAY, CAST-IRON
FRYING PAN OR 2 FOIL-WRAPPED BRICKS

2 boneless, skinless chicken breasts, each about 175 g/6 oz
Extra-virgin olive oil
½ teaspoon sea salt
¼ teaspoon ground black pepper

125 g/4 oz soft herb and garlic cheese
50 g/2 oz baby rocket
2 plum tomatoes, cut into 5-mm/¼-inch slices
500 g/1 lb wholegrain artisan bread, cut into 8 slices, each
about 5 mm/¼ inch thick

1 Prepare the grill for direct cooking over medium heat
(180–230°C/350–450°F).

2 Remove the piece of meat from the underside of each
chicken breast and save for another use. Cut each breast in
half lengthways, creating two long strips. One at a time, place
each breast strip, smooth side down, between two sheets of
clingfilm and pound to an even 5-mm/¼-inch thickness. Brush
both sides with oil and season evenly with the salt and pepper.

3 Brush the cooking grates clean. Grill the chicken breast
strips over *direct medium heat* for 4–5 minutes, with the lid
closed as much as possible and turning once, until firm to the
touch and opaque all the way to the centre. Remove from the
grill and let rest while you prepare the sandwiches.

4 Reduce the temperature of the grill to low heat
(130–180°C/250–350°F).

5 Spread the bread slices evenly with the soft cheese. Top
four slices with some rocket, three slices of tomato and a
chicken breast strip then add the remaining slices to make four
sandwiches. Press down on each sandwich so it is compacted
and then lightly brush each sandwich on both sides with oil.

6 Brush the cooking grates clean. Place the sandwiches
over *direct low heat* and put a roasting tray directly on top of
the sandwiches; weigh it down with a cast-iron frying pan or
two foil-wrapped bricks. Grill for 6–8 minutes, turning once
(carefully remove the weight and the roasting tray before
turning, then put the tray and weight back in place), until the
bread is toasted and golden. Remove the sandwiches from the
grill and serve immediately.

BOURBON-GLAZED TURKEY BREAST

SERVES: 4
PREP TIME: 15 MINUTES
GRILLING TIME: 13–16 MINUTES
SPECIAL EQUIPMENT: INSTANT-READ MEAT
    THERMOMETER

AÏOLI

2 applewood smoked bacon rashers, coarsely chopped
2 garlic cloves
1 spring onion, root end trimmed, chopped
1 tablespoon sherry
125 ml/4 fl oz mayonnaise
Sea salt

GLAZE

2 tablespoons soft brown sugar
2 tablespoons ketchup
2 tablespoons cider vinegar
2 tablespoons bourbon
1 teaspoon Worcestershire sauce

2 turkey breast fillets, about 625 g/1¼ lb in total
Ground black pepper

1 Fry the chopped bacon in a small sauté pan over a medium-high heat for about 6 minutes, stirring occasionally, until crisp but not burnt. Drain the bacon on kitchen paper and reserve the pan fat.

2 Whizz the garlic in a food processor or blender until finely chopped. Add the bacon, spring onion, sherry, mayonnaise and ¼ teaspoon salt and pulse until well combined.

3 Prepare the grill for direct cooking over medium heat (180–230°C/350–450°F).

4 Whisk the glaze ingredients in a bowl until the sugar has completely dissolved.

5 Lightly brush the turkey breasts on both sides with the reserved pan fat (if you do not have enough bacon fat, you can add, or substitute, vegetable oil). Season evenly with salt and pepper.

6 Brush the cooking grates clean. Grill the turkey over **direct medium heat** for about 8 minutes, with the lid closed as much as possible and turning once. Brush the fillets generously with the glaze and continue cooking for 5–8 minutes, turning and basting frequently with the glaze, until the meat is no longer pink in the centre and the internal temperature registers 70–74°C/160–165°F on an instant-read meat thermometer. Remove from the grill and leave to rest for 5–10 minutes (the internal temperature will rise 5–10 degrees during this time). Cut the turkey breasts crossways into slices and serve warm with the bacon aïoli.

TURKEY WRAPS WITH MINT CHUTNEY

SERVES: 4–6
PREP TIME: 30 MINUTES
GRILLING TIME: ABOUT 6 MINUTES

625 g/1¼ lb minced turkey thigh meat
2 teaspoons finely chopped garlic
1 small jalapeño chilli, deseeded and finely chopped
1 tablespoon finely chopped fresh ginger
1 tablespoon garam masala
1 teaspoon sea salt

4 tablespoons extra-virgin olive oil

CHUTNEY
75 g/3 oz mint
2 onions, coarsely chopped
15 g/½ oz fresh coriander
4 serrano chillies, deseeded and coarsely chopped
2 tablespoons fresh lime juice
½ teaspoon ground cumin
½ teaspoon sea salt

8 naan breads
2 firm ripe mangoes, peeled and cut into 5-mm/¼-inch slices

1 Gently mix the minced turkey with the garlic, jalapeño, ginger, garam masala and salt in a large bowl.

2 Pour the oil on to a roasting tray and brush it evenly all over the surface. Using two spoons, shape the turkey mixture into 24 small ovals or quenelles, placing them on the oiled tray as you make them. Turn them, making sure they are well coated with oil. Refrigerate until ready to grill.

3 Prepare the grill for direct cooking over medium heat (180–230°C/350–450°F).

4 Combine the chutney ingredients in a food processor or blender and pulse until the mixture is blended but still chunky.

5 Brush the cooking grates clean. Grill the quenelles over **direct medium heat** for about 6 minutes, with the lid closed as much as possible and turning once every 2 minutes, until the meat is firm and fully cooked but still moist. During the last minute of grilling time, lightly toast the naan over direct heat. Remove from the grill.

6 Place three quenelles on each piece of naan. Top generously with chutney and sliced mango to serve.

BEER-MARINATED MAHI-MAHI WITH GUACAMOLE

SERVES: 4
PREP TIME: 15 MINUTES
GRILLING TIME: 6–8 MINUTES

250 ml/8 fl oz beer
1 jalapeño chilli, thinly sliced
5 tablespoons fresh lime juice
4 skinless mahi-mahi fillets, each 175–250 g/6–8 oz and
    1.5 cm/¾ inch thick

2 avocados
1 plum tomato, chopped
1 tablespoon roughly chopped fresh coriander
Sea salt
Ground black pepper
Extra-virgin olive oil

1 Prepare the grill for direct cooking over high heat (230–290°C/450–550°F).

2 Combine the beer, jalapeño and 3 tablespoons of the lime juice in a glass baking dish. Place the fish fillets in the dish, cover and leave to marinate at room temperature for 15 minutes, turning once. (Do not leave the fillets in the marinade longer than 15 minutes as the lime juice will begin to cook the fish.)

3 Meanwhile, make the guacamole. Cut the avocados in half, remove the stones and scoop the flesh into a medium bowl. Add the remaining 2 tablespoons lime juice, the tomato, coriander, ½ teaspoon salt and ⅛ teaspoon pepper. Mash with the back of a fork.

4 Remove the fish from the dish and discard the marinade. Lightly brush the fillets on both sides with oil and season evenly with salt and pepper. Brush the cooking grates clean. Grill the fish over **direct high heat** for 6–8 minutes, with the lid closed as much as possible and turning once, until the flesh is opaque in the centre but still moist. Remove from the grill and serve warm with the guacamole.

PRAWN AND SHIITAKE MUSHROOMS WITH SOBA

SERVES: 4
PREP TIME: 30 MINUTES
GRILLING TIME: 2–4 MINUTES
SPECIAL EQUIPMENT: PERFORATED GRILL PAN

SAUCE
4 tablespoons soy sauce
2 tablespoons sake
1 tablespoon rice vinegar
1 tablespoon grated fresh ginger
1 teaspoon toasted sesame oil
1 teaspoon wasabi paste
1 garlic clove, finely chopped

250 g/8 oz soba noodles

125 g/4 oz fresh shiitake mushrooms, stalks removed
625 g/1¼ lb large prawns, peeled and deveined, tails removed
Vegetable oil
Sea salt
Ground black pepper

3 spring onions, thinly sliced
1 tablespoon toasted sesame seeds
1 sheet pre-toasted, ready-to-use nori, cut into 3-mm/⅛-inch strips (optional)

1 Whisk the sauce ingredients in a bowl until the wasabi paste dissolves.

2 Cook the soba noodles in a large saucepan of salted water according to the packet instructions. Drain, then rinse with cold water to stop the cooking process.

3 Prepare the grill for direct cooking over high heat (230–290°C/450–550°F) and preheat the grill pan.

4 Brush the mushrooms and prawns all over with vegetable oil and season evenly with salt and pepper.

5 Spread the mushrooms and prawns in a single layer on the grill pan. Grill over *direct high heat* for 2–4 minutes, with the lid closed as much as possible and turning once or twice, until the mushrooms are lightly browned and tender and the prawns are firm to the touch, lightly charred and just turning opaque in the centre. Remove from the grill and thinly slice the mushrooms.

6 Toss the soba noodles and mushrooms with the sauce in a large bowl. Divide evenly between plates and top with the grilled prawns, spring onions, sesame seeds and nori, if using. Serve immediately.

SUMMER ROLLS WITH HALIBUT, LEMONGRASS AND RADISHES

SERVES: 4–6
PREP TIME: 45 MINUTES
GRILLING TIME: 6–7 MINUTES

SUMMER ROLLS

375 g/12 oz halibut fillets, about 2.5 cm/1 inch thick
3 tablespoons hot chilli-garlic sauce
Extra-virgin olive oil
8 large round rice paper wrappers
1 cucumber, cut into very thin julienne strips
1 carrot, cut into very thin julienne strips
2 radishes, cut into very thin julienne strips
2 spring onions (white and light green parts only), cut into very thin julienne strips
75 g/3 oz lettuce leaves, roughly chopped
3 tablespoons chopped mint
3 tablespoons chopped fresh coriander

SAUCE

125 ml/4 fl oz fresh lime juice (from about 4 limes)
2 tablespoons granulated sugar
4½ teaspoons fish sauce *or* 1 tablespoon soy sauce
1 tablespoon finely chopped lemongrass
1 teaspoon grated fresh ginger
1 garlic clove, finely chopped

1 Prepare the grill for direct cooking over high heat (230–290°C/450–550°F).

2 Brush the fish fillets on both sides with 2 tablespoons of the chilli-garlic sauce then brush with oil.

3 Brush the cooking grates clean. Grill the fish over **direct high heat**, with the lid closed as much as possible, until you can lift them off the cooking grate without sticking, about 4 minutes for steaks, slightly less for fillets. Turn the fillets over and cook for 2–3 minutes until the centre is opaque. Remove and discard any skin. Break the fish into 1-cm/½-inch chunks. Lightly toss with the remaining tablespoon of chilli-garlic sauce.

4 To assemble the summer rolls, work with one rice paper wrapper at a time. Soak the wrapper in hot (but not boiling) water for 30 seconds, or until softened. Carefully lift out of the water. Place on a chopping board, blot dry and place a few pieces of halibut in a horizontal line just below the centre of the wrap. Top the halibut with some of the julienned vegetables, lettuce, mint and coriander. Fold the bottom of the wrapper over the filling and then fold in the sides; roll up tightly. Repeat with the remaining wrappers and fillings. Rolls may be covered and refrigerated for several hours at this point.

5 Combine the sauce ingredients in a small bowl. Cut the summer rolls diagonally in half and serve with the sauce for dipping.

PARMA-WRAPPED PRAWNS WITH PEAR CHUTNEY

SERVES: 6–8
PREP TIME: 20 MINUTES, PLUS 20–30 MINUTES FOR
   THE CHUTNEY
GRILLING TIME: 10–14 MINUTES

CHUTNEY
3–4 ripe pears, about 750 g/1½ lb in total
Extra-virgin olive oil
125 g/4 oz soft brown sugar
40 g/1½ oz dried cranberries
3 small shallots, finely chopped
4 tablespoons sherry vinegar
2 tablespoons grated lemon zest
2 tablespoons fresh lemon juice
1 tablespoon chopped crystallized ginger
15 g/½ oz unsalted butter
1 cinnamon stick
½ teaspoon sea salt
⅛ teaspoon ground cayenne pepper

125 g/4 oz Parma ham, about 10 slices
500 g/1 lb jumbo prawns, peeled and deveined, tails left on

1 Prepare the grill for direct cooking over medium heat
(180–230°C/350–450°F).

2 Peel the pears, cut them into quarters, core them and lightly brush all sides with oil.

3 Brush the cooking grates clean. Grill the pears over **direct medium heat** for 8–10 minutes, with the lid closed as much as possible and turning once or twice, until crisp-tender. Remove from the grill and, when cool enough to handle, put them in a food processor and pulse about 10 times (or cut them into small pieces). Combine the pears and the rest of the chutney ingredients in a saucepan over a medium heat. Cook for 20–30 minutes, stirring occasionally, until slightly thickened. Cool to room temperature.

4 Increase the temperature of the grill to high heat (230–290°C/450–550°F).

5 Cut the Parma ham slices in half lengthways. Starting at one end, lay a prawn on each ham slice and roll the ham around the prawn. Lightly brush with oil.

6 Grill the prawns over **direct high heat** for 2–4 minutes, with the lid closed as much as possible, until lightly charred, firm to the touch and just turning opaque in the centre. Remove from the grill and serve warm with the chutney.

SALMON SLIDERS WITH SPICY GINGER SAUCE AND PICKLED VEGETABLES

SERVES: 6–8
PREP TIME: 30 MINUTES
MARINATING TIME: 1 HOUR
CHILLING TIME: 30 MINUTES
GRILLING TIME: 6–8 MINUTES

250 ml/8 fl oz rice vinegar
2 tablespoons granulated sugar
1 teaspoon sea salt
½ cucumber, cut into paper-thin slices
½ red onion, halved
1 small red pepper

SAUCE
125 ml/4 fl oz mayonnaise
2 teaspoons grated fresh ginger
1 teaspoon hot chilli-garlic sauce

1 skinless salmon fillet, about 1 kg/2 lb, pin bones removed, patted dry and cut into 2.5-cm/1-inch pieces
6 spring onions (white and light green parts only), thinly sliced
15 g/½ oz fresh coriander, finely chopped
1 tablespoon grated fresh ginger
2 tablespoons fresh lime juice
2 tablespoons soy sauce
1 tablespoon toasted sesame oil
1 teaspoon hot chilli-garlic sauce
1 large egg
25 g/1 oz panko breadcrumbs

18 small burger buns or rolls, each about 5 cm/2 inches in diameter
Rapeseed oil spray

1 Stir the vinegar, sugar and salt in a bowl. Squeeze the cucumber slices until they are crushed and releasing liquid. Cut the onion into 3-mm/⅛-inch slices, then cut them into 2.5-cm/1-inch pieces. Cut the red pepper lengthways into 3-mm/⅛-inch slices, remove the seeds, then cut into 2.5-cm/1-inch pieces. Place the cucumber, onion and pepper in the vinegar mixture. Leave to marinate at room temperature for 1 hour, stirring occasionally. Drain well before assembling the sliders.

2 Combine the sauce ingredients in a small bowl. Cover and refrigerate.

3 Pulse the salmon pieces in a food processor until coarsely chopped. Add the spring onions, coriander, ginger, lime juice, soy sauce, sesame oil, chilli-garlic sauce and egg. Pulse a few times until just blended, being careful not to purée the mixture: some texture should remain. Transfer the mixture to a large bowl, gently stir in the breadcrumbs and form into 1-cm/½-inch-thick burgers roughly the size of the buns. Arrange the burgers on a roasting tray and refrigerate for 30 minutes before grilling.

4 Prepare the grill for direct cooking over medium heat (180–230°C/350–450°F).

5 Brush the cooking grates clean. Lay a single layer of heavy-duty aluminium foil over the grates. Generously spray the sliders on both sides with the rapeseed oil spray. Grill over **direct medium heat** for 6–8 minutes, with the lid closed as much as possible and turning once after about 4 minutes, until you can lift the burgers easily from the foil with a spatula. During the last minute of grilling time, grill the buns, cut side down, until lightly toasted.

6 To assemble the sliders, spread the sauce on to the bottom of each bun, place a burger on top and finish with some pickled vegetables. Serve immediately.

TUNA WITH CANNELLINI BEAN AND OLIVE SALAD

SERVES: 4–6
PREP TIME: 30 MINUTES
GRILLING TIME: ABOUT 4 MINUTES

1 tablespoon white balsamic vinegar
Extra-virgin olive oil
3 roasted red peppers (from a jar), drained and cut into
    1-cm/½-inch pieces
18 pitted brine-cured green olives, cut into 1-cm/½-inch pieces
8 pitted kalamata olives, cut into 1-cm/½-inch pieces
1 red onion, finely chopped
2 teaspoons finely grated lemon zest
475-g/15-oz can cannellini beans, rinsed
Sea salt
Ground black pepper

2 tuna steaks, each about 500 g/1 lb and 3 cm/1¼ inches thick
4 tablespoons roughly chopped basil
1 round lettuce

1 Whisk the vinegar with 2 tablespoons oil in a large bowl until well blended. Add the red peppers, olives, onion and lemon zest; stir to combine. Add the beans and stir gently to incorporate all the ingredients. Season with salt and pepper. Set aside.

2 Prepare the grill for direct cooking over high heat (230–290°C/450–550°F).

3 Coat the tuna steaks on both sides with oil and lightly season with salt and pepper. Brush the cooking grates clean. Grill the tuna over *direct high heat*, with the lid closed as much as possible and turning once, until cooked to your desired doneness, about 4 minutes for rare. Remove from the grill and cut each tuna steak into 8-mm/⅓-inch slices. Add the basil to the salad.

4 To serve, arrange two lettuce leaves on each plate. Spoon equal amounts of the bean salad on to the centre of the leaves and arrange the tuna slices on top of the bean salad.

CEDAR-SMOKED TUNA WITH CRISP VEGETABLES

SERVES: 4
PREP TIME: 20 MINUTES
GRILLING TIME: 21–28 MINUTES
SPECIAL EQUIPMENT: 1 UNTREATED CEDAR PLANK,
30–37 CM/12–15 INCHES LONG AND 1–1.5 CM/
½–¾ INCH THICK, SOAKED IN WATER FOR AT LEAST
1 HOUR

DRESSING
2 tablespoons balsamic vinegar
2 tablespoons fresh lemon juice
1 tablespoon wholegrain mustard
Sea salt
Ground black pepper
Extra-virgin olive oil

500 g/1 lb asparagus

4 tuna steaks, each about 250 g/8 oz and 2.5 cm/1 inch thick
½ teaspoon paprika

4 spring onions (white and light green parts only), thinly sliced
4–6 radishes, thinly sliced
100 g/3½ oz baby rocket

1 Prepare the grill for direct cooking over medium heat (180–230°C/350–450°F).

2 Whisk the vinegar, lemon juice, mustard, ¼ teaspoon salt and ½ teaspoon pepper in a small bowl. Then slowly whisk in 4 tablespoons oil until the dressing is emulsified. Set aside.

3 Remove and discard the tough bottom of each asparagus spear by grasping each end and bending it gently until it snaps at its natural point of tenderness, usually two-thirds of the way down the spear. Lightly coat the asparagus with oil and season evenly with salt and pepper.

4 Brush the tuna steaks on both sides with oil and season evenly with 1 teaspoon salt, ½ teaspoon pepper and the paprika.

5 Place the soaked plank over **direct medium heat** and close the lid. After 5–10 minutes, when the plank begins to smoke and char, turn the plank over. Place the tuna in a single layer on the plank. Close the lid and cook for about 10 minutes until the tuna is firm but still juicy. If the plank catches on fire, use a spray bottle to mist out the flames. Transfer the tuna to a serving plate. Discard the charred cedar plank once it cools.

6 Brush the cooking grates clean. Grill the asparagus over **direct medium heat** for 6–8 minutes, with the lid closed as much as possible and turning once, until crisp-tender. Remove from the grill and cut into 2.5-cm/1-inch pieces.

7 Combine the asparagus with the spring onions, radishes and rocket in a large bowl. Drizzle with the dressing and toss to coat. Arrange the vegetables on the serving plate with the tuna and serve immediately.

CINNAMON FRENCH TOAST

6 large eggs
350 ml/12 fl oz full-fat milk
1 tablespoon vanilla extract
1 tablespoon ground cinnamon
2 tablespoons granulated sugar
⅛ teaspoon sea salt
8 slices rustic white bread, each about 1.5 cm/¾ inch thick

Rapeseed oil spray
Icing sugar
Butter
Maple syrup

1 Whisk the eggs, milk, vanilla, cinnamon, sugar and salt in a large bowl. Arrange the bread in one layer in a large baking dish and pour the egg mixture over the bread. Let the bread stand for 10 minutes at room temperature, turning occasionally so that all the slices get a chance to sit in the liquid on both sides.

2 Prepare the grill for direct cooking over medium-low heat (about 180°C/350°F).

3 Brush the cooking grates clean. Tip one slice of bread on its side so that any extra liquid runs off. Spray both sides with the oil and then place on the grill. Repeat with the remaining slices. Grill over **direct medium-low heat** for 6–8 minutes, with the lid closed as much as possible and turning once, until firm on both sides and golden brown. Remove from the grill and dust with icing sugar. Serve immediately with butter and maple syrup.

PINEAPPLE WITH COCONUT POUND CAKE AND RASPBERRY SAUCE

SERVES: 6
PREP TIME: 40 MINUTES
BAKING TIME: ABOUT 50 MINUTES
GRILLING TIME: 4–6 MINUTES
SPECIAL EQUIPMENT: 23 × 12 CM/9 × 5 INCH LOAF TIN

CAKE
150 g/5 oz plain flour
3 tablespoons cornflour
¼ teaspoon baking powder
½ teaspoon sea salt
125 ml/4 fl oz buttermilk
4 tablespoons soured cream
175 g/6 oz unsalted butter, softened
175 g/6 oz granulated sugar
2 large eggs, at room temperature
40 g/1½ oz toasted desiccated coconut

SAUCE
250 g/8 oz fresh raspberries
3 tablespoons soft brown sugar
2 tablespoons balsamic vinegar
2 teaspoons cornflour

1 fresh pineapple, peeled, cored and cut into 1-cm/½-inch slices

1 Preheat the oven to 180°C/350°F/Gas Mark 4. Lightly grease the inside of a 23 × 12 cm/9 × 5 inch loaf tin.

2 Sift the flour, cornflour, baking powder and salt in a small bowl. Mix the buttermilk and soured cream in another small bowl.

3 Cream the butter and granulated sugar in a large bowl for about 5 minutes until the mixture is light and fluffy. Add the eggs, one at a time, beating well after each addition. Add the dry ingredients alternately with the wet ingredients. Mix just until the mixture is smooth. Stir in the coconut. Evenly spread the mixture into the prepared loaf tin and smooth the top. Bake for about 50 minutes, until a skewer inserted into the centre comes out clean. Remove from the oven and let cool. Cut six 1.5-cm/¾-inch slices.

4 Prepare the grill for direct cooking over medium heat (180–230°C/350–450°F).

5 Purée the sauce ingredients in a blender. Pour the sauce into a small saucepan and cook for about 3 minutes over a medium heat until thickened. Strain the sauce through a sieve into a small bowl and discard the seeds left behind. Set aside until ready to serve.

6 Brush the cooking grates clean. Grill the pineapple over **direct medium heat** for 4–6 minutes, with the lid open and turning once, until nicely marked. During the last 2 minutes of grilling time, grill the cake until lightly marked, turning once. Remove from the grill and cut the pineapple into bite-sized chunks.

7 Place a slice of the cake on each plate and top with pineapple chunks and raspberry sauce.

WARM BANANA CHOCOLATE SUNDAES

SERVES: 4
PREP TIME: 15 MINUTES
GRILLING TIME: 5–7 MINUTES

2 bananas, peeled and cut crossways into 1-cm/½-inch slices
8 tablespoons soft brown sugar
4 tablespoons whipping cream
4 tablespoons brandy *or* bourbon *or* fresh orange juice
Vanilla ice cream
25 g/1 oz plain chocolate, finely grated
50 g/2 oz pecans, finely chopped

1 Prepare the grill for direct cooking over medium heat (180–230°C/350–450°F).

2 Tear off two 30-cm/12-inch lengths of heavy-duty aluminium foil. Working with one piece of foil at a time, place a sliced banana in the centre of the foil. Sprinkle with 4 tablespoons brown sugar, then 2 tablespoons each cream and brandy. Fold in the sides of the foil, then the top and bottom to enclose the banana mixture. Repeat with the other banana.

3 Brush the cooking grates clean. Grill the foil packages, seam side up, over **direct medium heat** for 5–7 minutes with the lid closed, until the brown sugar is melted and the liquid is simmering and combined into a sauce (open a package to check). Transfer the packages to a roasting tray and leave to rest for 5 minutes to cool slightly.

4 Put two scoops of ice cream into each of four serving bowls. Snip the foil packages open with scissors. Pour the contents evenly over the ice cream in each bowl. Sprinkle each with equal amounts of the chocolate and then top with the nuts. Serve immediately.

LARGE GET-TOGETHERS

LARGE GET-TOGETHERS

FAMILY DO

143 HOT DOGS WITH AVOCADO AND CRISPS

155 HONEY-GINGER CHICKEN SATAYS

PARTY WITH FRIENDS

142 CHURRASCO MIXED GRILL WITH TOMATO-CITRUS
BLACK BEANS

151 PULLED PORK BARBECUE SANDWICHES

ONE DISH FEEDS MANY

147 TURKISH RACK OF LAMB WITH TABBOULEH

152 CHILLI-RUBBED PORK FILLET

167 CORIANDER-MARINATED PRAWNS

178 FOIL-WRAPPED BAKED POTATOES WITH
SAUTÉED WILD MUSHROOMS

164 TURKEY KOFTA WITH MAJOR GREY'S CHUTNEY

169 SWORDFISH AND TOMATO KEBABS

154 WHOLE HAM WITH PEAR CHUTNEY

168 PRAWN, SAUSAGE AND CLAM PAELLA

CHURRASCO MIXED GRILL WITH TOMATO-CITRUS BLACK BEANS

SERVES: 6
PREP TIME: 30 MINUTES
MARINATING TIME: 1 HOUR
GRILLING TIME: 15–20 MINUTES

BEANS
2 × 475-g/15-oz cans black beans, rinsed
300 g/10 oz cherry tomatoes, halved
2 onions, finely diced, rinsed under cold water
15 g/½ oz flat-leaf parsley, finely chopped
2 tablespoons extra-virgin olive oil
1 tablespoon fresh lime juice
2 teaspoons finely chopped garlic
Grated zest of 1 orange
½ teaspoon smoked paprika
½ teaspoon sea salt

MARINADE
15 g/½ oz flat-leaf parsley, finely chopped
4 tablespoons extra-virgin olive oil
4 tablespoons fresh orange juice
1 tablespoon fresh lime juice
1 tablespoon finely chopped garlic
2 teaspoons sea salt
1 teaspoon ground black pepper

1 pork fillet, 375–500 g/12 oz–1 lb, trimmed of excess fat
   and skin

3 boneless, skinless chicken breasts, each about 175 g/6 oz
250 g/8 oz fully cooked chorizo sausages

1 Gently mix the bean ingredients in a large bowl. Set aside at room temperature for at least 45 minutes.

2 Whisk the marinade ingredients in a bowl. Pour half the marinade into another bowl. Add the pork fillet to the first bowl and the chicken breasts to the second bowl. Turn to coat the meat evenly. Cover and refrigerate for 1 hour.

3 Prepare the grill for direct cooking over medium heat (180–230°C/350–450°F).

4 Brush the cooking grates clean. Remove the pork and chicken from the bowls and let any excess marinade drip back into the bowls. Discard the marinade. Grill the pork, chicken and chorizo over **direct medium heat**, with the lid closed as much as possible and turning occasionally, until the pork is evenly seared and the centre is barely pink, the chicken is firm to the touch and opaque all the way to the centre and the chorizo is browned. The pork will take 15–20 minutes, the chicken will take 8–12 minutes and the chorizo will take about 8 minutes. Remove from the grill as they are done.

5 Cut the meat into 1-cm/½-inch slices. Serve warm with the bean salad.

HOT DOGS WITH AVOCADO AND CRISPS

SERVES: 8
PREP TIME: 10 MINUTES
GRILLING TIME: 5–7 MINUTES

GUACAMOLE
2 ripe avocados
1 tablespoon fresh lime juice
½ teaspoon sea salt
¼ teaspoon ground black pepper

8 all-beef hot dogs, each about 125 g/4 oz
8 hot dog rolls
1 small onion, sliced
2 ripe plum tomatoes, deseeded and cut into 5-mm/
    ¼-inch pieces
50 g/2 oz potato crisps, crushed

1 Prepare the grill for direct cooking over medium heat (180–230°C/350–450°F).

2 Cut the avocados in half, remove the stones, and scoop the flesh into a bowl. Add the remaining guacamole ingredients and mash together with a fork. Cover with clingfilm, placing the film directly on the surface of the guacamole to prevent it from browning. Refrigerate until ready to serve.

3 Cut a few shallow slashes in each hot dog.

4 Brush the cooking grates clean. Grill the hot dogs over **direct medium heat** for 5–7 minutes, with the lid closed as much as possible and turning occasionally, until lightly marked on the outside and hot all the way to the centre. During the last minute of grilling time, toast the rolls, cut sides down, over direct heat.

5 Place the hot dogs in the rolls. Top each with the guacamole, sliced onions, tomatoes and crushed potato crisps. Serve warm.

PEPPERED BEEF SIRLOIN KEBABS WITH DIJON CREAM

1 tablespoon mixed peppercorns (black, white, pink and green) or 2 teaspoons black peppercorns
Sea salt
½ teaspoon ground cumin
1 kg/2 lb beef sirloin, about 3 cm/1¼ inches thick, cut into 3-cm/1¼-inch cubes
Extra-virgin olive oil
2 courgettes, cut lengthways and then crossways into 1-cm/½-inch pieces
2 large red peppers, cut into 3-cm/1¼-inch squares

CREAM
125 ml/4 fl oz crème fraîche or soured cream
2 tablespoons Dijon mustard
2 tablespoons finely chopped fresh chives
1 tablespoon red wine vinegar

1 Prepare the grill for direct cooking over high heat (230–290°C/450–550°F).

2 Coarsely grind the peppercorns in a spice mill. Pour the pepper into a large bowl and mix in 1½ teaspoons salt and the cumin. Place the meat in the bowl with the spices and add enough oil to coat the cubes lightly; toss to coat evenly. In another bowl lightly coat the courgettes and peppers with oil and season evenly with salt. Thread each skewer alternately with courgettes, meat cubes and peppers.

3 Whisk the cream ingredients in a small bowl. Cover and refrigerate until ready to serve.

4 Brush the cooking grates clean. Grill the kebabs over **direct high heat**, with the lid closed as much as possible and turning occasionally, until the vegetables are crisp-tender and the meat is cooked to your desired doneness, 6–8 minutes for medium rare. Remove the skewers from the grill and serve warm with the cream.

CHEESY NACHOS WITH STEAK AND BLACK BEANS

SERVES: 6–8; 12–15 AS A STARTER
PREP TIME: 30 MINUTES
GRILLING TIME: 14–16 MINUTES
SPECIAL EQUIPMENT: LARGE ROASTING TRAY

PASTE

1 tablespoon extra-virgin olive oil
1 tablespoon finely chopped garlic
1 teaspoon chilli powder
1 teaspoon soft brown sugar
½ teaspoon sea salt
½ teaspoon chipotle chilli powder
¼ teaspoon ground cumin

750 g/1½ lb skirt steak, 1–1.5 cm/½–¾ inch thick, trimmed of excess surface fat, cut into 30-cm/12-inch long pieces

SALSA

2 ripe avocados, chopped
3 ripe plum tomatoes, chopped
1 small red onion, finely chopped
5 tablespoons finely chopped fresh coriander
2–3 pickled jalapeño chillies, finely chopped
3 tablespoons fresh lime juice
1 tablespoon finely chopped garlic
Sea salt

375-g/12-oz bag tortilla chips

475-g/15-oz can black beans, rinsed
250 g/8 oz mature Cheddar cheese, grated
250 g/8 oz Monterey Jack or mild Cheddar cheese, grated

1 Mix the paste ingredients in a small bowl. Spread the paste on both sides of each steak. Allow the steaks to stand at room temperature for 15–30 minutes before grilling.

2 Combine the salsa ingredients in a bowl and season with salt. Let the salsa sit at room temperature for about 30 minutes to fully incorporate the flavours.

3 Prepare the grill for direct cooking over high heat (230–290°C/450–550°F).

4 Brush the cooking grates clean. Grill the steaks over **direct high heat**, with the lid closed as much as possible and turning once or twice (if flare-ups occur, move the steaks temporarily over indirect heat), until cooked to your desired doneness, 4–6 minutes for medium rare. Remove from the grill and leave to rest for 3–5 minutes. Cut the steak into bite-sized pieces.

5 Working in two batches, layer tortilla chips, steak, black beans and cheese on a large roasting tray. Place the tray over **direct high heat**, close the lid, and cook for about 5 minutes until the cheese is melted. Remove from the grill and serve immediately with the salsa.

TURKISH RACK OF LAMB WITH TABBOULEH

SERVES: 4
PREP TIME: 40 MINUTES
GRILLING TIME: 15–20 MINUTES

TABBOULEH
1 teaspoon sea salt
200 g/7 oz wholegrain quick-cooking bulgar wheat
75 g/3 oz shelled dry-roasted unsalted pistachios
15 g/½ oz chopped mint
50 g/2 oz currants
50 g/2 oz dried apricots, chopped

DRESSING
3 tablespoons extra-virgin olive oil
3 tablespoons fresh lemon juice
¾ teaspoon ground cumin
¼ teaspoon ground cinnamon

PASTE
2 tablespoons extra-virgin olive oil
1 tablespoon dried mint
½ teaspoon ground cumin
¼ teaspoon ground cinnamon
¼ teaspoon sea salt
¼ teaspoon ground black pepper

1 rack of lamb, 8 bones and about 750 g/1½ lb, frenched and
   trimmed of excess fat

1 Fill a large saucepan two-thirds full with water and bring to
the boil. Add the salt and bulgar. Boil for about 14 minutes,
stirring occasionally, until the bulgar is tender but still slightly
chewy. Drain, rinse under cold water to cool quickly, and drain
again. Squeeze one handful of bulgar at a time to remove the
excess water, transferring the dried grains to a large bowl. Add
the remaining tabbouleh ingredients and stir to combine.

2 Whisk the dressing ingredients in a small bowl. Pour the
dressing over the tabbouleh and mix thoroughly.

3 Prepare the grill for direct cooking over medium heat
(180–230°C/350–450°F).

4 Combine the paste ingredients in a small bowl. Spread the
paste all over the lamb. Allow to stand at room temperature for
15–30 minutes before grilling.

5 Brush the cooking grates clean. Grill the lamb, bone side
down first, over **direct medium heat**, with the lid closed as
much as possible, turning once or twice (if flare-ups should
occur, move the racks temporarily over indirect heat), until
cooked to your desired doneness, 15–20 minutes for medium
rare. Remove from the grill and leave to rest for 3–5 minutes.
Cut the rack between the bones into individual chops. Serve
warm with the tabbouleh.

BUTTERFLIED LEG OF LAMB WITH PESTO AÏOLI

SERVES: 6–8
PREP TIME: 15 MINUTES
GRILLING TIME: 30–45 MINUTES

AÏOLI
175 ml/6 fl oz ready-made pesto
125 ml/4 fl oz mayonnaise
1 garlic clove, finely chopped

1 boneless leg of lamb, about 1.5 kg/3 lb, butterflied and
    trimmed of excess fat
3 tablespoons extra-virgin olive oil
1 tablespoon sea salt
1½ teaspoons ground black pepper

1 Combine the aïoli ingredients in a small bowl. Set aside.

2 Coat the lamb on all sides with the oil and season evenly with the salt and pepper. Allow the lamb to stand at room temperature for 15–30 minutes before grilling.

3 Prepare the grill for direct and indirect cooking over medium heat (180–230°C/350–450°F).

4 Brush the cooking grates clean. Sear the lamb over **direct medium heat** for 10–15 minutes, with the lid closed as much as possible and turning once, until nicely browned on both sides. Slide the lamb over **indirect medium heat** and cook, with the lid closed, to your desired doneness, 20–30 minutes for medium rare. Remove from the grill and leave to rest for 5–10 minutes.

5 Cut the lamb crossways into 5-mm/¼-inch slices. Serve warm with the aïoli.

LAMB AND CHORIZO BURGERS WITH CHEESE AND POBLANO CHILLIES

SERVES: 6
PREP TIME: 30 MINUTES
GRILLING TIME: 14–18 MINUTES

MAYONNAISE
125 ml/4 fl oz mayonnaise
125 ml/4 fl oz Greek yogurt
1 tablespoon finely grated lime zest
2 teaspoons fresh lime juice
Sea salt
Ground black pepper

500 g/1 lb raw chorizo sausages, casings removed
500 g/1 lb minced lamb
Extra-virgin olive oil
3 large poblano chillies
12 thin slices Monterey Jack or Cheddar cheese
12 small pitta breads, tops cut off
6 thin slices mild onion

1 Combine the mayonnaise ingredients in a small bowl. Season with salt and pepper.

2 Sauté the chorizo for about 8 minutes in a heavy frying pan over a medium heat, stirring occasionally, until it is cooked through, breaking the meat into 1-cm/½-inch chunks. Transfer the chorizo to a large sieve set over a bowl. Drain and reserve the drippings.

3 Prepare the grill for direct cooking over medium-high heat (200–260°C/400–500°F).

4 Combine the minced lamb, 2 tablespoons water, ½ teaspoon salt, ¼ teaspoon pepper and 1 tablespoon of the chorizo drippings in a large bowl. Mix thoroughly. Add the drained chorizo and blend gently, taking care not to overwork the mixture. Using wet hands, form the mixture into 12 burgers, each about 1 cm/½ inch thick. Lightly brush both sides with oil.

5 Brush the cooking grates clean. Grill the chillies over **direct medium-high heat** for 8–10 minutes, with the lid closed as much as possible and turning occasionally, until charred and beginning to soften. Transfer to a bowl and cover with clingfilm to trap the steam.

6 Grill the burgers over **direct medium-high heat** for 6–8 minutes, with the lid closed as much as possible and turning once or twice, until cooked to medium doneness. During the last minute of grilling time, place a slice of cheese on top of each burger to melt.

7 Remove the chillies from the bowl and peel off and discard the skin, stems and seeds. Cut each chilli into four pieces. Serve the burgers in pitta breads with the mayonnaise, a few onion rings and a slice of chilli.

PULLED PORK BARBECUE SANDWICHES

SERVES: 10–12
PREP TIME: 30 MINUTES
GRILLING TIME: 3–4 HOURS
SPECIAL EQUIPMENT: INSTANT-READ MEAT
   THERMOMETER

SAUCE
475 ml/16 fl oz tomato ketchup
150 ml/¼ pint stout
125 ml/4 fl oz cider vinegar
4 tablespoons soft brown sugar
2 tablespoons black treacle
1 tablespoon Worcestershire sauce
1 tablespoon soy sauce
2 teaspoons Dijon mustard
1 teaspoon ground cayenne pepper

2–2.5 kg/4–5 lb boneless pork shoulder, rolled and tied
Sea salt
Ground black pepper

SLAW
½ head green cabbage, shredded
3 carrots, grated
1 red pepper, thinly sliced
½ mild onion, thinly sliced
125 ml/4 fl oz extra-virgin olive oil
2 tablespoons cider vinegar
¾ teaspoon Dijon mustard
2 tablespoons celery seeds
Burger buns

1 Whisk the sauce ingredients in a small saucepan. Bring the sauce to a simmer over a low heat and simmer gently for about 15 minutes, whisking occasionally. Set aside to cool at room temperature.

2 Season all sides of the pork generously with salt and pepper. Allow the meat to stand at room temperature for about 30 minutes before grilling.

3 Prepare the grill for indirect cooking over medium-low heat (about 170°C/325°F).

4 Brush the cooking grates clean. Grill the meat, fat side up, over *indirect medium-low heat* for 3–4 hours, with the lid closed, keeping the temperature of the grill as close to 170°C/325°F as possible, until the internal temperature registers 85–88°C/185–190°F on an instant-read meat thermometer. The meat should be so tender it pulls apart easily. Transfer to a carving board, cover loosely with foil and leave to rest for about 20 minutes. Toast the rolls over direct heat for about 1 minute.

5 Meanwhile, combine the cabbage, carrots, pepper and onion in a large bowl. Whisk the oil, vinegar, mustard and celery seeds in a small bowl. Add as much of the dressing to the slaw as you like. Mix well and set aside.

6 Using two forks or your fingers, pull the pork apart into shreds, discarding any pockets of fat. Place in a large bowl and moisten the pork with as much of the sauce as you like. Pile the warm pork on the toasted buns and top with coleslaw.

CHILLI-RUBBED PORK FILLET

SERVES: 4
PREP TIME: 10 MINUTES
GRILLING TIME: 15–20 MINUTES
SPECIAL EQUIPMENT: INSTANT-READ MEAT
    THERMOMETER

RUB
1 tablespoon soft brown sugar
1 tablespoon chilli powder
1 teaspoon ground cumin
¾ teaspoon sea salt
½ teaspoon garlic powder
¼ teaspoon ground black pepper

2 pork fillets, each 375–500 g/12 oz–1 lb, trimmed of excess
    fat and silver skin
2 teaspoons extra-virgin olive oil

1 tablespoon finely chopped oregano

1 Combine the rub ingredients in a small bowl, mashing with a fork to mix thoroughly. Coat the pork fillets with the oil then season evenly with the rub. Allow the meat to stand at room temperature for 15–30 minutes before grilling.

2 Prepare the grill for direct cooking over medium heat (180–230°C/350–450°F).

3 Brush the cooking grates clean. Grill the pork fillets over **direct medium heat** for 15–20 minutes, with the lid closed as much as possible and turning about every 5 minutes, until the outsides are evenly seared and the internal temperature registers 65°C/150°F on an instant-read meat thermometer. Remove from the grill and leave to rest for 3–5 minutes.

4 Season with the oregano then cut into 1-cm/½-inch slices. Serve warm.

WHOLE HAM WITH PEAR CHUTNEY

SERVES: 6–8

PREP TIME: 15 MINUTES, PLUS ABOUT 20 MINUTES FOR THE CHUTNEY

GRILLING TIME: 30–40 MINUTES

SPECIAL EQUIPMENT: LARGE DISPOSABLE ALUMINIUM FOIL ROASTING TRAY; 30-CM/12-INCH HEAVY FRYING PAN; INSTANT-READ MEAT THERMOMETER

1.5–2 kg/3–4 lb boneless smoked gammon joint, cooked
2 teaspoons vegetable oil
4 ripe pears, peeled and cored, cut into bite-sized pieces
375 g/12 oz soft brown sugar
175 ml/6 fl oz cider vinegar
1 tablespoon Dijon mustard
2 teaspoons grated fresh ginger
¼ teaspoon crushed red chilli flakes

1 Let the ham stand at room temperature for about 30 minutes before grilling.

2 Prepare the grill for indirect cooking over medium heat (180–230°C/350–450°F).

3 Brush the cooking grates clean. Put the ham, flat side down, in a large disposable foil tray and add 125 ml/4 fl oz water to help prevent the meat from drying out. Place the tray over *indirect medium heat*, close the grill lid and cook for 30–40 minutes, until the internal temperature registers 70°C/160°F on an instant-read meat thermometer.

4 While the ham is cooking, make the chutney. Warm the oil in a 30-cm/12-inch heavy frying pan over a medium-high heat. Add the pears, cooking and stirring them for 4–5 minutes until they are softened but not mushy. Using a slotted spoon, remove about half the pear pieces and set them aside. Add the sugar, vinegar, mustard, ginger and chilli flakes to the pears in the pan, combining thoroughly. Cook for 8–10 minutes, stirring occasionally, until the mixture thickens and begins to darken in colour. Return the reserved pears and any accumulated juices to the pan and continue cooking for 5 minutes, stirring occasionally to prevent the chutney from sticking. Transfer to a serving dish and cool slightly.

5 Remove the ham from the grill and leave to rest for 3–5 minutes. Cut into slices and serve warm with the chutney.

HONEY-GINGER CHICKEN SATAYS

SERVES: 4–6

PREP TIME: 20 MINUTES

GRILLING TIME: 4–6 MINUTES

SPECIAL EQUIPMENT: METAL OR BAMBOO SKEWERS
(IF USING BAMBOO, SOAK IN WATER FOR AT LEAST
30 MINUTES)

GLAZE

4 tablespoons honey

4 tablespoons soy sauce

2 tablespoons rice vinegar

1 tablespoon grated fresh ginger

2 teaspoons finely chopped garlic

½–1 teaspoon hot chilli-garlic sauce

1 kg/2 lb chicken strips *or* boneless, skinless chicken breasts,
cut into 1-cm/½-inch strips

Vegetable oil

½ teaspoon sea salt

½ teaspoon ground black pepper

1 lime, cut into wedges

1 Prepare the grill for direct and indirect cooking over high heat (230–290°C/450–550°F).

2 Combine the glaze ingredients in a small saucepan over a medium-high heat and bring to the boil. Reduce the heat to low and simmer for about 3 minutes. Set aside.

3 Thread the pieces of chicken lengthways on to skewers, making sure the skewers run through the centre of each piece. Lightly coat the chicken with oil and season evenly with the salt and pepper.

4 Brush the cooking grates clean. Grill the chicken over ***direct high heat*** for 2–3 minutes, with the lid closed as much as possible and turning once, until nicely marked. Move the chicken over ***indirect high heat***, brush with the glaze on both sides and continue grilling for 2–3 minutes, turning once, until the chicken is cooked through and the glaze looks glossy. Remove from the grill and serve warm with the lime wedges.

CHICKEN WINGS WITH HOT HONEY BARBECUE SAUCE

SERVES: 4–6
PREP TIME: 10 MINUTES
GRILLING TIME: 20–25 MINUTES

SAUCE
175 ml/6 fl oz tomato ketchup
4 tablespoons runny honey
2 tablespoons spicy brown mustard
3 tablespoons cider vinegar
1 teaspoon ground cayenne pepper

1.5 kg/3 lb chicken wings, each cut in half at the joint,
    wing tips removed
¾ teaspoon garlic powder
½ teaspoon sea salt

1 Prepare the grill for direct and indirect cooking over medium heat (180–230°C/350–450°F).

2 Combine the sauce ingredients in a small saucepan. Cook over a medium heat until the sauce comes to a simmer, stirring occasionally. Simmer for about 30 seconds to blend in the honey, stirring often, and then remove the saucepan from the heat.

3 Season the chicken wings evenly with the garlic powder and salt.

4 Brush the cooking grates clean. Grill the wings over **direct medium heat** for 10–15 minutes, with the lid closed as much as possible and turning once or twice, until golden brown. Move the wings over **indirect medium heat** and continue grilling for about 10 minutes more, until the skin is dark brown and crisp and the meat is no longer pink at the bone. During the final 5 minutes of grilling, brush the wings evenly with the sauce, turning once or twice. Serve warm.

Chicken wings are a super simple way to begin a casual barbecue. All you need to do is brown them over direct heat for 10 minutes or so and then finish them over indirect heat for about the same length of time. If they cook over indirect heat for 5 or 10 minutes more, no big deal. It's pretty hard to overcook them, and if any get a little too charred, use the sweet hot sauce here to gloss over the crispy edges.

SMOKED CHICKEN WITH HOMEMADE COLESLAW

SERVES: 4–6
PREP TIME: 30 MINUTES
GRILLING TIME: 45–50 MINUTES

SAUCE
250 ml/8 fl oz tomato ketchup
4 tablespoons red wine vinegar
4 tablespoons black treacle
2 tablespoons mild American mustard
1½ teaspoons Worcestershire sauce
1½ teaspoons ancho chilli powder
½ teaspoon liquid smoke
½ teaspoon garlic granules

Sea salt
Ground black pepper

6 whole chicken legs, each 300–375 g/10–12 oz, cut into
    thighs and drumsticks
Vegetable oil

2 handfuls hickory wood chips, soaked in water for at least
    30 minutes

COLESLAW
150 ml/¼ pint mayonnaise
1½ tablespoons cider vinegar
1 teaspoon granulated sugar
¼ teaspoon celery seeds
250 g/8 oz green cabbage, very thinly sliced
125 g/4 oz red cabbage, thinly sliced
50 g/2 oz carrots, peeled and coarsely grated

1 Prepare the grill for direct and indirect cooking over medium heat (180–230°C/350–450°F).

2 Bring the sauce ingredients to a simmer in a saucepan over a medium heat. Season with salt and pepper. Set aside.

3 Lightly coat the chicken on all sides with oil and season evenly with salt and pepper.

4 Brush the cooking grates clean. Grill the chicken, skin side down first, over *direct medium heat* for about 10 minutes, with the lid closed as much as possible and turning once or twice (watch for flare-ups), until golden brown. Move the chicken pieces over *indirect medium heat*. Drain and scatter the wood chips over the lit charcoal or put them in the smoker box of a gas grill, following manufacturer's instructions. Continue to grill the chicken, with the lid closed, for about 20 minutes.

5 Meanwhile, make the coleslaw. Whisk the mayonnaise, vinegar, sugar, celery seeds, ½ teaspoon salt and ¼ teaspoon pepper in a large bowl. Add the green and red cabbage and carrot and toss to coat. Refrigerate until ready to serve.

6 After the chicken pieces have cooked over indirect heat for 20 minutes, brush both sides with a thin layer of the sauce and continue cooking for 15–20 minutes, occasionally turning the chicken and brushing with the sauce, until the juices run clear and the meat is no longer pink at the bone. Serve warm or at room temperature with the remaining sauce and the coleslaw on the side.

CHICKEN AND HAM BROCHETTES WITH HONEY-MUSTARD DIPPING SAUCE

SERVES: 6
PREP TIME: 15 MINUTES
GRILLING TIME: 8–10 MINUTES
SPECIAL EQUIPMENT: METAL OR BAMBOO SKEWERS
   (IF USING BAMBOO, SOAK IN WATER FOR AT LEAST
   30 MINUTES)

3 tablespoons extra-virgin olive oil
1 teaspoon garlic granules
Sea salt
Ground black pepper
12 boneless, skinless chicken thighs, about 1 kg/2 lb in total,
   cut into 3.5-cm/1½-inch pieces
1 gammon steak, about 500 g/1 lb and 1.5 cm/¾ inch thick,
   cut into 1.5-cm/¾-inch cubes

SAUCE
150 ml/¼ pint mayonnaise
4 tablespoons Dijon mustard
3 tablespoons runny honey

1 Prepare the grill for direct cooking over medium heat (180–230°C/350–450°F).

2 Whisk the oil, garlic granules, ½ teaspoon salt and ¼ teaspoon pepper in a large bowl. Add the chicken pieces and gammon cubes and turn to coat them evenly. Thread the chicken and ham on to skewers, alternating the pieces and arranging them so they are touching (but not crammed together). You can also thread them separately on their skewers, if preferred.

3 Whisk the sauce ingredients in a small bowl then season with salt and pepper.

4 Brush the cooking grates clean. Grill the skewers over **direct medium heat** for 8–10 minutes, with the lid closed as much as possible and turning two or three times, until the chicken meat is firm and the juices run clear and the gammon is heated through. Serve the kebabs immediately with the dipping sauce.

EASY ROSEMARY-ROASTED CHICKEN

SERVES: 4
PREP TIME: 15 MINUTES
MARINATING TIME: UP TO 4 HOURS
GRILLING TIME: 40–50 MINUTES

MARINADE
2 tablespoons extra-virgin olive oil
1 tablespoon Dijon mustard
1 tablespoon Worcestershire sauce
1 tablespoon cider vinegar
1 tablespoon finely chopped rosemary
½ teaspoon sea salt
¼ teaspoon ground black pepper

1 chicken, about 2 kg/4 lb, giblets and any excess fat removed

1 Whisk all the marinade ingredients in a small bowl.

2 Cut the chicken into six pieces: two breast halves, two whole legs (thigh and drumstick) and two wings (remove and discard the wing tips). Brush each chicken piece on both sides with the marinade. If you have time, marinate the chicken in the refrigerator for as long as 4 hours. If not, you can roast the chicken straight away.

3 Prepare the grill for direct and indirect cooking over medium heat (180–230°C/350–450°F).

4 Brush the cooking grates clean. Grill the chicken pieces, skin side down, over *indirect medium heat*, with the lid closed as much as possible and turning once or twice, until fully cooked. The breasts and wing pieces will take 30–40 minutes and the whole legs will take 40–50 minutes. During the last 5 minutes of grilling time, move the chicken over *direct medium heat* and cook until well browned all over, turning once or twice. Remove from the grill and leave to rest for 3–5 minutes. Serve warm.

LEMON-PEPPER CHICKEN

SERVES: 4
PREP TIME: 15 MINUTES
GRILLING TIME: 40–50 MINUTES

PASTE
Finely grated zest of 2 lemons
2 tablespoons fresh lemon juice
2 tablespoons extra-virgin olive oil
2 tablespoons wholegrain mustard
1½ teaspoons sea salt
1 tablespoon dried oregano
2 garlic cloves, finely chopped
¾ teaspoon crushed red chilli flakes

1 chicken, about 2 kg/4 lb, giblets and any excess fat removed
1 lemon, cut into 8 wedges

1 Prepare the grill for indirect cooking over medium heat (180–230°C/350–450°F).

2 Whisk all the paste ingredients in a large bowl.

3 Cut the chicken into eight pieces: two breast halves, two thigh pieces, two drumsticks and two wings (cut off and discard the wing tips). Add the chicken pieces to the bowl with the paste and turn to coat evenly.

4 Brush the cooking grates clean. Grill the chicken pieces, skin side down, over **indirect medium heat** with the lid closed, until fully cooked. The breast and wing pieces will take 30–40 minutes. The drumstick and thigh pieces will take 40–50 minutes. If liked, to crisp the skin, grill the chicken over **direct medium heat** during the last 5–10 minutes of grilling time, turning once. Remove from the grill and leave to rest for 3–5 minutes. Serve warm with lemon wedges.

TURKEY KOFTA WITH MAJOR GREY'S CHUTNEY

SERVES: 6–8
PREP TIME: 15 MINUTES
GRILLING TIME: ABOUT 6 MINUTES
SPECIAL EQUIPMENT: 24 SHORT BAMBOO SKEWERS,
   SOAKED IN WATER FOR AT LEAST 30 MINUTES

KOFTA
625 g/1¼ lb minced turkey thigh meat
4 tablespoons finely chopped fresh coriander
1 tablespoon finely chopped garlic
1 tablespoon curry powder
½ teaspoon ground cayenne pepper
1 teaspoon sea salt

125 ml/4 fl oz Major Grey's mango chutney

1 Prepare the grill for direct cooking over medium heat (180–230°C/350–450°F).

2 Using your hands, gently mix the kofta ingredients in a large bowl. Shape into 24 small meatballs (kofta), each about 2.5 cm/1 inch in diameter. Place two kofta side by side. Push a skewer through the kofta and then another skewer parallel to the first one. Double skewer the remaining kofta.

3 Brush the cooking grates clean. Grill the kofta over **direct medium heat** for about 6 minutes, with the lid closed as much as possible and turning once, until the meat is firm and fully cooked but still moist. Remove from the grill and serve warm with the chutney.

GRILLED HALIBUT CEVICHE

SERVES: 4–6
PREP TIME: 20 MINUTES
MARINATING TIME: ABOUT 2 HOURS
GRILLING TIME: 4–5 MINUTES

500 g/1 lb skinless halibut fillets, about 2.5 cm/1 inch thick
Extra-virgin olive oil
175–250 ml/6–8 fl oz fresh lime juice (from 6–8 limes)
1 tomato, deseeded and chopped
1 small red onion, chopped
3 small radishes, trimmed and cut into very thin wedges
½–1 jalapeño chilli, stem and seeds removed, finely chopped
1 garlic clove, finely chopped
¼ teaspoon sea salt
⅛ teaspoon granulated sugar

375-g/12-oz bag tortilla chips

1 Prepare the grill for direct cooking over high heat (230–290°C/450–550°F).

2 Brush the halibut fillets on both sides with oil.

3 Brush the cooking grates clean. Grill the halibut over **direct high heat** for 4–5 minutes, with the lid closed as much as possible and turning once, just long enough to sear both sides. Remove from the grill and let cool. Break into 1-cm/½-inch pieces and place in a bowl with enough lime juice to cover the fish. Cover and refrigerate for 2 hours or until the fish is opaque, stirring once or twice.

4 Drain and discard the liquid from the bowl and then stir in the remaining ingredients (if not serving immediately, add radishes just before serving to prevent the ceviche turning pink). Serve immediately or cover and chill for several hours. Serve cold with tortilla chips.

SPICY CALAMARI AND CHICKPEA SALAD WITH ORANGE VINAIGRETTE

SERVES: 4–6
PREP TIME: 25 MINUTES
GRILLING TIME: 2–4 MINUTES

VINAIGRETTE
2 jalapeño chillies, halved lengthways, seeds and
    veins removed
1 tablespoon finely grated orange zest
4 tablespoons fresh orange juice
2 tablespoons white wine vinegar
½ teaspoon paprika
Sea salt
Extra-virgin olive oil

475-g/15-oz can chickpeas, rinsed
250 g/8 oz small cherry tomatoes, halved
1 shallot, thinly sliced into rings

750 g/1½ lb calamari, tubes and tentacles, cleaned and
    patted dry
½ teaspoon ground black pepper

4 tablespoons roughly chopped mint

1 Process the chillies in a food processor or blender until finely chopped. Add the orange zest and juice, vinegar, paprika and 2 teaspoons salt. Process to combine. With the motor running, slowly add 4 tablespoons oil and process until the vinaigrette is smooth and emulsified. Combine the chickpeas, tomatoes and shallot in a large bowl. Toss with 4 tablespoons of the vinaigrette and set aside.

2 Prepare the grill for direct cooking over high heat (230–290°C/450–550°F).

3 Slide a knife into each tube and make horizontal cuts on one side of the calamari (the knife inside the tube allows you to score each tube without cutting all the way through). Place the calamari in a bowl. Add 2 tablespoons oil, 1 teaspoon salt and the pepper and toss to coat evenly.

4 Brush the cooking grates clean. Grill the calamari over ***direct high heat*** for 2–4 minutes, with the lid closed as much as possible and turning once, until opaque and cooked through. Remove from the grill and slice the tubes into 1-cm/½-inch rings. Add the calamari rings and tentacles to the salad and drizzle with the remaining vinaigrette. Toss gently to combine. Top with the mint. Serve immediately.

CORIANDER-MARINATED PRAWNS

SERVES: 4
PREP TIME: 20 MINUTES
MARINATING TIME: 10–15 MINUTES
GRILLING TIME: 2–4 MINUTES
SPECIAL EQUIPMENT: METAL OR BAMBOO SKEWERS
   (IF USING BAMBOO, SOAK IN WATER FOR AT LEAST
   30 MINUTES)

MARINADE
1 onion, coarsely chopped
15 g/½ oz fresh coriander
2 tablespoons vegetable oil
2 tablespoons fresh lime juice
1 jalapeño chilli, deseeded and coarsely chopped
1 tablespoon finely chopped garlic
1½ teaspoons sea salt
1 teaspoon ground cumin

625 g/1¼ lb large prawns, peeled and deveined, tails left on

Salsa (optional)

1 Prepare the grill for direct cooking over high heat (230–290°C/450–550°F).

2 Combine the marinade ingredients in a blender and process until smooth. Put the prawns in a large, resealable plastic bag and pour in the marinade. Press the air out of the bag and seal tightly. Turn the bag to distribute the marinade, place in a bowl and marinate at room temperature for 10–15 minutes while the grill preheats.

3 Remove the prawns from the bag and discard the marinade. Thread the prawns on to skewers. Brush the cooking grates clean. Grill the prawns over **direct high heat** for 2–4 minutes, with the lid closed as much as possible and turning once or twice, until the prawns are firm to the touch, lightly charred and just turning opaque in the centre. Remove from the grill and serve warm with your favourite salsa, if liked.

PRAWN, SAUSAGE AND CLAM PAELLA

SERVES: 6
PREP TIME: 30 MINUTES
GRILLING TIME: 33–39 MINUTES
SPECIAL EQUIPMENT: 30-CM/12-INCH CAST-IRON
    FRYING PAN

250 g/8 oz large prawns, peeled and deveined, tails left on
3 tablespoons extra-virgin olive oil
Sea salt
Ground black pepper

250 g/8 oz fully cooked smoked spicy sausages

300 g/10 oz onions, finely chopped
1 large red pepper, finely chopped
1 tablespoon finely chopped garlic
1 teaspoon smoked paprika
¼ teaspoon crushed saffron threads
400 g/13 oz medium-grain rice, such as Arborio
1 litre/1¾ pints chicken stock
250 ml/8 fl oz clam juice

75 g/3 oz small pimento-stuffed green olives
12 small clams, rinsed and scrubbed

1 Prepare the grill for direct cooking over medium heat (180–230°C/350–450°F).

2 Combine the prawns with 1 tablespoon of the oil in a medium bowl and toss to coat. Season with salt and pepper.

3 Brush the cooking grates clean. Grill the prawns and sausages over **direct medium heat** for about 2 minutes, with the lid closed as much as possible and turning once, until the prawns are half-cooked and the sausages are beginning to colour. Remove from the grill and set aside to cool. When the sausages are cool enough to handle, cut crossways into 1-cm/½-inch slices.

4 Place a 30-cm/12-inch cast-iron frying pan over **direct medium heat**. Heat the remaining oil in the pan. Add the onion and pepper and cook for about 5 minutes until the onion is tender, stirring occasionally and rotating the pan for even cooking. Stir in the garlic, paprika, saffron, rice and 1 teaspoon salt and cook for 1–2 minutes until the rice is well coated. Slowly stir in the stock and clam juice. Close the grill lid and let the mixture cook at a brisk simmer for about 15 minutes, until the rice is al dente. Nestle the prawns, sausage slices and olives into the rice. Add the clams. Continue cooking for 10–15 minutes, with the grill lid closed, until the clams open and the prawns are opaque in the centre. Discard any clams that have not opened.

5 Wearing insulated barbecue mitts or oven gloves, transfer the pan from the grill to a heatproof surface. Serve the paella hot from the pan.

SWORDFISH AND TOMATO KEBABS

SERVES: 4
PREP TIME: 15 MINUTES
MARINATING TIME: 15–30 MINUTES
GRILLING TIME: 8–10 MINUTES
SPECIAL EQUIPMENT: 8 METAL OR BAMBOO SKEWERS
(IF USING BAMBOO, SOAK IN WATER FOR AT LEAST
30 MINUTES)

MARINADE
4 tablespoons finely chopped flat-leaf parsley
Grated zest and juice of 1 lemon
1 tablespoon red wine vinegar
1 small shallot, chopped
1 teaspoon sea salt
½ teaspoon ground black pepper

4 swordfish steaks, each 250–300 g/8–10 oz and about
2.5 cm/1 inch thick, cut into 2.5-cm/1-inch pieces
24 cherry tomatoes

1 Prepare the grill for direct cooking over medium heat
(180–230°C/350–450°F).

2 Combine the marinade ingredients in a bowl. Put the
swordfish steaks in the bowl, cover and marinate at room
temperature for 15–30 minutes while the grill preheats.

3 Thread the swordfish and tomatoes alternately on to eight
skewers. Discard any remaining marinade.

4 Brush the cooking grates clean. Grill the kebabs over **direct
medium heat** for 8–10 minutes, with the lid closed as much as
possible and turning several times, until the swordfish is opaque
in the centre but still juicy. Remove the kebabs from the grill
and serve immediately.

PINEAPPLE PRAWN KEBABS

SERVES: 4–6
PREP TIME: 30 MINUTES
GRILLING TIME: 16–21 MINUTES
SPECIAL EQUIPMENT: 30-CM/12-INCH CAST-IRON FRYING
    PAN OR WOK

750 g/1½lb large prawns, peeled and deveined, tails left on
Groundnut oil
Sea salt
Ground black pepper

2 red onions, sliced
1 tablespoon finely chopped garlic
2 teaspoons finely chopped serrano chillies, seeds removed
2 large eggs, lightly beaten
500 g/1 lb cooked jasmine rice, chilled
3 tablespoons soy sauce
1 teaspoon toasted sesame oil

400 g/13 oz fresh pineapple, coarsely chopped
4 tablespoons finely chopped mint
4 tablespoons finely chopped fresh coriander
75 g/3 oz roasted cashews, roughly chopped

1 Prepare the grill for direct cooking over high heat (230–290°C/450–550°F).

2 Lightly coat the prawns with groundnut oil in a large bowl and season evenly with salt and pepper.

3 Brush the cooking grates clean. Grill the prawns over **direct high heat** for 2–4 minutes, with the lid closed as much as possible and turning once or twice, until firm to the touch and just turning opaque in the centre. Remove from the grill and set aside. Decrease the temperature of the grill to medium heat (180–230°C/350–450°F).

4 Heat 4 tablespoons groundnut oil in a 30-cm/12-inch cast-iron frying pan over **direct medium heat**. Add the onion, garlic and chilli and cook for about 5 minutes until the onion is tender, stirring occasionally and rotating the pan for even cooking. Stir in the eggs and cook for 1–2 minutes. Add the rice, soy sauce and sesame oil, mix thoroughly, and cook for 8–10 minutes until lightly browned, stirring occasionally. Keep the lid closed as much as possible during cooking.

5 Remove from the heat and add the prawns, pineapple, mint and coriander. Toss to combine and season with salt and pepper. Top with the cashews. Serve hot from the pan.

LOBSTER BISQUE

SERVES: 6-8
PREP TIME: 20 MINUTES, PLUS ABOUT 45 MINUTES FOR
    THE BISQUE
GRILLING TIME: 7-11 MINUTES
SPECIAL EQUIPMENT: KITCHEN SHEARS

4 lobster tails, each 175–250 g/6–8 oz, thawed if necessary
Extra-virgin olive oil

750 ml/1¼ pints fish stock or clam juice

25 g/1 oz unsalted butter
1 onion, finely chopped
2 celery sticks, cut into 5-mm/¼-inch pieces
2 carrots, peeled and cut into 5-mm/¼-inch pieces
2 garlic cloves, finely chopped
Sea salt
Ground black pepper
125 ml/ 4 fl oz white wine
½ teaspoon smoked paprika
1 tablespoon tomato purée
475 ml/16 fl oz single cream
2 tablespoons finely chopped chives

1 Prepare the grill for direct cooking over medium heat (180–230°C/350–450°F).

2 Using kitchen shears, split each tail in half lengthways. (If liked, to prevent the lobster meat from curling on the grill, thread a skewer lengthways through the centre of the meat.) Lightly brush the exposed meat with oil.

3. Brush the cooking grates clean. Grill the lobster tails, meat side down, over **direct medium heat** for 2–3 minutes, with the lid closed (watch for flare-ups), until lightly marked. Turn the tails over and cook for 5–8 minutes, brushing occasionally with oil until the meat is white and firm but not dry. Remove from the grill. When cool enough to handle, remove the lobster meat from the shells and cut the meat into bite-sized pieces.

4 Melt the butter in a large saucepan over a medium heat. Add the onion, celery, carrots, garlic, ½ teaspoon salt and ¼ teaspoon pepper. Cook for about 5 minutes, stirring occasionally, until all the vegetables begin to soften and lightly brown. Add the wine and cook for about 3 minutes until it evaporates, stirring to scrape up any browned bits. Add the paprika and tomato purée and stir to combine. Stir in the fish stock and then the cream. Bring to a simmer and cook for about 10 minutes until the vegetables are tender.

5 Transfer to a blender (in two batches), or use a stick blender, and purée until smooth. Return the bisque to the saucepan and simmer until it has the consistency you like. Add the lobster meat and cook for 3–5 minutes until warm. Season with salt and pepper. Ladle into bowls and garnish with chives. Serve warm.

LEMON-STUFFED SNAPPER WITH ROASTED TOMATO SAUCE

SERVES: 4
PREP TIME: 30 MINUTES
GRILLING TIME: 53 MINUTES–1 HOUR
SPECIAL EQUIPMENT: KITCHEN STRING

SAUCE
1 large shallot, halved through the root and stem ends
500 g/1 lb plum tomatoes, halved lengthways
Extra-virgin olive oil
25 g/1 oz flat-leaf parsley
4 tablespoons toasted pine nuts
2 tablespoons fresh lemon juice
1 tablespoon sherry vinegar
¼ teaspoon ground cayenne pepper
Sea salt

1 red snapper or sea bass, 1.5–1.6 kg/3–3¼ lb, gutted
    and scaled
Ground black pepper
1 tablespoon tomato purée
1 lemon, cut into 4 slices
25 g/1 oz flat-leaf parsley

1 Prepare the grill for direct and indirect cooking over medium heat (180–230°C/350–450°F).

2 Lightly brush the shallot and tomatoes with oil. Brush the cooking grates clean. Grill them over **direct medium heat** for 8–10 minutes, with the lid closed as much as possible and turning once or twice, until the tomato skins blister and the shallot is tender. Cut off and discard the root ends of the shallot halves then roughly chop the shallot. Combine the shallot and tomatoes with the parsley, pine nuts, lemon juice, vinegar and cayenne pepper in a food processor. Pulse until you have a smooth consistency. Season with salt.

3 Season the inside of the fish evenly with 1 teaspoon salt and 1 teaspoon pepper then spread with the tomato purée. Fill the fish with the lemon slices and parsley, and tie with kitchen string to hold it closed. Lightly brush the fish with oil.

4 Brush the cooking grates clean. Grill the fish over **indirect medium heat** for 45–50 minutes, with the lid closed and turning once, until the flesh is opaque near the bone but still juicy. Transfer to a chopping board and leave to rest for 3–5 minutes.

5 Carefully remove the string from the fish and then cut off the head and tail. Cut along the backbone and open the fish like a book. Remove the bones, and lift the flesh off the skin. Serve warm with the sauce.

BABY ARTICHOKES WITH BASIL OIL

SERVES: 6
PREP TIME: 15 MINUTES
BOILING TIME: 5–10 MINUTES
GRILLING TIME: 6–8 MINUTES

Sea salt
12 baby artichokes
Juice of ½ lemon
125 ml/4 fl oz plus 1 tablespoon extra-virgin olive oil
Ground black pepper

15 g /½ oz basil leaves
4 tablespoons freshly grated Parmesan cheese
2 tablespoons pine nuts, preferably toasted
1 garlic clove, finely chopped

1 Bring a saucepan of lightly salted water to the boil. Rinse the artichokes under cold running water. Snap off the dark green outer leaves of the artichokes to reveal the yellowish leaves with pale green tips. Lay each artichoke on its side. With a sharp knife cut off the stalk end and the sharp tip of each artichoke.

Cut each artichoke in half lengthways. Pare off the green skin from the base and stalk. After each artichoke is trimmed, place in a bowl of water mixed with the lemon juice.

2 Prepare the grill for direct cooking over medium heat (180–230°C/350–450°F).

3 Drain the artichokes. Cook in the boiling water for 5–10 minutes, just until tender when pierced with the tip of a knife. Drain and rinse under cold water. Transfer to a bowl and toss with the 1 tablespoon oil. Season with salt and pepper.

4 Pulse the basil, cheese, pine nuts and garlic in a food processor until the basil is finely chopped. With the machine running, add the remaining 125 ml/4 fl oz oil through the feed tube. Season with ¼ teaspoon salt and ⅛ teaspoon pepper. Pour into a small bowl.

5 Brush the cooking grates clean. Grill the artichokes over **direct medium heat** for 6–8 minutes, with the lid closed as much as possible and turning occasionally, until golden brown. Remove from the grill and serve warm with the basil oil.

ROASTED PEPPER SALAD WITH PINE NUTS

SERVES: 6
PREP TIME: 15 MINUTES
GRILLING TIME: 6–8 MINUTES

6 peppers, preferably 2 red, 2 yellow and 2 orange
2 tablespoons pine nuts

2 teaspoons red wine vinegar
1 garlic clove, finely chopped
3 tablespoons extra-virgin olive oil
¼ teaspoon sea salt
¼ teaspoon ground black pepper
2 tablespoons small capers, rinsed
1 tablespoon chopped oregano

1 Prepare the grill for direct cooking over high heat (230–290°C/450–550°F).

2 Working with one pepper at a time, use a sharp knife, cut off the top and bottom of each pepper to make 'lids'. Remove the stalk. Cut each pepper down the side, and open each up into a large strip. Cut away the ribs and seeds (see page 15).

3 Brush the cooking grates clean. Grill the pepper strips and lids, shiny skin side down, over ***direct high heat*** for 6–8 minutes, with the lid closed, until the skin is blackened and blistered (do not turn). Place the pepper pieces in a bowl and cover with clingfilm to trap the steam. Leave to stand for 5–10 minutes.

4 Preheat a small frying pan over a medium heat. Add the pine nuts and cook for about 3 minutes, stirring often, until toasted. Transfer to a plate.

5 Remove the peppers from the bowl and peel away and discard the charred skins. Cut the long pepper strips into 2.5-cm/1-inch-wide pieces and coarsely chop the 'lids'. Arrange on a serving plate.

6 Whisk the vinegar and garlic in a small bowl. Gradually whisk in the oil, then season with the salt and pepper. Drizzle the vinaigrette over the peppers. Top with the toasted pine nuts, capers and oregano. Serve warm or at room temperature.

ASPARAGUS AND TOMATO SALAD WITH FETA

SERVES: 4–6
PREP TIME: 10 MINUTES
GRILLING TIME: 6–8 MINUTES
SPECIAL EQUIPMENT: PERFORATED GRILL PAN

VINAIGRETTE
1 tablespoon Dijon mustard
2 tablespoons champagne vinegar
¼ teaspoon sea salt
⅛ teaspoon ground black pepper
125 ml/4 fl oz extra-virgin olive oil

750 g/1½ lb asparagus
500 g/1 lb cherry tomatoes
3 slices rustic white bread, about 75 g/3 oz in total, cut into
    1-cm/½-inch cubes
125 g/4 oz feta cheese, crumbled
2 tablespoons chopped fresh chives

1 Prepare the grill for direct cooking over medium heat (180–230°C/350–450°F) and preheat the grill pan.

2 Whisk the mustard, vinegar, salt and pepper in a small bowl. Slowly drizzle and whisk in the oil until it is emulsified.

3 Remove and discard the tough bottom of each asparagus spear by grasping at each end and bending it gently until it snaps at its natural point of tenderness, usually about two-thirds of the way down the spear. Spread the asparagus on a large plate. Drizzle with 2 tablespoons of the vinaigrette and turn the spears until they are evenly coated. Toss the tomatoes and bread cubes with 2 tablespoons of the vinaigrette in a bowl.

4 Brush the cooking grates clean. Spread the tomatoes and bread cubes in a single layer on the grill pan and lay the asparagus on the cooking grate. Grill over **direct medium heat**, with the lid closed as much as possible and turning often, until the asparagus is tender, the tomatoes begin to soften and the bread cubes are toasted. The asparagus will take 6–8 minutes and the tomatoes and bread cubes will take 2–4 minutes.

5 Arrange the asparagus spears on a serving plate and top with the tomatoes, croutons, feta and chives. Serve with the remaining vinaigrette.

POTATO HASH WITH CABBAGE, HAM AND ONIONS

SERVES: 4
PREP TIME: 20 MINUTES
GRILLING TIME: 10–12 MINUTES

4 tablespoons extra-virgin olive oil
1 teaspoon sea salt
½ teaspoon onion granules
½ teaspoon ground black pepper
2 King Edward potatoes, about 750 g/1½ lb in total, cut lengthways into 8-mm/⅓-inch slices
½ head green cabbage, quartered
1 red onion, cut crossways into 1-cm/½-inch slices

25 g/1 oz unsalted butter, melted
1 teaspoon wholegrain mustard
2 teaspoons finely chopped thyme

1 gammon steak, 250–375 g/8–12 oz and about 1 cm/ ½ inch thick

1 Prepare the grill for direct cooking over medium heat (180–230°C/350–450°F).

2 Mix 2 tablespoons of the oil, the salt, onion granules and pepper in a bowl. Brush all sides of the potato slices, cabbage quarters and onion slices with the oil mixture.

3 Combine the remaining oil, the butter, mustard and thyme in a small bowl to make a dressing. Set aside.

4 Brush the cooking grates clean. Grill the potatoes, cabbage, onion and gammon steak over **_direct medium heat_** for 10–12 minutes, with the lid closed as much as possible and turning once or twice, until the potatoes are tender, the cabbage and onion are crisp-tender and the gammon is warmed through. Remove from the grill and roughly chop.

5 Place the vegetables and gammon in a serving bowl and drizzle with the dressing; stir until well combined. Serve warm.

FOIL-WRAPPED BAKED POTATOES WITH SAUTÉED WILD MUSHROOMS

SERVES: 4
PREP TIME: 20 MINUTES
GRILLING TIME: 40–50 MINUTES

4 large King Edward potatoes, pricked several times

500 g/1 lb mixed mushrooms, such as chanterelle, shiitake, porcini, portobello, brown chestnut or white button
2 tablespoons extra-virgin olive oil
Sea salt
10 garlic cloves, thinly sliced
6 tablespoons dry white wine
25 g/1 oz unsalted butter
1 tablespoon thyme

4 tablespoons freshly shaved Parmesan cheese
125 ml/4 fl oz crème fraîche or soured cream

1 Fill a chimney starter to the rim with charcoal and burn until it is lightly covered with ash. Spread the charcoal in a tightly packed, single layer across half of the charcoal grate. Close the lid. Leave all the vents open. If using a gas grill, prepare the grill for direct cooking over high heat (230–290°C/450–550°F).

2 Scrub the potatoes under cold running water and, while they're still wet, wrap each individually in heavy-duty aluminium foil. Place the potatoes directly on the coals of a charcoal grill or on the cooking grates over **direct high heat** on a gas grill. Close the lid, and cook for 40–50 minutes, turning occasionally, until the potatoes are tender when pierced with a fork or the tip of a knife.

3 While the potatoes are cooking, clean the mushrooms and cut them into 3.5–5-cm/1½–2-inch pieces.

4 Heat the oil for 2–3 minutes in a large frying pan over a high heat until it is shimmering. Add the mushrooms, season with 1 teaspoon salt, and stir them quickly to coat with oil. Sauté for 5–6 minutes until they are nicely browned, stirring as little as possible. Reduce the heat to medium, add the garlic and cook for 1–2 minutes until fragrant, stirring constantly to prevent browning. Add the wine and bring quickly to the boil. Stir in the butter until it melts. Turn off the heat. Add the thyme.

5 Remove the potatoes from the grill and carefully unwrap them.

6 To serve, cut the potatoes down the middle and put each on a plate. Squeeze them open and use a fork to fluff up the insides. Season with salt. Spoon the mushrooms evenly over the potatoes then top each with the cheese and crème fraîche. Serve warm.

TOASTED BREAD AND PEARS WITH CHOCOLATE FONDUE

SERVES: 6
PREP TIME: 15 MINUTES
GRILLING TIME: 3–5 MINUTES

FONDUE
250 g/8 oz good-quality plain chocolate, finely chopped
125 ml/4 fl oz whipping cream
1 tablespoon Grand Marnier *or* whisky *or* 2 teaspoons
    vanilla extract

3 ripe pears
4 tablespoons extra-virgin olive oil
Finely grated zest of 1 large orange
250 g/8 oz rustic white bread, cut into 3.5-cm/1½-inch chunks
1 teaspoon flaky sea salt *or* fleur de sel

1 Put the chocolate in a bowl. Using a microwave oven, heat the cream in a small bowl for about 1 minute on high until it just begins to bubble. Add the warm cream to the chocolate and stir constantly until the chocolate is melted and the sauce is smooth. Stir in the Grand Marnier. Keep warm.

2 Cut the pears in half lengthways, core, and then cut each half lengthways into thirds.

3 Prepare the grill for direct cooking over high heat (230–290°C/450–550°F).

4 Whisk the oil and orange zest in a large bowl. Add the bread chunks and carefully toss to coat them evenly.

5 Brush the cooking grates clean. Grill the bread chunks over **direct high heat** for 3–5 minutes, with the lid open and turning occasionally, until golden brown and crunchy. Remove from the grill and sprinkle with the sea salt.

6 Serve the fondue in bowls with the bread and pear slices on the side for dipping.

CHOCOLATE BROWNIES

SERVES: 8
PREP TIME: 15 MINUTES
GRILLING TIME: 25–35 MINUTES
SPECIAL EQUIPMENT: 20-CM/8-INCH SQUARE BAKING TIN

40 g/1½ oz cocoa powder
50 g/2 oz plain flour
¼ teaspoon sea salt
¼ teaspoon baking powder
2 large eggs
125 g/4 oz granulated sugar
½ teaspoon vanilla extract
½ teaspoon orange extract
125 g/4 oz unsalted butter, melted and cooled slightly
1 tablespoon orange marmalade

1 Prepare the grill for indirect cooking over medium heat (about 180°C/350°F). Generously grease a 20-cm/8-inch square baking tin.

2 Sift the cocoa, flour, salt and baking powder into a bowl. Beat the eggs with a wooden spoon in another bowl. Beat in the sugar and the vanilla and orange extracts. Slowly add in the melted butter and beat until completely incorporated.

3 Add the sifted dry ingredients to the butter mixture. Stir well until all the dry ingredients are completely moistened.

4 Scrape the mixture into the prepared baking tin. Drop spoonfuls of the marmalade on to the top of the mixture at even intervals across the centre. Drag the tip of a knife through each marmalade mound and pull it randomly through the mixture.

5 Place the tin over **indirect medium heat**, close the lid and bake for 25–35 minutes, until the brownies pull slightly away from the edges of the pan and a skewer inserted into the centre comes out clean. Keep the grill's temperature as close to 180°C/350°F as possible. Carefully remove the tin from the grill. Cool for about 15 minutes. Cut into 16 squares and serve.

FRIENDS FOR DINNER

FRIENDS FOR DINNER

SOMEONE TO IMPRESS

218 ROASTED PEPPER ROULADES WITH ITALIAN TUNA

208 ROASTED MUSSELS WITH GARLIC-PARSLEY BUTTER

SPECIAL OCCASIONS

202 MARINATED CHICKEN THIGHS WITH
MINT-TAHINI SAUCE

217 PESTO-MARINATED SEA BASS WITH WARM TOMATOES

PUSHING THE BOAT OUT

191 PEAR AND PARMA HAM BRUSCHETTA

207 SALMON FILLETS WITH FENNEL-OLIVE TAPENADE

188 PORTERHOUSE STEAKS WITH CREAMY PORCINI SAUCE

224 PLUMS WITH HONEY-LEMON YOGURT

186 MARINATED SIRLOIN STEAKS WITH GORGONZOLA SAUCE

211 SALMON AND SUN-DRIED TOMATOES EN PAPILLOTE

194 MARINATED PORK FILLET MEDALLIONS AU JUS

189 FILLET STEAKS WITH BROWN BUTTER SAUCE

FRIENDS FOR DINNER

MARINATED SIRLOIN STEAKS WITH GORGONZOLA SAUCE

SERVES: 4
PREP TIME: 20 MINUTES
MARINATING TIME: 2–4 HOURS
GRILLING TIME: 6–8 MINUTES

MARINADE
475 ml/16 fl oz beef stock
250 ml/8 fl oz dry red wine
1 onion, finely chopped
2 tablespoons tomato purée

4 sirloin steaks, each 300–375 g/10–12 oz and about
    2.5 cm/1 inch thick, trimmed of excess fat
Extra-virgin olive oil
Sea salt
Ground black pepper

SAUCE
15 g/½ oz unsalted butter
1 shallot, finely chopped
250 ml/8 fl oz soured cream
125 g/4 oz Gorgonzola cheese, crumbled

1 tablespoon finely chopped chives (optional)

1 Combine the marinade ingredients in a large glass baking dish. Whisk to dissolve the tomato purée. Submerge the steaks in the marinade. Cover and refrigerate for 2–4 hours.

2 Prepare the grill for direct cooking over high heat (230–290°C/450–550°F).

3 Lift the steaks from the dish and pat dry with kitchen paper. Discard the marinade. Lightly brush the steaks with oil and season evenly with salt and pepper. Allow to stand at room temperature for 15–30 minutes before grilling.

4 Meanwhile, make the sauce. Melt the butter in a saucepan over a medium heat. Add the shallot and cook for about 2 minutes until tender, stirring often. Mix in the soured cream and cheese and cook for about 3 minutes, stirring occasionally, until the sauce begins to simmer and the cheese has melted. Remove from the heat, add ¼ teaspoon pepper and cover to keep warm.

5 Brush the cooking grates clean. Grill the steaks over **direct high heat**, with the lid closed as much as possible and turning once or twice (if flare-ups occur, move the steaks temporarily over indirect heat), until cooked to your desired doneness, 6–8 minutes for medium rare. Remove from the grill and leave to rest for 3–5 minutes. Serve warm with the sauce. Garnish with chives, if liked.

PORTERHOUSE STEAKS WITH CREAMY PORCINI SAUCE

SERVES: 4–6

PREP TIME: 15 MINUTES, PLUS ABOUT 25 MINUTES FOR
    THE SAUCE

GRILLING TIME: 6–8 MINUTES

15 g/½ oz dried porcini mushrooms
250 ml/8 fl oz boiling water
15 g/½ oz unsalted butter
½ onion, finely chopped
2 tablespoons plus 2 teaspoons finely chopped thyme
250 ml/8 fl oz whipping cream

4 porterhouse steaks, each about 500 g/1 lb and 2.5 cm/1 inch
    thick, trimmed of excess fat
Extra-virgin olive oil
Sea salt
Ground black pepper

2 tablespoons finely grated Parmesan cheese
2 tablespoons finely chopped flat-leaf parsley

1 Soak the mushrooms in the boiling water in a bowl for about
15 minutes until they are soft. Drain, reserving the soaking
liquid. Finely chop the mushrooms.

2 Melt the butter in a saucepan over a medium heat. Add the
onion and 2 teaspoons of the thyme and cook for 3–5 minutes
until the onion is tender and just beginning to brown. Add the
reserved soaking liquid and cream and bring to a simmer. Add
the mushrooms. Simmer the sauce for about 15 minutes until
reduced to 250–350 ml/8–12 fl oz. Remove from the heat.

3 Prepare the grill for direct cooking over high heat
(230–290°C/450–550°F).

4 Lightly coat the steaks on both sides with oil and season
evenly with the remaining 2 tablespoons thyme, 2 teaspoons
salt and 1 teaspoon pepper. Allow the steaks to stand at room
temperature for 15–30 minutes before grilling.

5 Brush the cooking grates clean. Grill the steaks over **direct
high heat**, with the lid closed as much as possible and turning
once or twice (if flare-ups occur, move the steaks temporarily
over indirect heat), until cooked to your desired doneness,
6–8 minutes for medium rare. Remove from the grill and leave
to rest for 3–5 minutes.

6 While the steaks rest, reheat the sauce, add the cheese and
stir. Season with salt and pepper. Serve the steaks warm with
the sauce spooned over the top and garnished with the parsley.

FILLET STEAKS WITH BROWN BUTTER SAUCE

SERVES: 4
PREP TIME: 15 MINUTES
GRILLING TIME: 8–10 MINUTES

1½ tablespoons extra-virgin olive oil
2½ tablespoons finely chopped tarragon
Sea salt
Ground black pepper
4 fillet steaks, each about 250 g/8 oz and 3 cm/1¼ inches thick

75 g/3 oz unsalted butter, cut into 4 pieces
40 g/1½ oz chopped walnuts, preferably toasted
1 tablespoon white wine vinegar

1 Prepare the grill for direct cooking over medium heat (180–230°C/350–450°F).

2 Mix the oil, 1½ tablespoons of the tarragon, ¾ teaspoon salt and ¼ teaspoon pepper in a small bowl. Smear the paste on both sides of the steaks. Allow the steaks to stand at room temperature for 15–30 minutes before grilling.

3 Brush the cooking grates clean. Grill the steaks over **direct medium heat**, with the lid closed as much as possible and turning once or twice (if flare-ups occur, move the steaks temporarily over indirect heat), until cooked to your desired doneness, 8–10 minutes for medium rare. Remove the steaks from the grill and let rest while you make the sauce.

4 Melt the butter in a small frying pan over a medium heat. Let it foam and cook for 4–6 minutes, swirling the pan occasionally to prevent the butter from burning, until it turns a light golden brown. Remove the pan from the heat and add the nuts, vinegar (be careful, it will bubble up) and the remaining 1 tablespoon tarragon. Season with salt and pepper. Serve immediately with the steaks (the sauce will separate if it sits for more than a few minutes).

SIRLOIN STEAK WITH BROCCOLI

SERVES: 4
PREP TIME: 10 MINUTES
MARINATING TIME: 15–30 MINUTES
GRILLING TIME: 20–22 MINUTES

MARINADE
2 tablespoons balsamic vinegar
1 teaspoon prepared horseradish
¼ teaspoon ground black pepper
Extra-virgin olive oil
Sea salt

625 g/1¼ lb sirloin steak, about 2.5 cm/1 inch thick

250 g/8 oz tenderstem broccoli
1 red onion, cut crossways into 8-mm/⅓-inch slices

1 Prepare the grill for direct cooking over medium heat (180–230°C/350–450°F).

2 Whisk the vinegar, horseradish, pepper, 4 tablespoons oil and ½ teaspoon salt in a small bowl. Place the steak in the bowl and marinate at room temperature for 15–30 minutes.

3 Remove the steak from the bowl and discard the marinade. Brush the cooking grates clean. Grill the steak over ***direct medium heat***, with the lid closed as much as possible and turning once or twice (if flare-ups occur, transfer the steak temporarily to indirect heat), until cooked to your desired doneness, 12–14 minutes for medium rare. Remove from the grill and leave to rest for 3–5 minutes. Cut into thin slices.

4 Lightly brush the broccoli and onion slices with oil and season them with salt. Grill them over ***direct medium heat*** for about 8 minutes, with the lid closed as much as possible, until the vegetables are tender. Remove from the grill and chop the onion into small pieces.

5 Divide the steak slices and broccoli between four plates and top with the onions to serve.

PEAR AND PARMA HAM BRUSCHETTA

SERVES: 6–8
PREP TIME: 10 MINUTES
GRILLING TIME: 9–12 MINUTES

2 ripe pears, about 375 g/12 oz in total
1 tablespoon fresh lemon juice
Extra-virgin olive oil
1 baguette, cut into 20 slices
4 thin slices Parma ham

250 g/8 oz ricotta cheese
40 g/1½ oz blue cheese, crumbled
3 tablespoons runny honey

1 Prepare the grill for direct cooking over medium heat (180–230°C/350–450°F).

2 Peel the pears, cut them into quarters and core them. Put in a bowl, add the lemon juice and toss to coat. Lightly brush the pears on all sides with oil.

3 Lightly brush one side of each baguette slice with oil.

4 Brush the cooking grates clean. Grill the pears over **direct medium heat** for 8–10 minutes, with the lid closed as much as possible and turning occasionally, until crisp-tender. Remove from the grill and cut each pear quarter into about eight slices.

5 Grill the baguette slices and the Parma ham over **direct medium heat** for 1–2 minutes, with the lid open, until the bread is lightly toasted (grill one side only) and the ham is crisp. Remove from the grill and chop the ham.

6 Combine the ricotta and blue cheese in a small bowl. Spread about 1 tablespoon of the cheese mixture on the grilled side of each baguette slice. Place about three pear slices on top of the cheese and add some chopped Parma ham. Finish with a drizzle of honey and serve.

PORK CHOPS WITH HERB-GARLIC RUB

SERVES: 4
PREP TIME: 10 MINUTES
GRILLING TIME: 8–10 MINUTES

RUB
2 garlic cloves
1 teaspoon sea salt
3 tablespoons extra-virgin olive oil
2 teaspoons rosemary leaves
2 teaspoons sage leaves
½ teaspoon ground black pepper

4 bone-in pork loin chops, each about 250 g/8 oz and 2.5 cm/1 inch thick, trimmed of excess fat

Grill-roasted plum tomatoes (optional)

1 Prepare the grill for direct cooking over medium heat (180–230°C/350–450°F).

2 Smash the garlic with the back of a knife and finely chop it. Sprinkle with the salt and continue chopping and scraping the garlic against the board with the flat side of the knife to make a paste. Scrape up and transfer the garlic paste to a small bowl. Add the oil, rosemary, sage and pepper and stir well. Spread the rub on both sides of the chops. Allow the chops to stand at room temperature for 15–30 minutes before grilling.

3 Brush the cooking grates clean. Grill the chops over **_direct medium heat_** for 8–10 minutes, with the lid closed as much as possible and turning once or twice, until they are still slightly pink in the centre. Remove from the grill and leave to rest for 3–5 minutes. Serve warm with grill-roasted plum tomatoes, if liked.

Grilling pork chops with the bone still attached will always give you a little extra flavour, and your taste buds will really light up when the pork is rubbed with a fragrant combination of rosemary, sage and garlic. This Mediterranean blend opens the door to several French and Italian side dishes, from beans to grilled vegetables.

MARINATED PORK FILLET MEDALLIONS AU JUS

SERVES: 4
PREP TIME: 20 MINUTES, PLUS ABOUT 20 MINUTES FOR
    THE SAUCE
MARINATING TIME: 1–4 HOURS
GRILLING TIME: 4–6 MINUTES
SPECIAL EQUIPMENT: KITCHEN STRING

MARINADE
475 ml/16 fl oz dry white wine
125 ml/4 fl oz chicken stock
2 tablespoons soft brown sugar
1 tablespoon finely chopped garlic
3 tablespoons finely chopped rosemary

2 pork fillets, each 375–500 g/12 oz–1 lb, trimmed of excess fat
    and skin
1 tablespoon extra-virgin olive oil
½ teaspoon sea salt
½ teaspoon ground black pepper
15 g/½ oz unsalted butter

1 Mix the wine, stock, sugar, garlic and 2 tablespoons of the
rosemary in a large bowl.

2 Cut the pork fillets crossways into 3.5-cm/1½-inch
medallions, starting at the thicker ends. Tie the thinner ends
together. Add the medallions to the bowl, turn to coat, cover
and refrigerate for 1–4 hours.

3 Remove the meat from the bowl, reserving the marinade.
Pat dry with kitchen paper and lightly brush both sides with
the oil. Season evenly with the salt, pepper and the remaining
1 tablespoon rosemary. Allow to stand at room temperature for
15–30 minutes before grilling.

4 Prepare the grill for direct cooking over medium heat
(180–230°C/350–450°F).

5 Brush the cooking grates clean. Grill the medallions over **direct
medium heat** for 4–6 minutes, with the lid closed as much as
possible and turning once, until the outsides are evenly seared
and the centres are barely pink. Remove from the grill and leave
to rest for 3–5 minutes, reserving the juices that accumulate.

6 Strain the marinade into a small saucepan and bring it to the
boil. Lower the heat to maintain a steady simmer and cook for
15–17 minutes, skimming off any foam, until about 250 ml/8 fl oz
remain. Remove from the heat. Add the reserved meat juices
and stir in the butter. Serve the pork warm with the sauce.

FOIL-WRAPPED BABY BACK RIBS

SERVES: 4
PREP TIME: 15 MINUTES
GRILLING TIME: ABOUT 1¼ HOURS
SPECIAL EQUIPMENT: 45-CM/18-INCH-WIDE HEAVY-DUTY
    ALUMINIUM FOIL

RUB
1 tablespoon sea salt
2 teaspoons paprika
2 teaspoons garlic granules
2 teaspoons dried thyme
½ teaspoon ground black pepper

2 racks baby back pork ribs, each 1–1.25 kg/2–2½ lb

2 handfuls hickory wood chips, soaked in water for at least
    30 minutes
250 ml/8 fl oz ready-made barbecue sauce

1 Prepare the grill for direct cooking over medium heat
(180–230°C/350–450°F).

2 Mix the rub ingredients in a small bowl.

3 Remove the membrane from the back of each rack of ribs
(see photo at bottom right). Cut each rack crossways in the
middle to create two smaller racks.

4 Season each half-rack evenly with the rub. Using eight
45 x 60 cm/18 x 24 inch sheets of heavy-duty aluminium foil,
double wrap each half-rack in its own package.

5 Brush the cooking grates clean. Place the ribs on the grill
over ***direct medium heat*** and cook for 1 hour, with the lid
closed and occasionally turning the packages over for even
cooking, making sure not to pierce the foil.

6 Remove the packages from the grill and leave to rest for
about 10 minutes. Carefully open the foil, remove the ribs and
discard the rendered fat and foil.

7 Drain and add the wood chips directly on to burning coals
or to the smoker box of a gas grill, following manufacturer's
instructions. When the wood begins to smoke, return the ribs
to the grill, bone side down. Grill over ***direct medium heat*** for
10–12 minutes, with the lid closed as much as possible and
turning and basting once or twice with the barbecue sauce,
until they are sizzling and lightly charred. Remove from the
grill and leave to rest for about 5 minutes. Cut into individual
ribs and serve warm with any remaining sauce on top.

JERK PORK MEDALLIONS WITH GRILLED CORN AND CUCUMBER SALSA

SERVES: 4
PREP TIME: 30 MINUTES
GRILLING TIME: 14–21 MINUTES

SALSA

2 fresh corn cobs, outer leaves and silk removed
Extra-virgin olive oil
½ cucumber, chopped
½ red pepper, finely chopped
65 g/2½ oz feta cheese, crumbled
2 tablespoons cider vinegar
2 tablespoons finely chopped oregano
½ teaspoon sea salt
¼ teaspoon ground cayenne pepper
¼ teaspoon ground black pepper

PASTE

3 tablespoons extra-virgin olive oil
2 tablespoons soy sauce
1 tablespoon onion powder
1 tablespoon soft brown sugar
2 teaspoons dried thyme
2 teaspoons ground allspice
1 teaspoon ground cayenne pepper
1 teaspoon ground black pepper
1 teaspoon garlic powder
½ teaspoon grated nutmeg
½ teaspoon ground cinnamon

2 pork fillets, each 375–500 g/12 oz–1 lb, trimmed of excess fat and skin

1 Prepare the grill for direct cooking over medium heat (180–230°C/350–450°F).

2 Lightly brush the corn cobs with oil. Brush the cooking grates clean. Grill the corn over *direct medium heat* for 10–15 minutes, with the lid closed as much as possible and turning occasionally, until the corn is browned in spots and tender. Remove from the grill and, when cool enough to handle, cut the corn kernels off the cobs into a bowl. Add the remaining salsa ingredients to the bowl, including 2 tablespoons oil, and set aside until ready to use.

3 Mix the paste ingredients in a small bowl.

4 Cut off the thin, tapered end from each pork fillet and reserve for another use, or grill along with the medallions. Cut each fillet crossways into six equal pieces, each about 3.5 cm/1½ inches thick. Brush the paste all over the medallions, cover with clingfilm and allow to stand at room temperature for 15–30 minutes before grilling.

5 Grill the medallions over *direct medium heat* for 4–6 minutes, with the lid closed as much as possible and turning once, until the outsides are evenly seared and the centres are barely pink. Remove from the grill and leave to rest for 3–5 minutes. Serve warm with the salsa.

CHICKEN BREASTS WITH WHITE WINE-CAPER SAUCE

SERVES: 4
PREP TIME: 10 MINUTES
GRILLING TIME: 8–12 MINUTES

4 boneless, skinless chicken breasts, each about 175 g/6 oz
2 tablespoons extra-virgin olive oil
¾ teaspoon sea salt
Ground black pepper

SAUCE
4 tablespoons dry white wine
1 shallot, finely chopped
2 teaspoons Dijon mustard
50 g/2 oz unsalted butter, cut into 4 pieces
2 tablespoons small capers, rinsed
1 tablespoon finely chopped flat-leaf parsley

1 Prepare the grill for direct cooking over medium heat (180–230°C/350–450°F).

2 Lightly coat the chicken on both sides with the oil and season evenly with the salt and ½ teaspoon pepper. Brush the cooking grates clean. Grill the chicken, smooth (skin) side down first, over **direct medium heat** for 8–12 minutes, with the lid closed as much as possible and turning once or twice, until the meat is firm to the touch and opaque all the way to the centre. Remove from the grill and cover with foil to keep warm while you make the sauce.

3 Mix the wine, shallot and mustard in a small frying pan over a medium heat. Cook until the mixture comes to a simmer. Simmer for about 30 seconds then remove the pan from the heat. Add the butter, one piece at a time, whisking it into the sauce and waiting until it is almost completely melted before adding the next piece. After all the butter has melted into the sauce add the capers and parsley. Season with pepper.

4 Transfer the chicken to plates, top with the sauce and serve warm.

LEMON-MARINATED CHICKEN AND OLIVE SKEWERS

SERVES: 4
PREP TIME: 15 MINUTES
MARINATING TIME: 15–30 MINUTES
GRILLING TIME: 8–10 MINUTES
SPECIAL EQUIPMENT: METAL OR BAMBOO SKEWERS
    (IF USING BAMBOO, SOAK IN WATER FOR AT LEAST
    30 MINUTES)

MARINADE
2 tablespoons extra-virgin olive oil
1 teaspoon finely grated lemon zest
1 tablespoon fresh lemon juice
1 teaspoon sea salt
½ teaspoon ground black pepper

6 boneless, skinless chicken thighs, each about 125 g/4 oz, cut
    into 3.5-cm/1½-inch pieces
175-g/6-oz can pitted large black olives, drained

1 Combine the marinade ingredients in a bowl. Add the chicken thigh pieces and toss to coat thoroughly. Let the chicken marinate at room temperature for 15–30 minutes before grilling.

2 Prepare the grill for direct cooking over medium heat (180–230°C/350–450°F).

3 Thread the chicken on to skewers, alternating chicken pieces with olives. Brush the cooking grates clean. Grill the skewers over *direct medium heat* for 8–10 minutes, with the lid closed as much as possible and turning once or twice, until the meat is firm and the juices run clear. Remove from the grill and leave to rest for 3–5 minutes. Serve warm.

GARAM MASALA SPICED CHICKEN SPREAD

SERVES: 4, OR 5 AS A STARTER
PREP TIME: 15 MINUTES
GRILLING TIME: 8–10 MINUTES

6 boneless, skinless chicken thighs, each about 75 g/3 oz, or
    500 g/1 lb in total
Extra-virgin olive oil
Sea salt
Ground black pepper

4 tablespoons Greek yogurt
4 tablespoons mayonnaise
Grated zest and juice of 1 lemon
1 teaspoon garam masala
40 g/1½ oz feta cheese, crumbled
2 tablespoons finely chopped flat-leaf parsley

Pitta chips
Whole basil leaves
Sliced fresh vegetables, such as cucumber and red pepper

1 Prepare the grill for direct cooking over medium heat (180–230°C/350–450°F).

2 Lightly coat the chicken on both sides with oil and season evenly with salt and pepper.

3 Brush the cooking grates clean. Grill the chicken over **direct medium heat** for 8–10 minutes, with the lid closed as much as possible and turning once or twice, until the meat is firm and the juices run clear. Remove from the grill and leave to rest for 3–5 minutes. Coarsely chop the chicken.

4 Combine the yogurt, mayonnaise, lemon zest and juice, garam masala, cheese and parsley in a medium bowl.

5 Put the chicken in a food processor and pulse until it is finely chopped. Add the chicken to the yogurt mixture and mix. Season with salt.

6 Serve the chicken spread warm or chilled with pitta chips, whole basil leaves and sliced fresh vegetables.

CREAMY CHICKEN LINGUINE WITH WILTED TOMATOES

SERVES: 4
PREP TIME: 30 MINUTES
GRILLING TIME: 10–15 MINUTES
SPECIAL EQUIPMENT: PERFORATED GRILL PAN

2 slices wholegrain artisan bread, each about ½ inch thick, torn into pieces
Extra-virgin olive oil
1 tablespoon lemon zest
Sea salt

50 g/2 oz soft brown sugar
50 g/2 oz dry sherry
300 g/10 oz baby plum tomatoes

4 boneless, skinless chicken breasts, each about 175 g/6 oz
Ground black pepper

250 g/8 oz dried linguine, fettuccine or spaghetti
175 g/6 oz baby spinach leaves
125 g/4 oz herb and garlic spreadable cheese

1 Prepare the grill for direct cooking over medium heat (180–230°C/350–450°F) and preheat the grill pan.

2 Pulse the bread in a food processor until coarse crumbs form. In a small skillet over medium-high heat, toss the crumbs with 1 tablespoon oil and toast for 3–4 minutes until crisp and golden, . Remove from the heat and stir in the lemon zest and ¼ teaspoon salt. Set aside. In a small bowl whisk the brown sugar and sherry until the sugar dissolves. Combine the tomatoes with 2 tablespoons of the brown sugar-sherry mixture in a bowl and toss to coat. Set aside the rest of the brown sugar-sherry mixture to use for basting the chicken. Using a slotted spoon, spread the tomatoes onto the preheated grill pan in a single layer. Grill over *direct medium heat* for 2–3 minutes with the lid open, stirring frequently, just until the tomatoes are soft and caramelized. Using a spatula, remove the tomatoes from the grill and return to the bowl with the brown sugar-sherry mixture. Season with ¼ teaspoon salt and stir. Wearing insulated barbecue mitts, remove the grill pan.

3 Lightly coat the chicken on both sides with oil and season evenly with salt and pepper. Brush the cooking grates clean. Grill the chicken, smooth (skin) side down first, over *direct medium heat* for 8–12 minutes, with the lid closed as much as possible, turning once or twice and basting with the reserved brown sugar-sherry mixture several times, until the meat is firm to the touch and opaque all the way to the centre. Remove from the grill and let rest for 3–5 minutes. Cut the chicken into ½-inch cubes.

4 Meanwhile, cook the pasta in a large saucepan of boiling, salted water according to package directions. About 1 minute before the pasta is done, add the spinach to the saucepan and stir until wilted. Drain the pasta and spinach, reserving some of the pasta water, and then return the pasta and spinach to the pan. Immediately toss the hot pasta and spinach with the tomatoes, chicken and cheese and stir to melt. If the sauce is too thick, add a little of the reserved pasta water. Divide the pasta evenly among serving plates and top with the breadcrumbs. Serve immediately.

MARINATED CHICKEN THIGHS WITH MINT-TAHINI SAUCE

SERVES: 4
PREP TIME: 30 MINUTES
MARINATING TIME: 1–2 HOURS
GRILLING TIME: 36–40 MINUTES

PASTE
125 ml/4 fl oz Greek yogurt
4 tablespoons grated red onion
1 tablespoon fresh lemon juice
1 tablespoon garam masala
2 teaspoons finely chopped garlic
2 teaspoons chilli powder
Sea salt

8 chicken thighs (with bone and skin), each about 150 g/5 oz,
    trimmed of excess fat and skin
Extra-virgin olive oil

SAUCE
1 large garlic clove
4 tablespoons Greek yogurt
4 tablespoons tahini
2 tablespoons fresh lemon juice
75 g/3 oz mint leaves

1 Combine the paste ingredients in a bowl, including
1 teaspoon salt.

2 Place the chicken in a large, resealable plastic bag and
spoon in the marinade. Press the air out of the bag and seal
tightly. Turn the bag to distribute the marinade. Refrigerate for
1–2 hours, turning occasionally.

3 Prepare the grill for direct and indirect cooking over medium
heat (180–230°C/350–450°F). Process the garlic in a food
processor until finely chopped. Add the yogurt, tahini, lemon
juice and 4 tablespoons water and process to combine. Add
the mint and ½ teaspoon salt, and pulse until the mint is finely
chopped and the sauce is smooth.

4 Remove the chicken from the bag and wipe off most of the
marinade. Lightly brush the chicken on both sides with oil.

5 Brush the cooking grates clean. Grill the chicken, skin side
down first, over **direct medium heat** for 6–10 minutes, turning
once or twice, until golden brown. Then move the chicken over
indirect medium heat and cook for about 30 minutes, until
the juices run clear and the meat is no longer pink at the bone.
Keep the lid closed as much as possible during grilling. Remove
from the grill and leave to rest for 3–5 minutes. Serve warm with
the sauce.

ROASTED CHICKEN BREASTS WITH MANGO-GINGER SALSA

SERVES: 4
PREP TIME: 30 MINUTES
GRILLING TIME: 23–35 MINUTES

SALSA
750 g/1½ lb ripe mangoes *or* peaches, chopped
1 red pepper, finely chopped
½ small onion, finely chopped
1 jalapeño chilli, stem and seeds removed, finely chopped
2 tablespoons finely chopped fresh coriander
1 tablespoon fresh lime juice
1 teaspoon grated fresh ginger
¼ teaspoon ground cayenne pepper
¼ teaspoon sea salt

RUB
1 teaspoon sea salt
1 teaspoon dried thyme
½ teaspoon ground black pepper

4 chicken breasts (with bone and skin), each
    300–375 g/10–12 oz
2 tablespoons extra-virgin olive oil

1 Prepare the grill for direct and indirect cooking over medium heat (180–230°C/350–450°F).

2 Mix the salsa ingredients in a large bowl. Cover and refrigerate until ready to serve.

3 Mix the rub ingredients in a small bowl. Lightly brush the chicken on both sides with the oil and season evenly with the rub.

4 Brush the cooking grates clean. Grill the chicken, skin side down first, over **direct medium heat** for 3–5 minutes, with the lid closed, until the skin is browned. Turn the chicken over and continue to grill over **indirect medium heat** for 20–30 minutes, with the lid closed, until the meat is opaque all the way to the bone. Remove from the grill and leave to rest for 3–5 minutes. Serve warm with the salsa.

CHICKEN BREASTS WITH MOLE RUB

SERVES: 4
PREP TIME: 10 MINUTES
GRILLING TIME: 33–45 MINUTES

RUB
2 tablespoons chilli powder
2 teaspoons unsweetened cocoa powder
2 teaspoons soft brown sugar
1 teaspoon sea salt
1 teaspoon ground black pepper

2 limes, halved
4 plum tomatoes, halved lengthways
2 courgettes, cut diagonally into 8-mm/⅓-inch slices
4 chicken breasts (with bone and skin), each 300–375 g/
    10–12 oz
2 tablespoons extra-virgin olive oil

1 Prepare the grill for direct and indirect cooking over medium heat (180–230°C/350–450°F).

2 Combine the rub ingredients in a small bowl. Season the cut sides of the limes, tomatoes, and courgette slices with the rub. Lightly coat the chicken on both sides with the oil and season evenly with the remaining rub.

3 Brush the cooking grates clean. Grill the chicken, bone side down, over **indirect medium heat** for 30–40 minutes, with the lid closed, until the meat is opaque all the way to the bone. If desired, to crisp the skin, grill the chicken over **direct medium heat** during the last 5–10 minutes of grilling time, turning once. Remove from the grill and leave to rest for 3–5 minutes.

4 While the chicken rests, grill the limes, tomatoes and courgettes over **direct medium heat** for 3–5 minutes, with the lid closed and turning once, until the limes and tomatoes are warm and the courgettes are crisp-tender.

5 Squeeze the grilled limes over the chicken and serve with the tomatoes and courgettes.

OYSTERS WITH APPLE-TARRAGON MIGNONETTE

SERVES: 4–6

PREP TIME: 5 MINUTES, PLUS ABOUT
    30 MINUTES TO SHUCK THE OYSTERS

GRILLING TIME: 2–4 MINUTES

SPECIAL EQUIPMENT: OYSTER KNIFE

MIGNONETTE

3 tablespoons finely chopped shallot

125 ml/4 fl oz cider vinegar

125 ml/4 fl oz apple cider

1 tablespoon finely chopped fresh
    tarragon leaves

⅛ teaspoon sea salt

⅛ teaspoon ground black pepper

24 large, fresh oysters, each about 7.5 cm/3 inches long

1 Whisk the mignonette ingredients in a small bowl. Refrigerate until ready to use.

2 Shuck the oysters: Grip each oyster, flat side up, in a folded kitchen towel. Find the small opening between the shells near the hinge and pry it open with an oyster knife. Try not to spill the delicious juices, known as the 'oyster liquor', in the bottom shell. Cut the oyster meat loose from the top shell and then loosen the oyster from the bottom shell by running the oyster knife carefully under the body. Discard the top, flatter shell, keeping the oyster and juices in the bottom, deeper shell.

3 Prepare the grill for direct cooking over high heat (230–290/450–550°F).

4 Brush the cooking grates clean. Grill the oysters, shell sides down, over **direct high heat** for 2–4 minutes, with the lid closed as much as possible, until the oyster juices start to bubble and the edges curl. (The oysters should be warmed but not actually cooked through.) Using tongs, carefully remove the oysters from the grill. Serve with the apple-tarragon mignonette.

SALMON FILLETS WITH FENNEL-OLIVE TAPENADE

SERVES: 4
PREP TIME: 15 MINUTES
GRILLING TIME: 8-12 MINUTES

TAPENADE
1 fennel bulb, about 625 g/1¼ lb, with stalks attached
20 garlic-stuffed green olives
Finely grated zest of 1 orange
2 tablespoons fresh orange juice
2 teaspoons roughly chopped tarragon
Extra-virgin olive oil
Sea salt
Ground black pepper

6 salmon fillets (with skin), each 175–250 g/6–8 oz and about
    3 cm/1¼ inches thick, pin bones removed

1 Cut the stalks from the fennel. If liked, finely chop and reserve the fronds for garnish. Cut out and discard the tough core from the bulb. Roughly chop the bulb. Cook the fennel for 3 minutes in a saucepan of boiling salted water. Drain in a sieve, then run cold water over it to stop the cooking.

2 Combine the fennel with the olives, orange zest and juice, tarragon and 3 tablespoons oil in the bowl of a food processor. Pulse the mixture and scrape down the side of the bowl occasionally until you have a coarse texture. Season with salt and pepper.

3 Prepare the grill for direct cooking over high heat (230–290°C/450–550°F).

4 Generously coat the salmon fillets with oil and season evenly with salt and pepper.

5 Brush the cooking grates clean. Grill the salmon over **direct high heat** for 6–8 minutes, with the lid closed as much as possible, until you can lift the fillets off the cooking grate with tongs. Turn the fillets over and continue cooking to your desired doneness, 2–4 minutes for medium rare. Slip a spatula between the skin and the flesh and transfer the fillets to individual plates. Serve warm with the tapenade and garnish with chopped fennel fronds, if liked.

ROASTED MUSSELS WITH GARLIC-PARSLEY BUTTER

SERVES: 2; 4 AS A STARTER
PREP TIME: 10 MINUTES PLUS SOAKING TIME FOR
    WILD MUSSELS: 30 MINUTES–1 HOUR
GRILLING TIME: 21–25 MINUTES
SPECIAL EQUIPMENT: 30-CM/12-INCH CAST-IRON
    FRYING PAN

50 g/2 oz unsalted butter, softened
4 large garlic cloves, finely chopped
4 tablespoons finely chopped flat-leaf parsley

2 tablespoons extra-virgin olive oil
1 small onion, finely chopped
¼ teaspoon sea salt
⅛ teaspoon ground black pepper
175 ml/6 fl oz dry white wine
1 kg/2 lb live mussels, scrubbed and beards removed

Crusty bread (optional)

1 Mash the butter, garlic and parsley with a fork in a small bowl until evenly blended. Set aside.

2 Prepare the grill for direct cooking over medium heat (180–230°C/350–450°F).

3 Combine the oil, onion, salt and pepper in a 30-cm/12-inch cast-iron frying pan. Place the pan over **direct medium heat**, close the grill lid, and cook for about 5 minutes, stirring once or twice, until the onion begins to soften. Add the wine, stir to combine, and cook with the grill lid closed until the wine comes to the boil. Simmer for 5 minutes.

4 Add the mussels to the pan, cover the pan with a roasting tray (or use foil), close the grill lid, and cook for 8–10 minutes. Check to see if the mussels are open. If not, continue to cook for 3–5 minutes more. Wearing insulated barbecue mitts or oven gloves, carefully remove the roasting tray from the pan and remove the pan from the grill. Remove and discard any unopened mussels. Add the butter mixture to the pan, dropping bits of it all over, and use a large spoon to stir the mussels around as the butter melts. Serve the mussels and sauce in bowls with crusty bread, if liked.

Although many farmed mussels don't develop large 'beards', the small bunch of threads that connect them to their habitat, most wild ones do. Just before cooking, prepare wild mussels by first soaking them for 30 minutes to 1 hour in cold, salted water (this removes any extra sand) then scrubbing them and removing the beards, discarding any mussels that are chipped or that don't close when you tap the shells. To 'debeard' a mussel, use your thumb and first finger to grasp the beard, and pull sharply, perpendicular to the mussel.

SALMON WITH CREAMY CITRUS SAUCE

SERVES: 4–6
PREP TIME: 30 MINUTES
GRILLING TIME: 3–6 MINUTES
SPECIAL EQUIPMENT: 12 METAL OR BAMBOO SKEWERS
    (IF USING BAMBOO, SOAK IN WATER FOR AT LEAST
    30 MINUTES)

SAUCE
1 orange
1 teaspoon cornflour
125 ml/4 fl oz clam juice
4 large egg yolks
2 tablespoons finely chopped tarragon
15 g/½ oz unsalted butter
Finely grated zest of 1 lemon
2 tablespoons fresh lemon juice
Sea salt
Ground black pepper

1 centre-cut, skinless salmon fillet, about 1 kg/2 lb, pin bones
    removed
Extra-virgin olive oil

1 Finely grate the zest from the orange and set aside. Squeeze 125 ml/4 fl oz juice from the orange and pour it into a heavy saucepan. Add the cornflour and whisk until it has dissolved. Whisk in the clam juice and egg yolks. Cook over a medium heat for about 4 minutes, whisking almost constantly, until the sauce thickens and comes to a gentle boil. Remove from the heat and stir in the tarragon, butter, grated orange and lemon zests and the lemon juice. Stir to melt the butter. Season with salt and pepper. Cover to keep warm, whisking the sauce occasionally.

2 Prepare the grill for direct cooking over high heat (230–290°C/450–550°F).

3 Cut the salmon into 1.5-cm/¾-inch slices. Thread the slices on to 12 skewers. Generously brush the salmon on all sides with oil and season evenly with salt and pepper.

4 Brush the cooking grates clean. Grill the salmon skewers over ***direct high heat*** for 2–4 minutes, with the lid closed as much as possible, until you can lift them off the cooking grate with tongs without sticking. Turn the salmon skewers over and continue cooking to your desired doneness, 1–2 minutes for medium. Reheat the sauce gently over a low heat and whisk again. Spoon the sauce over the salmon. Serve warm.

SALMON AND SUN-DRIED TOMATOES EN PAPILLOTE

SERVES: 4
PREP TIME: 20 MINUTES
GRILLING TIME: 27–35 MINUTES

1 red pepper
3 tablespoons sun-dried tomatoes in olive oil, drained
    and chopped
3 tablespoons chopped kalamata olives
2 tablespoons small capers, drained
2 teaspoons finely chopped oregano
1 garlic clove, finely chopped

4 salmon steaks, each 175–250 g/6–8 oz and about 2.5 cm/
    1 inch thick, pin bones removed
Sea salt
Ground black pepper
1 large courgette, ends trimmed, cut in half lengthways then
    into 5-mm/¼-inch slices
4 teaspoons extra-virgin olive oil
1 lemon, quartered

1 Prepare the grill for direct cooking over medium heat (180–230°C/350–450°F).

2 Brush the cooking grates clean. Grill the pepper over **direct medium heat** for 12–15 minutes, with the lid closed as much as possible and turning occasionally, until it is blackened and blistered all over. Place the pepper in a bowl and cover with clingfilm to trap the steam. Set aside for 10 minutes. Remove

from the bowl, peel away and discard the skin, cut off and discard the stalk and seeds, then roughly chop the pepper.

3 Combine the pepper, tomatoes, olives, capers, oregano and garlic in a bowl.

4 Season the salmon evenly with salt and pepper. Put the courgette slices in a bowl and add ¼ teaspoon salt and ⅛ teaspoon pepper. Toss to coat evenly.

5 Tear four 45-cm/18-inch lengths of heavy-duty aluminium foil. Place one piece of foil on a work surface. Fold the foil in half crossways to make a crease and reopen the foil to lie flat. Pour 1 teaspoon of oil in the centre of the bottom half of the foil. Place a salmon steak in the oil and turn to coat on both sides. Add a quarter of the red pepper mixture and a quarter of the courgettes over and around the salmon. Fold the foil over and crimp the three open sides tightly. Repeat with the remaining foil and ingredients.

6 Brush the cooking grates clean. Grill the packages over **direct medium heat** for 15–20 minutes, with the lid closed as much as possible, until the salmon is barely opaque in the thickest part of the flesh (cut a small hole in the top of one package and pull the fish apart with the tip of a knife to check). Remove the packages from the grill.

7 Open each foil parcel and transfer its contents to a plate. Squeeze a lemon quarter over each salmon steak. Serve warm.

COCONUT-CURRY SALMON WITH PATTYPAN SQUASH

SERVES: 4
PREP TIME: 15 MINUTES
MARINATING TIME: 15–30 MINUTES
GRILLING TIME: 14–19 MINUTES

MARINADE
400 ml/14 fl oz full-fat unsweetened coconut milk
Grated zest and juice of 2 large limes
2 tablespoons soft light brown sugar
2 tablespoons Thai green curry paste
1 tablespoon soy sauce
1 teaspoon hot chilli-garlic sauce

4 salmon fillets (with skin), each 175–250 g/6–8 oz and about
    2.5 cm/1 inch thick, pin bones removed
625 g/1¼ lb small pattypan squash, halved lengthways
1 teaspoon extra-virgin olive oil

1 Prepare the grill for direct cooking over high heat (230–290°C/450–550°F).

2 Combine the marinade ingredients in a glass baking dish just large enough to hold all the salmon fillets. Add the salmon and turn to coat all sides. Marinate at room temperature for 15–30 minutes while the grill preheats.

3 Remove the fillets from the dish, allowing any excess marinade to drip off. Reserve the marinade. Brush the cooking grates clean. Grill the salmon, flesh side down, over **direct high heat** for 6–8 minutes, with the lid closed as much as possible, until you can lift the fillets off the cooking grate with tongs without sticking. Turn the fillets over and continue cooking to your desired doneness, 2–3 minutes for medium rare. Slip a spatula between the skin and the flesh, and transfer the fillets to individual plates.

4 While the salmon is cooking, pour the reserved marinade into a small saucepan. Bring to the boil over a medium-high heat. Reduce the heat to maintain a steady simmer and cook for 6–8 minutes, stirring occasionally, until the sauce has thickened and coats the back of a spoon.

5 Lightly brush the squash with the oil. Grill over **direct high heat** for 6–8 minutes, with the lid closed as much as possible and turning occasionally, until crisp-tender and lightly browned. Serve the squash and salmon drizzled with the coconut sauce.

SWORDFISH STEAK WITH SICILIAN SALSA

SERVES: 4
PREP TIME: 30 MINUTES
GRILLING TIME: 8–10 MINUTES

SALSA
1 large slice rustic white bread, about 40–50 g/1½ –2 oz
Extra-virgin olive oil
500 g/1 lb cherry tomatoes, halved or quartered, depending
    on their size
4 tablespoons pine nuts, lightly toasted
4 tablespoons finely chopped flat-leaf parsley
½ red onion, finely chopped
2 tablespoons currants *or* raisins
Finely grated zest of 1 lemon
2 tablespoons fresh lemon juice
1 tablespoon red wine vinegar
Sea salt

4 swordfish steaks, each 250–300 g/8–10 oz and about
    2.5 cm/1 inch thick
Ground black pepper

1 Prepare the grill for direct cooking over medium heat (180–230°C/350–450°F).

2 Brush the bread on both sides with oil. Set aside. Mix the remaining salsa ingredients, including 1 teaspoon salt, in a bowl.

3 Brush the swordfish steaks on both sides with oil and season evenly with salt and pepper.

4 Brush the cooking grates clean. Grill the bread and swordfish steaks over **direct medium heat**, with the lid closed as much as possible and turning once, until the bread is golden brown and crispy and the swordfish is just opaque in the centre but still juicy. The bread will take 4–6 minutes and the swordfish will take 8–10 minutes. Remove from the grill as they are done.

5 Cut the bread into 5-mm/¼-inch cubes and add to the bowl with the salsa. Serve the swordfish steaks warm with the salsa.

HALIBUT WITH WARM POTATO AND BACON SALAD

SERVES: 4
PREP TIME: 20 MINUTES
GRILLING TIME: 23–27 MINUTES

4 waxy potatoes, about 625 g/1¼ lb in total, cut into
    1-cm/½-inch slices
4 halibut fillets (with or without skin), each 175–250 g/6–8 oz
    and about 2.5 cm/1 inch thick
Extra-virgin olive oil
Sea salt
Ground black pepper
12 rosemary sprigs, each 12–15 cm/5–6 inches long, soaked in
    water for about 30 minutes

4 thick bacon rashers, cooked and coarsely chopped
1 red pepper, finely chopped
4 tablespoons finely chopped flat-leaf parsley
1 tablespoon small capers, drained and coarsely chopped
2 tablespoons cider vinegar

1 Prepare the grill for direct and indirect cooking over medium heat (180–230°C/350–450°F).

2 Brush the potato slices and halibut fillets on all sides with oil; season the potatoes with salt and the fillets with salt and pepper. Drain the rosemary sprigs and arrange them into four beds of three sprigs each. Place one fish fillet, skin or skinned side down, on top of each bed of sprigs.

3 Brush the cooking grates clean. Grill the potato slices over **direct medium heat** for 3–5 minutes, with the lid closed as much as possible and turning once, until marked by the grill. Then move them over **indirect medium heat** and continue cooking for about 10 minutes, turning once or twice, until golden brown and tender. Remove from the grill and cut into bite-sized pieces.

4 Combine the potatoes, bacon, pepper, parsley and capers in a bowl. Add 2 tablespoons oil and the vinegar. Toss gently to combine. Season with pepper.

5 Grill the rosemary-bedded halibut over **indirect medium heat** for 10–12 minutes, with the lid closed, until the flesh is opaque in the centre and just beginning to flake (do not turn). Lift the fillets off the rosemary and serve warm with the salad.

MAHI-MAHI WITH PEPITA PESTO AND AVOCADO CREAM

SERVES: 4
PREP TIME: 30 MINUTES
GRILLING TIME: 6–8 MINUTES

2 garlic cloves, roughly chopped
2 jalapeño chillies, stems and seeds removed, roughly chopped
1 avocado, roughly chopped
125 ml/4 fl oz buttermilk
1 tablespoon white wine vinegar
1 tablespoon fresh lime juice
¼ teaspoon ground cumin
Sea salt

PESTO
50 g/2 oz pumpkin seeds
25 g/1 oz fresh coriander
25 g/1 oz flat-leaf parsley
2 tablespoons freshly grated Parmesan cheese
2 teaspoons fresh lime juice
¼ teaspoon Tabasco® sauce
Extra-virgin olive oil

4 skinless mahi-mahi fillets, each 175–250 g/6–8 oz and about 1.5 cm/¾ inch thick
Ground black pepper

1 Prepare the grill for direct cooking over high heat (230–290°C/450–550°F).

2 Pulse half the garlic and half the chillies in a blender or food processor until finely chopped. Add the avocado, buttermilk, vinegar, lime juice, cumin and ½ teaspoon salt. Process until smooth. Add 2–4 tablespoons of water, if liked, for a smoother, looser consistency. Transfer to a serving bowl, cover, and refrigerate until ready to serve.

3 Toast the pumpkin seeds in a large frying pan over a medium heat for 1–2 minutes, stirring occasionally, until lightly browned. Remove from the heat and set aside to cool.

4 Combine the remaining garlic and chillies with the pumpkin seeds, coriander, parsley, cheese, lime juice, Tabasco and ⅛ teaspoon salt in a food processor or blender. Pulse until finely chopped. With the motor running, add 75 ml/3 fl oz oil in a steady stream.

5 Lightly brush the fish fillets on both sides with oil and season evenly with salt and pepper. Brush the cooking grates clean. Grill the fillets over **direct high heat** for 4–5 minutes, with the lid closed, until nice grill marks appear and the fillets release easily from the cooking grate. Turn the fish over and generously spoon the pesto over the tops of the fillets. Continue cooking for 2–3 minutes, with the lid closed, until the flesh is opaque in the centre but still moist. Remove from the grill.

6 Spoon 3–4 tablespoons of the avocado sauce on each plate and top with a fish fillet. Serve with any remaining sauce on the side.

PESTO-MARINATED SEA BASS WITH WARM TOMATOES

SERVES: 4
PREP TIME: 15 MINUTES
MARINATING TIME: ABOUT 20 MINUTES
GRILLING TIME: ABOUT 6 MINUTES
SPECIAL EQUIPMENT: PERFORATED GRILL PAN

MARINADE
125 ml/4 fl oz white wine
4 tablespoons ready-made pesto
1 teaspoon crushed red chilli flakes
½ teaspoon sea salt

4 sea bass fillets (with skin), each about 175 g/6 oz and 1 cm/
   ½ inch thick
750 g/1½ lb cherry tomatoes

1 Mix the marinade ingredients in a small bowl. Place the fish fillets on a roasting tray and spoon the marinade over. Allow the fish to marinate at room temperature for about 20 minutes while you preheat the grill.

2 Prepare the grill for direct cooking over medium heat (180–230°C/350–450°F) and preheat the grill pan.

3 Using a spatula, transfer the fish from the roasting tray directly to the grill and discard any remaining marinade left on the tray. Arrange the tomatoes on the grill pan in a single layer and grill the fish and tomatoes over *direct medium heat* for about 6 minutes, with the lid closed as much as possible and turning the tomatoes once or twice, until the fish is just opaque at the centre and the tomatoes are warm and have collapsed. Do not turn the fish. Remove from the grill and serve the fillets warm with the tomatoes.

ROASTED PEPPER ROULADES WITH ITALIAN TUNA

SERVES: 6
PREP TIME: 30 MINUTES
GRILLING TIME: 6–8 MINUTES

2 × 150-g/5-oz cans tuna chunks in olive oil, drained
2 tablespoons small capers, rinsed
2 tablespoons finely chopped red onion
1 tablespoon chopped oregano
Zest and juice of 1 lemon
¼ teaspoon crushed red chilli flakes
Sea salt

6 peppers, preferably 2 red, 2 yellow and 2 orange

VINAIGRETTE
2 tablespoons fresh lemon juice
¼ teaspoon ground black pepper
4 tablespoons extra-virgin olive oil

150 g/5 oz gourmet salad mix

1 Prepare the grill for direct cooking over high heat (230–290°C/450–550°F).

2 Flake the tuna with a fork in a bowl and then mix in the capers, onion, oregano, lemon zest and chilli flakes. Season with salt and set aside.

3 Working with one pepper at a time, use a sharp knife to cut off the top and bottom of each pepper (save for another use). Cut each pepper down the side, and open each up into a large strip. Cut away the ribs and seeds (see page 15).

4 Brush the cooking grates clean. Grill the pepper strips, shiny skin side down, over **direct high heat** for 6–8 minutes, with the lid closed, until the skin is blackened and blistered (do not turn). Place the peppers in a bowl and cover with clingfilm to trap the steam. Leave to stand for 5–10 minutes.

5 Remove the peppers from the bowl and peel away and discard the charred skins. Cut each pepper strip in half to make 12 rectangles about 7.5 cm/3 inches long. Place in a bowl and drizzle with the lemon juice to coat all the peppers. Spread the tuna mixture evenly on to each pepper strip. Roll up the strips and secure with cocktail sticks. Transfer to a plate, cover with clingfilm and refrigerate for 15 minutes or up to 12 hours.

6 Whisk the lemon juice, pepper and ¼ teaspoon salt in a small bowl. Gradually whisk in the oil. Toss the salad leaves in a large bowl with half the vinaigrette.

7 To serve, divide the dressed salad and roulade pieces evenly between six plates. Drizzle the roulades with the remaining vinaigrette.

PORTOBELLO TOSTADOS WITH AVOCADO CREMA AND TOMATO SALSA

SERVES: 4
PREP TIME: 30 MINUTES
GRILLING TIME: 12-15 MINUTES

CREMA
1 ripe avocado, chopped
125 ml/4 fl oz soured cream
2 tablespoons fresh lime juice

Sea salt

SALSA
200 g/7 oz ripe tomatoes, finely chopped
½ red onion, thinly sliced
1 small jalapeño chilli, deseeded and finely chopped
2 tablespoons finely chopped fresh coriander
1 tablespoon red wine vinegar

4 large portobello mushrooms, stalks and gills removed
1 large red onion, cut crossways into 1-cm/½-inch slices
Extra-virgin olive oil
2 tablespoons ready-made fajita seasoning
2 large peppers, 1 red and 1 yellow, each cut into 4 pieces
8 flour tortillas, about 20 cm/8 inches in diameter
200 g/7 oz Monterey Jack or Cheddar cheese, grated

1 Blend the crema ingredients in a food processor until smooth. Season with salt. Cover and refrigerate until ready to serve.

2 Mix all the salsa ingredients in a bowl and season with salt. Set aside at room temperature.

3 Prepare the grill for direct cooking over medium heat (180–230°C/350–450°F).

4 Generously brush the mushroom caps and onion slices with oil and season evenly with the fajita seasoning.

5 Brush the cooking grates clean. Grill the mushrooms, onion and peppers over *direct medium heat*, with the lid closed as much as possible and turning occasionally, until browned and tender. The mushrooms will take 12–15 minutes, the onion will take 8–10 minutes and the peppers will take 6–8 minutes. If necessary, to prevent the mushrooms from drying out, occasionally brush them with a bit more oil. Remove the vegetables from the grill and scrape off any blackened areas of the peppers. Cut the vegetables into thin strips.

6 Grill the tortillas on one side over *direct medium heat* for 10–20 seconds, with the lid open, just until warm. Turn them over, top each one with 4 tablespoons of the cheese, and grill just until the cheese melts. Remove from the grill and assemble the tostados with the grilled vegetables, salsa and crema.

AUBERGINE PARMESAN

SERVES: 4
PREP TIME: 20 MINUTES
GRILLING TIME: 8–10 MINUTES

475-g/15-oz jar good-quality marinara sauce
2 large egg whites
3 oz Parmesan cheese, freshly grated
25 g/1 oz plus 2 tablespoons panko breadcrumbs
1 large rounded aubergine, cut into 12 slices, each about
     8 mm/$\frac{1}{3}$ inch thick and 7.5–10 cm/3–4 inches in diameter
Sea salt
Ground black pepper
Olive oil spray
300 g/10 oz fontina cheese, grated
12 large basil leaves

1 Warm the marinara sauce in a heavy saucepan over a medium heat. Set aside.

2 Prepare the grill for direct cooking over medium-high heat (200–260°C/400–500°F).

3 Whisk the egg whites in a shallow bowl until very light and foamy. Combine the Parmesan and breadcrumbs in another shallow bowl.

4 Dip one aubergine slice into the egg whites, covering thoroughly, and then place it in the breadcrumb mixture. Turn to coat, patting the crumbs to help them adhere, then gently shake off the excess. Place on a large roasting tray and repeat with the remaining aubergine slices. Season the slices with salt and pepper and generously spray both sides with olive oil.

5 Brush the cooking grates clean. Grill the aubergine slices over ***direct medium-high heat*** for 4–5 minutes, with the lid closed as much as possible, until the bottoms are golden. Turn the slices over, using a thin spatula. Place about 4 tablespoons of fontina cheese on each aubergine slice. Continue cooking for 4–5 minutes, with the lid closed, until the aubergine bottoms are golden brown and the cheese is melted.

6 Slightly overlap three aubergine slices on each of four plates. Serve warm with the sauce spooned over the aubergines and a basil leaf on top of each slice.

SPINACH SALAD WITH GRILLED TOMATOES AND ONIONS

SERVES: 4
PREP TIME: 10 MINUTES
GRILLING TIME: ABOUT 8 MINUTES

DRESSING
125 ml/4 fl oz ready-made pesto
3 tablespoons buttermilk
½ teaspoon ground black pepper

1 red onion, cut crossways into 1-cm/½-inch slices
6 plum tomatoes, halved lengthways

200 g/7 oz baby spinach
250 g/8 oz fresh mozzarella balls

1 Prepare the grill for direct cooking over medium heat (180–230°C/350–450°F).

2 Whisk the dressing ingredients in a small bowl. Cover and refrigerate until ready to use.

3 Brush the cooking grates clean. Grill the onion and tomatoes over **direct medium heat** for about 8 minutes, with the lid closed as much as possible and turning once or twice, until the onion is tender and the tomatoes are warmed through. Remove from the grill and cut the onion slices into bite-sized pieces.

4 Place a quarter of the spinach on each plate and top with equal amounts of the onion, tomatoes and mozzarella balls. Drizzle with the dressing. Serve immediately.

SPICY GRILLED TOFU WITH MARINATED VEGETABLES

SERVES: 4
PREP TIME: 15 MINUTES
MARINATING TIME: 3–12 HOURS
GRILLING TIME: 12–16 MINUTES

MARINADE
125 ml/4 fl oz low-sodium soy sauce
125 ml/4 fl oz vegetable oil
4 tablespoons rice vinegar
3 tablespoons toasted sesame oil
2 teaspoons hot chilli-garlic sauce

2 × 425-g/14-oz blocks extra-firm tofu, drained
175 g/6 oz button or chestnut mushrooms, cleaned, ends trimmed flat
2 small courgettes, cut lengthways into quarters
2 red peppers, cut into 2.5-cm/1-inch strips

1 Combine the marinade ingredients in a small bowl, whisking until combined. Cut each tofu block lengthways into four slices, each about 1.5 cm/¾ inch thick. Place the tofu in a large glass baking dish. Place the mushrooms, courgettes and peppers in a large bowl. Pour half the marinade into the dish with the tofu and the remainder into the bowl with the vegetables. Cover and refrigerate for at least 3 hours or up to 12 hours, turning the tofu and vegetables once or twice.

2 Prepare the grill for direct cooking over high heat (230–290°C/450–550°F).

3 Brush the cooking grates clean. Lay a large sheet of heavy-duty aluminium foil, about 30 × 40 cm/12 × 16 inches, directly on the cooking grates. Lift the tofu slices out of the dish, letting any extra marinade drip off, and arrange them in a single layer on the foil. Reserve the marinade. Grill the tofu over **direct high heat** for 6–8 minutes, with the lid closed as much as possible, turning once with a wide spatula and brushing occasionally with some of the reserved marinade, until both sides are nicely browned and the slices are hot. Transfer the tofu slices to a serving plate and tent them with foil to keep them warm while grilling the vegetables. Remove the foil from the grill.

4 Grill the mushrooms, courgettes and peppers over **direct high heat** for 3–4 minutes, with the lid closed as much as possible, until nicely marked. Turn, brush with the reserved marinade and continue cooking for 3–4 minutes until tender. Remove from the grill and cut the courgettes and peppers into bite-sized pieces. Transfer the vegetables to the serving plate with the tofu and serve immediately.

WARM POTATO SALAD WITH ROCKET, RED ONION AND GRAINY MUSTARD

SERVES: 4
PREP TIME: 20 MINUTES
GRILLING TIME: 15–20 MINUTES
SPECIAL EQUIPMENT: PERFORATED GRILL PAN

VINAIGRETTE
1 tablespoon sherry vinegar *or* red wine vinegar
½ small shallot, finely chopped
1½ teaspoons fresh lemon juice
¾ teaspoon wholegrain mustard
½ teaspoon finely chopped garlic
Sea salt
Ground black pepper
Extra-virgin olive oil

500 g/1 lb small new potatoes, each 3.5–5 cm/1½ –2 inches in diameter, scrubbed and halved
200 g/7 oz baby rocket
¼ red onion, very thinly sliced
250 g/8 oz cherry tomatoes, halved or quartered, depending on their size
4 tablespoons freshly shaved Parmesan cheese

1 Prepare the grill for direct cooking over medium heat (180–230°C/350–450°F) and preheat the grill pan.

2 Whisk the vinaigrette ingredients, including ¼ teaspoon salt and ⅛ teaspoon pepper, in a large bowl. Slowly add 3 tablespoons of oil, whisking constantly to emulsify the vinaigrette. Set aside.

3 Lightly coat the potatoes with oil and season them with salt in a large bowl. Spread the potatoes in a single layer on the grill pan. Grill over **direct medium heat** for 15–20 minutes, with the lid closed as much as possible and turning with a wide spatula about every 5 minutes, until they are golden brown and tender. Remove from the grill.

4 Combine the rocket, onion and tomatoes in a large bowl. Drizzle the salad with 3 tablespoons of the vinaigrette, season with salt and pepper and toss gently. Divide the salad between four plates.

5 Put the potatoes in the bowl with the remaining vinaigrette and toss to coat them well. Using a slotted spoon to allow excess vinaigrette to drip off, mound an equal portion of the potatoes on top of each salad and then top with the cheese. Drizzle more vinaigrette over the salad, if liked, and serve immediately.

PLUMS WITH HONEY-LEMON YOGURT

SERVES: 6
PREP TIME: 15 MINUTES
GRILLING TIME: ABOUT 6 MINUTES

250 ml/8 fl oz Greek yogurt
2 tablespoons runny honey
2 teaspoons fresh lemon juice
¼ teaspoon ground cardamom

6 firm but ripe plums, about 1 kg/2 lb in total, halved
Vegetable oil or rapeseed oil
1 tablespoon granulated sugar
40 g/1½ oz pistachios, coarsely chopped

1 Whisk the yogurt, honey, lemon juice and cardamom in a small bowl. Refrigerate until ready to use.

2 Prepare the grill for direct cooking over medium heat (180–230°C/350–450°F).

3 Lightly brush the cut side of each plum half with oil. Brush the cooking grates clean. Grill the plum halves, cut side down first, over *direct medium heat* for about 3 minutes, with the lid open, until slightly charred and grill marks appear. Turn the plums over, sprinkle evenly with the sugar, and continue cooking for 3 more minutes.

4 Place two plum halves in each of six cups or bowls. Spoon the honey yogurt over the plums. Sprinkle the pistachios on top to serve.

PINEAPPLE WITH TOASTED COCONUT AND RASPBERRY CREAM

SERVES: 4
PREP TIME: 15 MINUTES
GRILLING TIME: 4–6 MINUTES

4 tablespoons desiccated coconut
4 tablespoons chopped macadamia nuts
125 ml/4 fl oz chilled whipping cream
2 tablespoons raspberry jam
1 fresh pineapple, peeled, cored and cut into
    1-cm/½-inch slices

1 Prepare the grill for direct cooking over medium heat (180–230°C/350–450°F).

2 Toast the coconut for about 3 minutes in a small frying pan over a low heat. Watch it closely as it can burn quickly. Pour the coconut into a small bowl. Add the nuts to the same pan and cook for about 3 minutes, shaking the pan occasionally, until golden. Pour the nuts into the bowl with the coconut.

3 Whisk the cream for about 2 minutes in a bowl. Add the jam and whisk for 2–3 minutes more until soft peaks form.

4 Brush the cooking grates clean. Grill the pineapple slices over *direct medium heat* for 4–6 minutes, with the lid open and turning once, until nicely marked. Remove from the grill and cut into bite-sized pieces.

5 Divide the pineapple between four dessert dishes. Top with the coconut, nuts and cream.

BARBECUING OFF SEASON

BARBECUING OFF SEASON

WINTER COMFORTS

255 **ROASTED BUTTERNUT SQUASH HASH**

245 **BACON-WRAPPED TURKEY BREAST WITH APPLE-SAGE STUFFING**

ALL YEAR ROUND

230 **SPAGHETTI AND MEATBALLS**

257 **AUBERGINE AND TOMATO PASTA WITH TOASTED SESAME SEEDS**

SOUPS & STEWS

256 **BUTTERNUT SQUASH SOUP**

237 **GRILLED PORK POSOLE**

259 MIXED BERRY CRISP WITH CRÈME ANGLAISE

234 STEAK AND ALE CHILLI WITH BEANS

253 BACON-WRAPPED HALIBUT FILLETS

240 WHISKY-MUSTARD PORK CHOPS WITH
   GRILLED APPLES

244 CHICKEN AND CORN CHOWDER WITH
   PARMESAN-GARLIC TOAST

233 STEAK AND CHEESE TAMALE CASSEROLE

SPAGHETTI AND MEATBALLS

SERVES: 4
PREP TIME: 15 MINUTES
GRILLING TIME: ABOUT 10 MINUTES

MEATBALLS
500 g/1 lb minced beef (80% lean)
25 g/1 oz panko breadcrumbs
1 large egg
2 tablespoons finely chopped flat-leaf parsley
1 tablespoon finely chopped oregano
½ teaspoon sea salt
¼ teaspoon ground black pepper
¼ teaspoon garlic powder

750-g/1½-lb jar tomato-basil pasta sauce
500 g/1 lb spaghetti
Freshly grated Parmesan cheese

1 Prepare the grill for direct cooking over medium heat (180–230°C/350–450°F).

2 Bring a large saucepan of water to the boil for the pasta.

3 Blend the meatball ingredients thoroughly but gently in a large bowl. Using 4 tablespoons of the mixture for each, gently make eight meatballs slightly larger than a golf ball.

4 Brush the cooking grates clean. Grill the meatballs over **direct medium heat** for about 10 minutes, with the lid closed as much as possible and turning two or three times, until cooked on all sides.

5 Meanwhile, heat the pasta sauce in a large saucepan over low heat. Cook the spaghetti in the large saucepan of boiling water according to packet instructions. When the meatballs are done, add them to the hot pasta sauce and simmer gently while the pasta finishes cooking. Drain the pasta, toss it with the sauce and meatballs and serve hot with freshly grated cheese.

SAUSAGE-STUFFED COURGETTES WITH ROASTED PEPPER PURÉE

SERVES: 4-6
PREP TIME: 30 MINUTES
GRILLING TIME: 25-30 MINUTES

PURÉE
4 large plum tomatoes, about 500 g/1 lb in total
1 small onion, cut crossways into 1-cm/½-inch slices
2 small peppers, 1 red and 1 yellow
2 tablespoons finely chopped basil
2 tablespoons finely chopped oregano
2 garlic cloves
2 tablespoons red wine vinegar
1 teaspoon sea salt
¼ teaspoon ground black pepper
4 tablespoons extra-virgin olive oil

4 courgettes, about 1 kg/2 lb in total, halved lengthways
500 g/1 lb uncooked Italian sausages, casings removed
125 g/4 oz Romano cheese, grated
15 g/½ oz panko breadcrumbs

Cooked rice or pasta (optional)

1 Prepare the grill for direct cooking over medium heat (180–230°C/350–450°F).

2 Brush the cooking grates clean. Grill the tomatoes, onion and peppers over **direct medium heat**, with the lid closed as much as possible and turning every few minutes, until the tomatoes and onions are soft and the peppers are blackened. The tomatoes and onions will take 8–10 minutes, and the peppers will take 10–15 minutes. Remove from the grill as they are done. Place the peppers in a bowl and cover with clingfilm to trap the steam. Leave to stand for about 10 minutes.

3 When the vegetables are cool enough to handle, pull the skins from the tomatoes and cut out the stalk ends. Peel, core and deseed the peppers. Combine the tomatoes, onion, peppers, basil, oregano, garlic, vinegar, salt and pepper in the bowl of a food processor. Pulse until a semi-smooth purée is created. With the motor running, slowly add the oil. Warm the purée for 3–5 minutes in a saucepan over a low heat, stirring occasionally, until slightly thickened. Remove from the heat.

4 With the cut sides of the courgettes facing up, lightly score the flesh 3–5 mm/⅛–¼ inch in from the edges all the way round. Using a small spoon or melon baller, and using the scored edges as guides, carefully scoop out and discard the flesh and seeds, leaving a boat shape with uniformly thick sides.

5 Gently combine the sausage meat, cheese, breadcrumbs and 125 ml/4 fl oz of the purée in a bowl. Divide the mixture between the courgette boats, spreading it to fill them completely.

6 Brush the cooking grates clean. Grill the courgette boats over **direct medium heat** for about 15 minutes, with the lid closed as much as possible, until the sausage is cooked through and no longer pink. Using a wide spatula under the courgettes for support, carefully remove them from the grill. Serve on a bed of rice or pasta, if liked, and top each with some of the warm purée. Serve any remaining purée separately.

NOT YOUR MOTHER'S MEAT LOAF

SERVES: 6
PREP TIME: 30 MINUTES
GRILLING TIME: 45 MINUTES–1 HOUR
SPECIAL EQUIPMENT: 23 × 12-CM/9 × 5-INCH LOAF TIN,
   30-CM/12-INCH CAST-IRON FRYING PAN

Extra-virgin olive oil
1 onion, finely chopped
4 garlic cloves, finely chopped
1½ tablespoons finely chopped thyme
1 tablespoon finely chopped rosemary
500 g/1 lb minced beef (80% lean)
250 g/8 oz minced pork
250 g/8 oz minced lamb
50 g/2 oz panko breadcrumbs
75 g/3 oz Parmesan cheese, freshly grated
300 ml/½ pint jar ready-made tomato sauce
2 large eggs
½ teaspoon sea salt
¼ teaspoon ground black pepper

2 large tomatoes, about 500 g/1 lb in total, roughly chopped
2 tablespoons dry red wine or balsamic vinegar
1 teaspoon crushed red chilli flakes
2 garlic cloves, finely chopped

1 Prepare the grill for direct cooking over medium-low heat (150–200°C/300–400°F).

2 Heat a 30-cm/12-inch cast-iron frying pan on the hob over a medium heat. When hot, add 1 tablespoon oil and the onion and cook for about 5 minutes, stirring occasionally, until the onion is soft. Add the garlic and herbs. Cook for another minute and then transfer the mixture to a large bowl. (No need to clean the pan; it will be reused.) Add the minced beef, pork, lamb, breadcrumbs, cheese, 125 ml/4 fl oz of the tomato sauce, the eggs, salt and pepper to the bowl and blend well.

3 Line a 23 × 12-cm/9 × 5-inch loaf tin by placing a 23-cm/9-inch-wide strip of aluminium foil across the tin, leaving some foil hanging over the sides. There is no need to line the short ends of the tin. Pat the meat loaf into the lined tin. Brush the cooking grates clean. Turn the loaf tin upside-down on to the grill, lift off the tin and carefully remove the foil by pulling gently on what was the foil overhang. Grill the meat loaf over **direct medium-low heat** for about 15 minutes, with the lid closed, until one side begins to brown.

4 Meanwhile, mix the remaining tomato sauce, the tomatoes, wine, chilli flakes, garlic and 1 tablespoon oil in the cast-iron frying pan. Push the tomato chunks to the edges of the pan. Using a long spatula, lift the meat loaf off the grill and turn it into the frying pan, grilled side up. Spoon some of the sauce over the top of the meat loaf. Place the pan over **direct medium-low heat**, close the lid, and cook for 30–45 minutes, spooning the sauce over the meat every 15 minutes, until the meat is cooked through and the sauce is thick. Wearing insulated barbecue mitts or oven gloves, carefully remove the pan from the grill. Cut the meat loaf into thick slices and serve hot topped with the sauce.

STEAK AND CHEESE TAMALE CASSEROLE

SERVES: 6–8
PREP TIME: 30 MINUTES
GRILLING TIME: 53 MINUTES–1 HOUR
SPECIAL EQUIPMENT: 30-CM/12-INCH CAST-IRON
    FRYING PAN

RUB
1 teaspoon sea salt
1 teaspoon chilli powder
½ teaspoon ground cumin
¼ teaspoon ground black pepper

Piece of flank or skirt steak, 500–625 g/1–1¼ lb and about
    1.5 cm/¾ inch thick
Vegetable oil

DOUGH
350 g/11½ oz masa harina flour (fine Mexican cornmeal)
1 teaspoon sea salt
1 teaspoon ground cumin
½ teaspoon baking powder
50 g/2 oz unsalted butter, melted

250 ml/8 fl oz ready-made red or green salsa, preferably
    medium or hot
125 ml/4 fl oz chopped roasted red peppers
300 g/10 oz pepper Jack or Cheddar cheese, grated

1 Combine the rub ingredients in a small bowl. Lightly brush the steak on both sides with oil and season with the rub. Allow the steak to stand at room temperature for 15–30 minutes.

2 Prepare the grill for direct and indirect cooking over medium heat (180–230°C/350–450°F). Brush the cooking grates clean. Grill the steak over **direct medium heat**, with the lid closed as much as possible and turning once or twice (if flare-ups occur, move the steak temporarily to **indirect heat**), until cooked to desired doneness, 8–10 minutes for medium rare. Remove from the grill and leave to rest for 3–5 minutes. Cut the steak into 1-cm/½-inch pieces. Mix the flour, salt, cumin and baking powder in a bowl. Pour in 475 ml/16 fl oz water, the melted butter and stir for 2–3 minutes until the dough is thick and paste-like.

3 Lightly brush the inside of a 30-cm/12-inch cast-iron frying pan with oil. Spoon the dough into the pan and spread it out evenly to cover the bottom and 2.5 cm/1 inch up the sides. Combine steak pieces, salsa, roasted peppers and 250 g/8 oz of the cheese in a bowl. Pour into the pan, spreading evenly and leaving a 1-cm/½-inch rim of the crust uncovered. Grill the casserole over **indirect medium heat** for about 40 minutes, with the lid closed, rotating the pan for even cooking, until the crust begins to brown. Top with the remaining cheese and cook for 5–10 minutes until the cheese has melted and the crust turns golden brown along the edges. Remove the pan from the grill. Leave to cool for 10 minutes. Cut into slices and serve.

STEAK AND ALE CHILLI WITH BEANS

SERVES: 6–8

PREP TIME: 30 MINUTES

GRILLING TIME: 4–6 MINUTES, PLUS 1–1¼ HOURS FOR
    THE CHILLI

RUB

2 teaspoons ground cumin
Sea salt
Ground black pepper

500 g/1 lb skirt steak, about 1.5 cm/¾ inch thick, trimmed of
    excess fat, cut into 30-cm/12-inch-long pieces
Vegetable oil

CHILLI

3 onions, finely chopped
1 tablespoon finely chopped garlic
2 tablespoons chilli powder
2 teaspoons dried oregano
1 kg/2 lb canned chilli beans, such as pinto beans, with liquid
875 g/1¾ lb canned chopped tomatoes
350 ml/12 fl oz stout
2 tablespoons cider vinegar
½ teaspoon Worcestershire sauce

250 g/8 oz Cheddar cheese, finely grated

1 Prepare the grill for direct cooking over medium heat (180–230°C/350–450°F).

2 Combine the cumin, 1 teaspoon salt and 1 teaspoon pepper in a small bowl. Lightly brush the steaks on both sides with oil and season evenly with the rub. Allow the steaks to stand at room temperature for 15–30 minutes before grilling.

3 Brush the cooking grates clean. Grill the steaks over **direct medium heat** for 4–6 minutes, with the lid closed as much as possible and turning once, until cooked to medium-rare doneness. Remove from the grill and leave to rest for 3–5 minutes. Cut the steaks into 1-cm/½-inch pieces.

4 Heat 1 tablespoon oil in a large saucepan over a medium heat. Add the onion and garlic and cook for about 5 minutes, stirring occasionally, until the onion is tender. Stir in the chilli powder and oregano and cook for 1–2 minutes until fragrant. Add the remaining chilli ingredients and increase the heat to bring the chilli to the boil. Reduce the heat to low, add the steak, cover and simmer for 20 minutes. Uncover the pan and continue to simmer for 40–50 minutes, stirring to the bottom of the pan occasionally, until the chilli thickens to your preferred consistency. Season with salt and pepper. Serve warm topped with the grated cheese.

PORK FILLET ROULADES WITH GARLICKY SWEET POTATOES

SERVES: 4
PREP TIME: 30 MINUTES
GRILLING TIME: 40–45 MINUTES
SPECIAL EQUIPMENT: KITCHEN STRING, INSTANT-READ
    MEAT THERMOMETER

1 tablespoon finely chopped garlic
Extra-virgin olive oil
Sea salt
Ground black pepper
750 g/1½ lb small sweet potatoes, cut crossways into 1.5-cm/
    ¾-inch slices, skin left on

125 g/4 oz breadcrumbs
Zest and 75 ml/3 fl oz juice from 2 lemons
2 teaspoons finely chopped thyme

2 pork fillets, each 375–500 g/12 oz–1 lb, butterflied, trimmed
    of excess fat and skin

1 Combine the garlic, 1 tablespoon oil, ½ teaspoon salt and
¼ teaspoon pepper in a bowl. Add the sweet potatoes and turn
to coat evenly. Place the potatoes on one long half of a 60-cm/
24-inch long piece of aluminium foil. Fold the other side of
the foil over the potatoes and crimp the edges so that they are
securely sealed in a package.

2 Add the breadcrumbs, lemon zest and juice, thyme, ½
teaspoon salt, ¼ teaspoon pepper and 2 tablespoons oil to the
same bowl and toss until the breadcrumbs are evenly moistened.

3 Place the butterflied pork fillets on a work surface between
two sheets of clingfilm and pound to an even thickness until the
pork is about 1 cm/½ inch thick all over.

4 Prepare the grill for direct and indirect cooking over medium
heat (180–230°C/350–450°F).

5 Press half of the stuffing on to each piece of meat, spreading
it all the way to the edges. Roll the meat up from one long edge
to the other so the fillets generally regain their original shape.
Secure each roll with kitchen string at 5-cm/2-inch intervals.
Brush with oil and season evenly with salt and pepper.

6 Brush the cooking grates clean. Grill the potato package over
indirect medium heat and the pork rolls over **direct medium
heat**, with the lid closed as much as possible and turning
occasionally, until the potatoes are tender and the outside of
the pork is evenly seared and the internal temperature registers
65°C/150°F on an instant-read meat thermometer. The potatoes
will take 40–45 minutes and the pork will take 25–30 minutes,
so start the potatoes 15–20 minutes before the pork. Cut the
pork into 1-cm/½-inch slices. Serve with the hot sweet potatoes.

GRILLED PORK POSOLE

SERVES: 4–6
PREP TIME: 25 MINUTES, PLUS ABOUT 35 MINUTES ON
   THE HOB
GRILLING TIME: ABOUT 6 MINUTES
SPECIAL EQUIPMENT: PERFORATED GRILL PAN,
   5–7-LITRE CAST-IRON CASSEROLE

2 pork fillets, each 375–500 g/12 oz–1 lb, trimmed of excess
   fat and skin, or 750-g/1½-lb boneless pork joint, trimmed
   of excess fat
Extra-virgin olive oil
1 teaspoon sea salt
¼ teaspoon ground black pepper
3 Anaheim chillies
1 onion, chopped
2 garlic cloves, finely chopped
2 teaspoons ground cumin
¼ teaspoon ground cloves
2 canned chipotle chillies in adobo sauce, chopped
1 tablespoon adobo sauce (from the canned chipotle chillies)
1 litre/1¾ pints chicken stock
2 × 475-g/15-oz cans hominy, rinsed
475-g/15-oz can chopped tomatoes

Chopped avocado
Thinly sliced cabbage
Soured cream
Lime wedges
Corn tortillas

1 Prepare the grill for direct cooking over high heat
(230–290°C/450–550°F) and preheat the grill pan.

2 Cut the pork into 2.5–3-cm/1–1¼-inch pieces and place
them in a bowl. Add 1 tablespoon oil, ½ teaspoon of the salt
and the pepper and toss until evenly coated. Lightly brush the
Anaheim chillies with oil.

3 Spread the pork in a single layer on the grill pan and cook
over **direct high heat** for 3–5 minutes, with the lid closed as
much as possible and turning occasionally, until the pork is
seared but not completely cooked. At the same time, grill the
chillies over **direct high heat** for about 6 minutes, turning
occasionally to char all sides. Carefully remove the grill pan
from the grill and transfer the pork to a bowl; set aside. Transfer
the chillies to a bowl and cover tightly with clingfilm to trap the
steam. Leave to stand for 10–15 minutes.

4 Heat a large cast-Iron casserole over a medium heat. Add
1 tablespoon oil and the onion and cook for about 10 minutes,
stirring occasionally, until the onion is soft. Add the remaining
½ teaspoon salt, the garlic, cumin, cloves, chipotle chillies and
adobo sauce and cook for another minute, stirring constantly.
Add the chicken stock, hominy, tomatoes and pork, bring to
a low boil, reduce the heat and simmer for about 15 minutes.
While the posole is simmering, peel, deseed and chop the
Anaheim chillies and add them to the casserole.

5 Serve the posole hot with avocado, cabbage, soured cream,
lime wedges and grilled tortilla chips.

ROASTED PORK LOIN WITH PLUMS AND MINT SAUCE

SERVES: 6–8
PREP TIME: 30 MINUTES
DRY BRINING TIME: 12–24 HOURS
GRILLING TIME: 43–57 MINUTES
SPECIAL EQUIPMENT: INSTANT-READ MEAT
    THERMOMETER

1.5–2-kg/3–4-lb boneless centre-cut pork loin roasting joint
2 teaspoons sea salt
2 teaspoons vegetable oil *or* rapeseed oil

1 serrano chilli
125 g/4 oz mint
2 teaspoons grated fresh ginger
2 garlic cloves
2 tablespoons fresh lemon juice
6 tablespoons extra-virgin olive oil

6 ripe plums, halved

1 Sprinkle the joint all over with 1 teaspoon of the salt. Place it in a bowl, cover and refrigerate for 12–24 hours.

2 Remove the meat from the bowl and pat dry with kitchen paper. Coat the joint all over with 1 teaspoon of the vegetable oil and allow to stand at room temperature for about 30 minutes before grilling.

3 Prepare the grill for direct and indirect cooking over high heat (230–290°C/450–550°F).

4 Brush the cooking grates clean. Sear the joint over ***direct high heat*** for 10–12 minutes, with the lid closed as much as possible and turning occasionally, until the surface is well marked but not burnt. Watch for flare-ups, especially when searing the fatty side. Move the meat over ***indirect high heat*** and cook, fat side up, for 25–35 minutes, with the lid closed, until the internal temperature registers 63–65°C/145–150°F on an instant-read meat thermometer. Transfer the joint to a carving board, tent loosely with aluminium foil and leave to rest for about 15 minutes.

5 Remove and discard the stem from the chilli and cut it into a few large pieces (if a milder sauce is preferred, remove the seeds). Whizz the chilli, mint, ginger, garlic, lemon juice, olive oil and the remaining 1 teaspoon salt in a blender or food processor until smooth. Set aside.

6 Brush both sides of the plums with the remaining 1 teaspoon vegetable oil. Grill the plums, cut side down, over ***indirect high heat*** for 8–10 minutes, with the lid closed as much as possible, until grill marks appear and the plums are tender when poked with the tip of a knife; do not turn the plums. Remove from the grill and cut each plum half in half.

7 Carve the pork crossways into 1-cm/½-inch slices. Serve warm with the grilled plums and the mint sauce.

WHISKY-MUSTARD PORK CHOPS WITH GRILLED APPLES

SERVES: 4
PREP TIME: 15 MINUTES
GRILLING TIME: 12–16 MINUTES

GLAZE
4 tablespoons whisky
4 tablespoons soft brown sugar
2 tablespoons wholegrain mustard
1 teaspoon vanilla extract

4 bone-in pork loin chops, each about 250 g/8 oz and 2.5 cm/1
    inch thick, trimmed of excess fat
Vegetable oil
Sea salt
Ground black pepper
4 Granny Smith apples, cored and cut into 1-cm/½-inch
    wedges
1 tablespoon finely chopped tarragon

1 Whisk the glaze ingredients in a small bowl until the brown sugar
dissolves. Reserve 3 tablespoons of the glaze in a large bowl.

2 Lightly coat the pork chops on both sides with oil, season
evenly with salt and pepper, and brush with the whisky glaze in
the small bowl. Allow the chops to stand at room temperature
for 15–30 minutes before grilling.

3 Prepare the grill for direct cooking over medium heat
(180–230°C/350–450°F).

4 Lightly coat the apple slices on both sides with oil.

5 Brush the cooking grates clean. Grill the apples over **direct
medium heat** for 4–6 minutes, with the lid closed as much as
possible and turning once or twice, until crisp-tender and lightly
charred. Transfer the apple slices to the large bowl with the
reserved whisky glaze, add the tarragon and toss to coat.

6 Grill the chops over **direct medium heat** for 8–10 minutes,
with the lid closed as much as possible and turning once or
twice, until they are still slightly pink in the centre. Remove
from the grill and leave to rest for 3–5 minutes. Serve the chops
warm with the grilled apples.

TOMATO AND SAUSAGE STRATA

SERVES: 8
PREP TIME: 20 MINUTES
REFRIGERATION TIME: OVERNIGHT
GRILLING TIME: 10–12 MINUTES FOR THE SAUSAGES,
    PLUS 30–40 MINUTES FOR THE STRATA
SPECIAL EQUIPMENT: 30-CM/12-INCH CAST-IRON
    FRYING PAN

2–3 uncooked mild Italian sausages, each about 125 g/4 oz,
    pierced a few times with a fork
8 large eggs
300 ml/½ pint full-fat milk
2 teaspoons finely chopped rosemary
2 teaspoons finely chopped oregano
½ teaspoon sea salt
¼ teaspoon ground black pepper
400-g/13-oz loaf Italian bread, cut into 1.5-cm/¾-inch cubes
500 g/1 lb cherry tomatoes
1 roasted red pepper (from a jar), cut lengthways into
    5-mm/¼-inch slices
175 g/6 oz mozzarella cheese, cut into 5-mm–1-cm/
    ¼–½-inch cubes
5 g/¼ oz unsalted butter
50 g/2 oz Parmesan cheese, freshly grated

1 Prepare the grill for direct cooking over medium heat
(180–230°C/350–450°F).

2 Brush the cooking grates clean. Grill the sausages over ***direct
medium heat*** for 10–12 minutes, with the lid closed as much
as possible and turning occasionally, until they are cooked
through and no longer pink in the centre. Remove from the grill
and turn off the grill.

3 Cut the cooked sausages in half lengthways and then cut
them crossways into thin slices. Whisk the eggs, milk, rosemary,
oregano, salt and pepper in a large bowl. Add the sausage
slices, bread cubes, tomatoes, roasted pepper and mozzarella
cheese to the bowl and toss to coat evenly.

4 Grease a 30-cm/12-inch cast-iron frying pan with the butter.
Put the mixture in the pan and top with the Parmesan cheese.
Cover with foil and refrigerate overnight. Allow the pan to stand
at room temperature for about 30 minutes before grilling.

5 Prepare the grill for direct cooking over medium-low heat
(about 180°C/350°F).

6 Remove and discard the foil from the pan. Grill over ***direct
medium-low heat*** for 30–40 minutes, with the lid closed as
much as possible, until the centre of the strata is firm (a knife
inserted into the centre should come out free of uncooked egg)
and the bread is toasted. Towards the end of the cooking time
some liquid may accumulate as the cheese melts. The liquid
will reabsorb upon resting. Remove from the grill and let the
strata cool for about 10 minutes. Serve warm.

PORK CHOPS WITH WHITE BEAN RAGOUT

SERVES: 4
PREP TIME: 15 MINUTES, PLUS ABOUT 25 MINUTES FOR
THE RAGOUT
GRILLING TIME: 8–10 MINUTES

PASTE
2 tablespoons Dijon mustard
Extra-virgin olive oil
Sea salt
Ground black pepper

4 bone-in pork loin chops, each about 250 g/8 oz and 2.5 cm/
1 inch thick, trimmed of excess fat

RAGOUT
50 g/2 oz pancetta, sliced 3 mm/⅛ inch thick *or* 2 thick bacon
rashers, cut into 5-mm/¼-inch dice
1 shallot, finely chopped
2 × 475-g/15-oz cans cannellini beans, rinsed
175 ml/6 fl oz chicken stock
1 ripe plum tomato, deseeded and diced
3 tablespoons dry white wine *or* dry vermouth
½ teaspoon chopped rosemary
½ teaspoon chopped sage

2 slices wholegrain artisan bread, each about 1 cm/½ inch
thick, torn into pieces
1 garlic clove, finely chopped

1 Mix the mustard with 3 tablespoons oil, 1 teaspoon salt and ½ teaspoon pepper in a small bowl. Lightly brush the pork chops on both sides with the paste. Allow the chops to stand at room temperature for 15–30 minutes before grilling.

2 Prepare the grill for direct cooking over medium heat (180–230°C/350–450°F).

3 Cook the pancetta in 2 teaspoons oil in a saucepan over a medium heat for about 5 minutes, stirring often, until it is lightly browned. Add the shallot and cook for about 2 minutes until softened. Stir in the beans, stock, tomato, wine, rosemary and sage and bring to the boil. Reduce the heat to medium-low and simmer for about 15 minutes until the liquid is reduced by half. Season with salt and pepper. Remove from the heat and cover.

4 Pulse the bread in a food processor until coarse crumbs form. Heat 2 tablespoons oil and the garlic in a large frying pan over a medium heat for about 3 minutes, stirring often, until the garlic begins to turn golden. Add the breadcrumbs and cook for about 2 minutes, stirring often, until they are crispy.

5 Brush the cooking grates clean. Grill the chops over **direct medium heat** for 8–10 minutes, with the lid closed as much as possible and turning once or twice, until they are still slightly pink in the centre. Remove from the grill and leave to rest for 3–5 minutes.

6 Serve the chops warm with the ragout and topped with the breadcrumbs.

CHICKEN AND CORN CHOWDER WITH PARMESAN-GARLIC TOAST

SERVES: 4–6
PREP TIME: 30 MINUTES, PLUS ABOUT 30 MINUTES FOR
    THE CHOWDER
GRILLING TIME: 10–16 MINUTES

3 boneless, skinless chicken breasts, each about 175 g/6 oz
1½ tablespoons extra-virgin olive oil
1½ tablespoons finely chopped thyme
Sea salt
Ground black pepper
4 fresh corn cobs, outer leaves and silk removed
25 g/1 oz unsalted butter
1 onion, finely chopped
2 teaspoons finely chopped garlic
475 ml/16 fl oz full-fat milk
3 large potatoes, about 1 kg/2 lb in total, cut into 1-cm/
    ½-inch cubes
1 litre/1¾ pints chicken chicken stock

TOAST
50 g/2 oz unsalted butter, melted
2 large garlic cloves, finely chopped
½ baguette
4 tablespoons freshly grated Parmesan cheese

1 Prepare the grill for direct cooking over medium heat (180–230°C/350–450°F).

2 Lightly coat the chicken on both sides with the oil and season evenly with the thyme, ½ teaspoon salt and ¼ teaspoon pepper.

3 Brush the cooking grates clean. Grill the chicken, smooth (skin) side down first, over *direct medium heat* for 8–12 minutes, with the lid closed as much as possible and turning once or twice, until the meat is firm to the touch and opaque all the way to the centre. At the same time, grill the corn over *direct medium heat* for 8–10 minutes, turning occasionally, until the kernels turn brown in spots all over. Remove from the grill.

4 Melt the butter in a large saucepan over a medium heat. Add the onion and garlic, season with salt and pepper and cook for about 5 minutes, stirring occasionally, until soft. Add the milk, potatoes and stock. Bring to a simmer and cook for 15–20 minutes, uncovered, until the potatoes are tender.

5 While the chowder simmers, chop the chicken into 1-cm/½-inch pieces, cut the kernels from the cobs and make the toast. Mash the butter and garlic in a small bowl with a fork. Season with salt and pepper. Cut the baguette into slices about 2.5 cm/1 inch thick and spread the butter mixture evenly on both sides of each slice. Grill over *direct medium heat* for 1–2 minutes, with the lid open (watch for flare-ups), until lightly toasted. Turn the slices over and sprinkle the sides with a thin layer of cheese. Grill for 1–2 minutes more, until the cheese begins to melt. Stir the chicken and corn into the soup. Serve warm with the toast.

BACON-WRAPPED TURKEY BREAST WITH APPLE-SAGE STUFFING

SERVES: 6
PREP TIME: 30 MINUTES
GRILLING TIME: ABOUT 1½ HOURS
SPECIAL EQUIPMENT: KITCHEN STRING, LARGE
    DISPOSABLE ALUMINIUM FOIL ROASTING TRAY,
    INSTANT-READ MEAT THERMOMETER

40 g/1½ oz unsalted butter
1 onion, roughly chopped
1 large apple, peeled, cored and roughly chopped
1 tablespoon finely chopped sage
1 tablespoon finely chopped garlic
½ teaspoon sea salt
¼ teaspoon ground black pepper
1 boneless, skinless turkey breast, about 1.5 kg/3 lb, butterflied
12 bacon rashers

SAUCE
250 g/8 oz fresh cranberries, rinsed and drained
250 ml/8 fl oz apple juice
3 tablespoons soft dark brown sugar
¼ teaspoon sea salt
¼ teaspoon ground black pepper

1 Melt the butter in a large frying pan over a medium-high heat. Add the onion and apple and cook for 3–4 minutes, stirring. Add the sage, garlic, salt and pepper. Cook for 2 more minutes, stirring. Transfer to a bowl to cool.

2 Place the butterflied turkey breast on a work surface between two sheets of clingfilm and pound to an even thickness. Evenly spread the stuffing over the turkey breast and then roll up the breast lengthways to create a cylinder. Wrap the turkey in the bacon as shown in the photo below and tie it with kitchen string to create a uniform roast and to secure the bacon.

3 Before you light the grill, place a large disposable foil roasting tray under the cooking grate to catch any grease. Prepare the grill for indirect cooking over medium heat (about 200°C/400°F).

4 Brush the cooking grates clean. Centre the turkey over the foil tray and grill over *indirect medium heat* for about 1½ hours, with the lid closed and turning once or twice to ensure the bacon gets crispy on all sides, until the internal temperature registers 70–74°C/160–165°F on an instant-read meat thermometer.

5 Meanwhile, make the sauce. Bring the sauce ingredients to the boil in a saucepan over a medium-high heat. Lower the heat to a simmer and cook for 10–12 minutes, stirring occasionally, until the cranberries pop and the sauce thickens. Let cool to room temperature.

6 Transfer the turkey to a carving board and leave to rest for 5–10 minutes (the internal temperature will rise 5–10 degrees during this time). Remove the string and carve into 2.5-cm/1-inch slices. Serve warm or at room temperature with the sauce.

TURKEY BREAST WITH ITALIAN SALSA VERDE

SERVES: 6–8

PREP TIME: 15 MINUTES

GRILLING TIME: 1½–2 HOURS

SPECIAL EQUIPMENT: LARGE DISPOSABLE ALUMINIUM FOIL ROASTING TRAY, INSTANT-READ MEAT THERMOMETER

SALSA VERDE

125 g/4 oz flat-leaf parsley

2 tablespoons small capers, rinsed

1 teaspoon anchovy paste

1 garlic clove, finely chopped

Sea salt

Ground black pepper

Extra-virgin olive oil

2 tablespoons red wine vinegar

1 turkey breast (with bone and skin), 3–3.5 kg/6–7 lb, thawed if necessary

1 Carefully place a large disposable foil roasting tray underneath the cooking grate to catch the turkey drippings. Prepare the grill for indirect cooking over medium-low heat (about 180°C/350°F).

2 Combine the parsley, capers, anchovy paste, garlic, ¼ teaspoon salt and ¼ teaspoon pepper in a food processor and pulse until the parsley is finely chopped. With the machine running, gradually add 125 ml/4 fl oz oil and process to a fairly smooth sauce. Transfer to a bowl, cover, and set aside at room temperature while the turkey is grilling.

3 Brush the turkey breast all over with oil and season evenly with salt and pepper. Brush the cooking grates clean. Centre the turkey above the foil tray and grill over *indirect medium-low heat* for 1½–2 hours, with the lid closed, until an instant-read meat thermometer inserted into the thickest part of the breast (not touching the bone), registers 70–74°C/160–165°F. Keep the temperature of the grill as close to 180°C/350°F as possible. Transfer to a carving board and leave to rest for 5–10 minutes (the internal temperature will rise 5–10 degrees during this time).

4 Remove each half of the turkey breast by cutting lengthways along both sides of the breastbone. Pull each breast half away from the breastbone, using a sharp knife to carefully release the meat from the rib cage. Cut the meat across the grain into 1-cm/½-inch slices. Stir the vinegar into the salsa verde. Serve the turkey warm or at room temperature with the salsa verde on the side.

GLAZED DUCK BREASTS WITH SPICED MINT AND PISTACHIO PILAF

SERVES: 4
PREP TIME: 30 MINUTES, PLUS 10–15 MINUTES FOR
    THE GLAZE
GRILLING TIME: 10–12 MINUTES

350 ml/12 fl oz refrigerated pomegranate juice
4 tablespoons soft light brown sugar
2 tablespoons balsamic vinegar
1½ teaspoons ground cumin

3 duck breast halves (with skin), each about 175 g/6 oz,
    patted dry
½ teaspoon sea salt
¼ teaspoon ground black pepper

PILAF
1 tablespoon vegetable oil
1½ onions, chopped
¼ teaspoon ground turmeric
¼ teaspoon ground cardamom
200 g/7 oz basmati rice
400 ml/14 fl oz chicken stock
½ teaspoon sea salt
50 g/2 oz raisins *or* currants

4 tablespoons chopped mint
4 tablespoons chopped unsalted pistachios

1 Combine the pomegranate juice, brown sugar and vinegar in a small saucepan; bring to the boil over a high heat, stirring until the sugar dissolves. Lower the heat to a simmer and cook for 10–15 minutes, stirring often, until the glaze is slightly thickened and reduced to 125 ml/4 fl oz. Add ½ teaspoon of the cumin. Remove from the heat and reserve 4 tablespoons of the glaze to serve with the duck.

2 Prepare the grill for direct cooking over medium-low heat (about 180°C/350°F).

3 Using a sharp knife, score the skin of each duck breast on the diagonal in a crisscross pattern (do not cut through the breast meat). Rub both sides of each breast evenly with the remaining 1 teaspoon of cumin, the salt and pepper. Brush the duck with some of the glaze.

4 Heat the oil in a heavy saucepan over a medium-high heat. Add the onion and sauté for 4–5 minutes until tender and golden. Add the turmeric and cardamom; stir for 15 seconds. Add the rice and stir for 30 seconds. Add the stock and salt and bring to the boil. Reduce the heat to low. Cover and simmer for about 15 minutes until the rice is tender and the liquid is absorbed. Remove from the heat and add the raisins. Leave to stand, covered, for 5 minutes.

5 Brush the cooking grates clean. Grill the duck breasts, skin side down first, over **direct medium-low heat**, with the lid closed as much as possible, turning once or twice and occasionally brushing the duck with the glaze (if flare-ups occur, move the breasts temporarily over indirect heat), until cooked to your desired doneness, 10–12 minutes for medium rare. Remove from the grill and leave to rest for 3–5 minutes.

6 Divide the pilaf between four plates and top with the mint and pistachios. Cut the duck breasts crossways into 8-mm/⅓-inch slices. Divide the duck slices between the plates. Serve warm with the reserved glaze.

SEARED SCALLOPS WITH PROSCIUTTO BITS

SERVES: 4
PREP TIME: 10 MINUTES
GRILLING TIME: 5–9 MINUTES

12 scallops, each 25–40 g/1–1½ oz
1 tablespoon extra-virgin olive oil
Sea salt
Ground black pepper

2 paper-thin slices Parma ham

250 ml/8 fl oz good-quality marinara sauce
2 tablespoons finely chopped flat-leaf parsley or basil

1 Prepare the grill for direct cooking over medium heat (180–230°C/350–450°F).

2 Remove and discard the small tough side muscle that might be left on each scallop. Lightly brush the scallops with the oil and season evenly with salt and pepper.

3 Brush the cooking grates clean. Grill the Parma ham over **direct medium heat** for 1–3 minutes, with the lid open and turning once or twice, until the meat browns on the edges and turns crispy. Remove from the grill and let cool. Roughly chop the ham into pieces.

4 Grill the scallops over **direct medium heat** for 4–6 minutes, with the lid closed as much as possible and turning once or twice, until just opaque in the centre. Remove from the grill.

5 Warm the marinara sauce in a small saucepan over a medium heat. To serve, divide the marinara sauce evenly between four plates. Arrange three scallops on top. Garnish with the chopped Parma ham and fresh herbs. Serve warm.

BACON-WRAPPED HALIBUT FILLETS

SERVES: 4
PREP TIME: 10 MINUTES
MARINATING TIME: 15–30 MINUTES
GRILLING TIME: ABOUT 10 MINUTES

MARINADE
2 tablespoons extra-virgin olive oil
1 teaspoon finely chopped rosemary
1 teaspoon finely chopped oregano
1 teaspoon finely chopped garlic
¼ teaspoon sea salt
¼ teaspoon ground black pepper

4 skinless halibut fillets, each about 175 g/6 oz and 2.5 cm/
    1 inch thick
1 lemon, thinly sliced
8 thin bacon rashers

1 Prepare the grill for direct and indirect cooking over medium heat (180–230°C/350–450°F).

2 Combine the marinade ingredients in a bowl. Add the halibut and turn to coat each fillet thoroughly. Leave to marinate at room temperature for 15–30 minutes.

3 Place one or two lemon slices on each fish fillet. Using two bacon rashers, wrap a fillet by starting with one end of a rasher on the underside of the fillet. Wrap it around in a slight spiral, bringing it back to the bottom so the edges of the bacon overlap only minimally. Wrap the second rasher the same way to cover the rest of the fillet as much as possible. Secure the bacon with cocktail sticks. Repeat with the remaining fish fillets.

4 Brush the cooking grates clean. Grill the halibut, underside down, over **direct medium heat** for about 10 minutes, with the lid closed as much as possible and turning once or twice (when flare-ups occur, move the halibut temporarily over indirect heat), until the bacon is browned and the halibut is opaque in the centre. Remove from the grill and serve warm.

ROASTED BRUSSELS SPROUTS

SERVES: 4
PREP TIME: 10 MINUTES
GRILLING TIME: 10–15 MINUTES
SPECIAL EQUIPMENT: PERFORATED GRILL PAN

MARINADE
1 tablespoon lemon-infused olive oil
1 teaspoon finely chopped thyme
½ teaspoon sea salt
¼ teaspoon ground black pepper

500 g/1 lb Brussels sprouts, each one trimmed at the root end and cut in half lengthways

Finely grated zest of 1 lemon
1 teaspoon champagne vinegar

1 Prepare the grill for direct cooking over low heat (130–180°C/250–350°F) and preheat the grill pan.

2 Mix the marinade ingredients in a bowl. Add the Brussels sprouts and turn to coat them evenly.

3 Spread the sprouts in a single layer on the grill pan and grill over *direct low heat* for 10–15 minutes, with the lid closed as much as possible and turning several times, until crisp-tender. Transfer to a serving bowl and add the lemon zest and vinegar. Toss to coat evenly. Season with salt, if liked. Serve warm.

ROASTED BUTTERNUT SQUASH HASH

SERVES: 4
PREP TIME: 35 MINUTES
GRILLING TIME: 20–30 MINUTES
SPECIAL EQUIPMENT: PERFORATED GRILL PAN

4 tablespoons extra-virgin olive oil
1 tablespoon finely chopped sage
1 tablespoon finely chopped thyme
1 teaspoon sea salt
1 teaspoon ground black pepper
1 butternut squash, about 1 kg/2 lb, peeled, deseeded and cut
    into 2.5-cm/1-inch chunks
1 large Granny Smith apple, peeled, cored and cut into
    2.5-cm/1-inch chunks
1 sweet potato, peeled and cut into 2.5-cm/1-inch chunks
1 red onion, peeled and cut into wedges

Finely grated zest of 1 orange

1 Prepare the grill for direct cooking over low heat (130–180°C/250–350°F) and preheat the grill pan.

2 Whisk the oil, sage, thyme, salt and pepper in a large bowl. Add the squash, apple, sweet potato and onion pieces and toss to coat evenly.

3 Spread the vegetables and apple in a single layer on the grill pan. Grill over **_direct low heat_** for 20–30 minutes, with the lid closed as much as possible and turning occasionally, until tender. Transfer to a serving bowl and stir in the orange zest. Serve warm.

BUTTERNUT SQUASH SOUP

SERVES: 4
PREP TIME: 20 MINUTES
GRILLING TIME: ABOUT 20 MINUTES
SPECIAL EQUIPMENT: PERFORATED GRILL PAN

2 tablespoons extra-virgin olive oil
1 teaspoon finely chopped sage
Sea salt
Ground black pepper
1 butternut squash, about 1 kg/2 lb, peeled, deseeded and cut
    into 2.5-cm/1-inch cubes
1 large Granny Smith apple, peeled, cored and chopped
1 small shallot, peeled and cut into quarters

475 ml/16 fl oz chicken stock
1 tablespoon champagne vinegar
4 tablespoons whipping cream
Finely grated zest of 1 small orange

Finely chopped chives (optional)

1 Prepare the grill for direct cooking over low heat (130–180°C/250–350°F) and preheat the grill pan.

2 Whisk the oil, sage, 1 teaspoon salt and ½ teaspoon pepper in a large bowl. Add the squash, apple and shallot and toss to coat evenly.

3 Spread the squash, apple and shallot in a single layer on the grill pan. Grill over *direct low heat* for about 20 minutes, with the lid closed as much as possible and turning occasionally, until the vegetables and apple are fork tender. Remove the squash mixture from the grill and place in a food processor or blender and pulse until finely chopped.

4 Warm the stock in a saucepan over a medium heat. Add the stock, vinegar, cream and orange zest to the food processor and process until smooth. Pour the soup back into the saucepan and season with salt and pepper. Keep warm over a low heat.

5 Serve the soup warm, garnished with chives, if liked.

AUBERGINE AND TOMATO PASTA WITH TOASTED SESAME SEEDS

SERVES: 4-6
PREP TIME: 25 MINUTES
GRILLING TIME: 8–10 MINUTES

2 rounded aubergines, cut crossways into 1-cm/½-inch slices
1 onion, cut crossways into 1-cm/½-inch slices
4 tablespoons extra-virgin olive oil
Sea salt
6 plum tomatoes

375 g/12 oz short pasta such as gemelli

5 tablespoons chopped flat-leaf parsley
1 tablespoon finely chopped garlic
5 tablespoons small capers, rinsed
4 tablespoons sesame seeds, toasted

1 Prepare the grill for direct cooking over medium heat (180–230°C/350–450°F).

2 Brush the aubergine and onion slices with the oil and season with salt. Brush the cooking grates clean. Grill the aubergines, onion and tomatoes over **direct medium heat** for 8–10 minutes, with the lid closed as much as possible and turning as needed, until the vegetables are tender. Remove from the grill. Slip the tomatoes from their skins then chop the tomatoes, aubergines and onion.

3 Bring a large saucepan of salted water to the boil. Add the pasta and cook until al dente, following packet instructions. Drain well.

4 Combine the chopped vegetables with the parsley, garlic and capers in a large bowl. Add the hot pasta and toss to combine. Sprinkle with toasted sesame seeds. Serve immediately.

CHOCOLATE PUDDING WITH GRILLED BANANAS

SERVES: 6
PREP TIME: 20 MINUTES
CHILLING TIME: AT LEAST 8 HOURS
GRILLIING TIME: 2–3 MINUTES
SPECIAL EQUIPMENT: 6 X 175-ML/6-FL OZ RAMEKINS

PUDDING
1 sachet (about 2¼ teaspoons) unflavoured gelatine powder
350 ml/2 fl oz whipping cream
175 ml/6 fl oz full-fat milk
4 tablespoons granulated sugar
175 g/6 oz plain chocolate, finely chopped (or chocolate chips)
½ teaspoon vanilla extract

325 g/11 oz raspberry jam
3 bananas
Vegetable oil

1 Sprinkle gelatine over 4 tablespoons water in a small bowl. Leave to stand for about 5 minutes until the gelatine softens. Bring the cream, milk and sugar to a simmer in a saucepan over a medium-high heat, stirring to dissolve the sugar. Remove the pan from the heat and add the gelatine; stir for 2 full minutes until completely dissolved. Put the chocolate in a bowl (or a 1-litre/1¾-pint heatproof measuring jug) and pour the hot cream mixture over the chocolate. Leave to stand for 3 minutes then whisk until the chocolate is melted. Whisk in the vanilla. Let cool at room temperature.

2 Pour equal amounts of the chocolate mixture into each ramekin. Place the ramekins on a roasting tray and loosely cover with clingfilm. Refrigerate for 8 hours, or up to 1 day, until the puddings are chilled and set. Heat the raspberry jam in a saucepan over a medium heat, and stir until warmed through and melted. Place a small sieve over a bowl and strain the seeds out, extracting by pressing the jam through. Set aside.

3 Prepare the grill for direct cooking over medium heat (180–230°C/350–450°F). Cut each banana in half lengthways, but do not peel. Lightly brush the cut side of the bananas with oil. Brush the cooking grates clean. Grill the bananas, cut side down, over ***direct medium heat*** for 2–3 minutes, with the lid open, until warm and well marked; not too soft. Remove from the grill. Peel the bananas and cut into 1-cm/½-inch slices. Serve the pudding and banana slices with jam on the top.

MIXED BERRY CRISP WITH CRÈME ANGLAISE

SERVES: 6–8
PREP TIME: 30 MINUTES
GRILLING TIME: 35–40 MINUTES
SPECIAL EQUIPMENT: 25-CM/10-INCH CAST-IRON
    FRYING PAN

FILLING
175 g/6 oz granulated sugar
2 tablespoons cornflour
¼ teaspoon ground cinnamon
¼ teaspoon ground cardamom
250 g/8 oz fresh blueberries
125 g/4 oz fresh raspberries
200 g/7 oz fresh strawberries, thinly sliced

TOPPING
40 g/1½ oz plain flour
3 tablespoons soft light brown sugar
½ teaspoon ground cinnamon
25 g/1 oz unsalted butter, cold, cut into pieces

CRÈME ANGLAISE
4 large egg yolks
75 g/3 oz granulated sugar
250 ml/8 fl oz whipping cream
2 teaspoons vanilla extract

1 Prepare the grill for indirect cooking over medium heat (about 200°C/400°F).

2 Combine the sugar, cornflour, cinnamon and cardamom in a saucepan. Slowly stir in 175 ml/6 fl oz water then bring to the boil over a medium-high heat, stirring constantly. Remove from the heat. Place the berries in a 25-cm/10-inch cast-iron frying pan. Pour the liquid over the berries. Brush the cooking grates clean. Bake the berries over *indirect medium heat* for about 10 minutes, with the lid closed.

4 Meanwhile, combine the flour, brown sugar and cinnamon in a bowl. Using a fork, cut the butter into the flour mixture until it has the consistency of fine breadcrumbs. Remove the pan from the grill and sprinkle the topping evenly over the berries. Place the pan over *indirect medium heat*, close the lid, and continue to bake for 25–30 minutes until the berries are bubbling and the topping is just beginning to brown. Keep the grill's temperature as close to 200°C/400°F as possible. Carefully remove the pan from the grill and allow to cool for about 15 minutes.

5 Whisk the egg yolks and sugar in a bowl to a rich yellow colour. Heat the cream in a medium saucepan over a medium heat until scalded but not boiling (bubbles will begin to form around the edge of the pan). Whisking constantly, slowly pour 125 ml/4 fl oz of the hot cream into the egg-sugar mixture. Then, using a wooden spoon, gradually add the egg mixture into the saucepan containing the cream, stirring constantly. Cook for 1–2 minutes until the mixture thickens and coats the back of the spoon. Remove the saucepan from the heat. Stir in the vanilla. Spoon the warm crisp into bowls and top with the crème anglaise.

BALSAMIC TOASTED CARAMELIZED PECANS

SERVES: 6
PREP TIME: 5 MINUTES
GRILLING TIME: 11–15 MINUTES
SPECIAL EQUIPMENT: 30-CM/12-INCH CAST-IRON
    FRYING PAN

175 g/6 oz granulated sugar
4 tablespoons balsamic vinegar

500 g/1 lb pecan halves
½ teaspoon sea salt

1 Prepare the grill for direct cooking over medium heat (180–230°C/350–450°F).

2 Mix the sugar with the vinegar in a cast-iron frying pan until the sugar is evenly moistened. Place the pan on the grill over **direct medium heat**, close the lid, and cook for 5–7 minutes, stirring occasionally, until the sugar has dissolved and the mixture comes to a strong simmer.

3 Add the pecans, stir to coat them evenly, and continue cooking over **direct medium heat** for 6–8 minutes, with the lid closed, until the liquid has reduced to a thick glaze that coats the nuts and almost no liquid remains on the bottom of the pan. Sprinkle the salt over the pecans and stir to coat evenly. Carefully transfer the nuts to a wire rack, spreading them into one thin layer.

4 Leave the nuts to cool for 10 minutes, then break apart the clusters into individual nuts. Let cool completely, then serve.

APRICOT MASCARPONE TARTS WITH CARAMEL SAUCE

SERVES: 6
PREP TIME: 15 MINUTES, PLUS 45 MINUTES FOR PASTRY
GRILLING TIME: 6–8 MINUTES EQUIPMENT: PASTRY
  BRUSH

6 frozen puff pastry cases, about 300 g/10 oz in total
250 g/8 oz granulated sugar
125 ml/4 fl oz whipping cream
125 ml/4 fl oz canned apricot nectar
25 g/1 oz unsalted butter
½ teaspoon vanilla extract
125 g/4 oz mascarpone cheese
1 tablespoon icing sugar
9 firm but ripe apricots, halved lengthways
25 g/1 oz unsalted butter, melted
¼ teaspoon grated nutmeg
3 tablespoons flaked almonds, toasted and chopped

1 Preheat the oven to 200°C/400°F/Gas Mark 6. Prepare the grill for direct cooking over medium heat (180–230°C/350–450°F). Place the pastry cases about 5 cm/2 inches apart on a baking sheet. Bake for 20–25 minutes until puffed and golden brown. Remove from the oven and cool for 5 minutes. Remove the centres of the pastries to make shells and return to the oven for 3–5 minutes to crisp. Cool.

2 Combine the granulated sugar and 3 tablespoons water in a heavy saucepan. Cook over a high heat, stirring constantly. Once the sugar is just dissolved, cook for 3–5 minutes without stirring, occasionally swirling the pan and using a damp pastry brush to remove any sugar crystals from the side, until the caramel is amber with a sharp (but not acrid) aroma. Watch the sauce carefully; once it darkens, it caramelizes quickly. Remove from the heat.

3 Heat the cream and apricot nectar in a pan over a medium-low heat until steaming, then pour into the caramel. It will bubble up and some solid pieces may form. Return to a medium-low heat and stir constantly for about 1 minute until completely melted. Simmer for about 3 minutes, stirring occasionally, until the sauce is slightly reduced. Remove from the heat. Whisk in 25 g/1 oz butter until it is completely incorporated, and stir in the vanilla. Set aside at room temperature to cool and thicken. Combine the mascarpone and icing sugar in a small bowl. Set aside.

4 Toss the apricots, melted butter and nutmeg in a bowl. Brush the cooking grates clean. Grill the apricots, cut side down, over **direct medium heat** for 6–8 minutes, with the lid closed as much as possible and turning once, until hot through. Remove from the grill and cut each apricot piece in half. Place each shell on a plate, spoon in the mascarpone, top with apricot, caramel sauce and almonds.

RECIPES FOR THE ADVENTUROUS BARBECUER

RECIPES FOR THE ADVENTUROUS BARBECUER

I NEVER THOUGHT I COULD COOK THAT ON A BARBECUE

288 OYSTERS WITH SPINACH AND
BACON BREADCRUMBS

291 EGGS PROVENÇALE

SOMETHING TO GET YOUR TEETH INTO

281 ROSEMARY-BRINED ROTISSERIE CHICKEN

284 BRINED TURKEY WITH HERBED PAN GRAVY

ULTIMATE SHOW-OFF RECIPES

272 PORK CHOPS STUFFED WITH APRICOTS
AND SULTANAS

277 MOLE-RUBBED BUTTERFLY CHICKEN WITH
MEXICAN CREMA

293 SOBA NOODLES WITH GRILLED TOFU
AND PEANUTS

298 CHOCOLATE CAKE WITH ORANGE GLAZE

266 WHOLE BEEF FILLET WITH BÉARNAISE
AND ASPARAGUS

270 SLOW SPARERIBS WITH MEDITERRANEAN HERB BASTE

286 LOBSTERS AND SWEETCORN

297 PEACH TART TATIN WITH CARDAMOM

WHOLE BEEF FILLET WITH BÉARNAISE AND ASPARAGUS

SERVES: 4
PREP TIME: 30 MINUTES
GRILLING TIME: 36–43 MINUTES

1 kg/2 lb beef fillet, trimmed of excess fat and skin
Extra-virgin olive oil
Sea salt
Ground black pepper
500 g/1 lb asparagus, woody ends removed

SAUCE
1 shallot, finely chopped
1 tablespoon finely chopped tarragon
4 tablespoons dry white wine *or* dry vermouth
4 tablespoons white wine vinegar
250 g/8 oz unsalted butter
4 large egg yolks

1 Prepare the grill for direct and indirect cooking over medium heat (180–230°C/350–450°F).

2 Lightly brush the beef on all sides with oil and season evenly with salt and pepper. Lightly coat the asparagus with oil. Allow the meat to stand at room temperature for 15–30 minutes before grilling.

3 Remove and discard the tough bottom of each asparagus spear by grasping at each end and bending it gently until it snaps at its natural point of tenderness, usually about two-thirds of the way down the spear. Lightly coat the asparagus with oil.

4 Brush the cooking grates clean. Sear the beef over *direct medium heat* for about 15 minutes, with the lid closed as much as possible and turning a quarter turn every 3–4 minutes, until well marked. Continue grilling over *indirect medium heat*, with the lid closed and turning once, until cooked to your desired doneness, 15–20 minutes for medium rare.

5 Meanwhile, make the sauce. Bring the shallot, tarragon, wine and vinegar to the boil in a small saucepan over a high heat. Cook for 4–6 minutes, until the liquid is reduced to about 2 tablespoons. Strain through a wire sieve into a small bowl and set both the liquid and the strained shallot mixture aside.

6 Melt the butter in another saucepan over a medium heat until it is bubbling hot (so that it will cook the egg yolks). Place the yolks and the wine mixture in a blender. Pulse to combine. With the blender running, in a slow, steady stream, pour one-third of the hot butter into the blender and process until the sauce has emulsified. Then add the remaining butter and blend on high for 5 seconds until it is thick and smooth. Transfer to a heatproof bowl. Stir in the reserved shallot mixture and season with salt and pepper. Place the bowl in a pan of hot (but not simmering) water over a very low heat to keep warm.

7 Remove the meat from the grill and leave to rest for 5–10 minutes. Meanwhile, grill the asparagus over *direct medium heat* for 6–8 minutes, with the lid closed as much as possible and rolling the spears a couple of times, until browned in spots but not charred.

8 Cut the beef fillet crossways into slices. Serve warm with the asparagus and sauce.

MEATBALLS WITH GRILLED ROMAINE AND FETA DRESSING

SERVES: 4
PREP TIME: 30 MINUTES
GRILLING TIME: ABOUT 8 MINUTES

MEATBALLS
500 g/1 lb minced beef (80% lean)
125 g/4 oz mozzarella cheese, grated
65 g/2½ oz dried breadcrumbs
2 large eggs
2 tablespoons tomato ketchup
Sea salt
Ground black pepper

2 romaine lettuce hearts, halved lengthways

DRESSING
125 ml/4 fl oz buttermilk
4 tablespoons mayonnaise
50 g/2 oz feta cheese
Juice of ½ lemon
½ teaspoon ground black pepper

1 tablespoon chopped chives
1 teaspoon chopped thyme

1 Prepare the grill for direct cooking over medium heat (180–230°C/350–450°F).

2 Using your hands, gently mix the meatball ingredients in a bowl, adding ½ teaspoon salt and ½ teaspoon pepper. Do not overwork the mixture or the meatballs will be tough. Shape into 12 balls, and then flatten the meatballs with the palm of your hand.

3 Drizzle oil on the cut sides of the lettuce hearts and season evenly with salt and pepper.

4 Combine the dressing ingredients in a food processor and process until smooth. Add the chives and thyme. Set aside.

5 Brush the cooking grates clean. Grill the meatballs and the lettuce hearts over **direct medium heat**, with the lid closed as much as possible and turning once, until the meatballs are cooked to medium doneness and the lettuce just starts to wilt and has nice grill marks. The meatballs will take about 8 minutes and the lettuce will take about 2 minutes. Remove from the grill as they are done.

6 Spoon about 4 tablespoons of the dressing on each plate and top with a grilled romaine half and three meatballs. Drizzle with a little more dressing and serve immediately.

BUTTERMILK-BRINED PORK CHOPS WITH WHISKY-BRAISED CABBAGE AND APPLES

SERVES: 4
PREP TIME: 30 MINUTES
BRINING TIME: 1–1½ HOURS
GRILLING TIME: 8–10 MINUTES

BRINE
475 ml/16 fl oz cold buttermilk
250 ml/8 fl oz water
8 tablespoons sea salt
1 tablespoon wholegrain mustard
1 tablespoon finely chopped tarragon

4 boneless pork loin chops, each about 250 g/8 oz and
    2.5 cm/1 inch thick, trimmed of excess fat
Extra-virgin olive oil

25 g/1 oz unsalted butter
500 g/1 lb red cabbage, shredded
1 kg/2 lb tart green apples, such as Granny Smith, coarsely grated
75 ml/3 fl oz whisky
2 tablespoons balsamic vinegar
¼ teaspoon celery seeds
¾ teaspoon sea salt
¼ teaspoon ground black pepper

1 Whisk the brine ingredients together in a bowl until the salt dissolves.

2 Put the chops in a large, resealable plastic bag and pour in the brine. Press the air out of the bag and seal tightly. Place the bag in a bowl or a rimmed dish and refrigerate for 1–1½ hours, turning the bag every 30 minutes.

3 Remove the chops from the bag and discard the brine. Rinse the chops under cold water and pat dry with kitchen paper. Lightly brush or spray the chops on both sides with oil and allow to stand at room temperature for 15–30 minutes before grilling.

4 Prepare the grill for direct cooking over medium heat (180–230°C/350–450°F).

5 Melt the butter in a large lidded frying pan over a medium-high heat. Add the cabbage and apples and sauté for 2–3 minutes until the cabbage just starts to wilt. Stir in the whisky, vinegar and celery seeds. Cover and cook for 10–12 minutes, stirring occasionally, until the cabbage is tender. Remove from the heat, season with the salt and pepper and cover to keep warm.

6 Brush the cooking grates clean. Grill the chops over **direct medium heat** for 8–10 minutes, with the lid closed as much as possible and turning once or twice, until they are still slightly pink in the centre. Remove the chops from the grill and let rest for 3–5 minutes. Serve warm on a bed of the braised cabbage and apples.

SLOW SPARERIBS WITH MEDITERRANEAN HERB BASTE

SERVES: 6
PREP TIME: 30 MINUTES
GRILLING TIME: 3–4 HOURS

RUB
2 tablespoons sea salt
2 tablespoons chilli powder
2 tablespoons soft light brown sugar
1 tablespoon dried thyme
2 teaspoons ground black pepper

3 racks trimmed pork spareribs, each 1.5–1.75 kg/3–3½ lb

BASTE
125 g/4 oz parsley, leaves and tender stalks
25 g/1 oz oregano
75 g/3 oz sun-dried tomatoes packed in oil
3 garlic cloves
1 teaspoon sea salt
½ teaspoon crushed red chilli flakes
350 ml/12 fl oz dry white wine
4 tablespoons extra-virgin olive oil
2 tablespoons white wine vinegar

3 fist-sized chunks hickory or apple wood (dry)

1 Prepare the smoker, following the manufacturer's instructions, for cooking over low heat.

2 Mix the rub ingredients in a bowl.

3 Using a round-bladed knife, slide the tip under the membrane covering the back of each rack of ribs. Lift and loosen the membrane until it breaks, then grab a corner of it with kitchen paper and pull it off. Season the ribs all over with the rub, putting more on the meaty sides than the bone sides.

4 Process the parsley, oregano, sun-dried tomatoes, garlic, salt and chilli flakes in a food processor or blender until the herbs are finely chopped. Add the wine, oil and vinegar. Process briefly to mix.

5 Place the spareribs on the cooking grates and add two wood chunks to the coals. Close the lid and smoke the spareribs for 3–4 hours, keeping the temperature inside the smoker at 130–150°C/250–300°F, until the meat has shrunk back from the bones at least 1 cm/½ inch in several places and tears easily when you lift each rack (not all racks will cook in the same amount of time). Maintain the temperature of the grill by opening and closing the vents. After the first hour, add the last wood chunk and then begin basting the ribs on both sides with the baste once every hour.

6 Remove the racks from the smoker and let rest at room temperature for about 10 minutes. If you cover them with foil, they will stay warm for about 30 minutes. If you wrap them tightly in foil, they will stay warm for at least 1 hour. When ready to serve, cut the racks between the bones into individual ribs. Serve warm.

PORK CHOPS STUFFED WITH APRICOTS AND SULTANAS

SERVES: 6
PREP TIME: 30 MINUTES
GRILLING TIME: 12–16 MINUTES

RUB

1 tablespoon mild curry powder
2 teaspoons soft brown sugar
¾ teaspoon sea salt
½ teaspoon ground ginger
½ teaspoon ground black pepper

6 boneless pork loin chops, each about 250 g/8 oz and
    3 cm/1¼ inches thick, trimmed of excess fat
Extra-virgin olive oil

STUFFING

75 g/3 oz dried apricots, finely chopped
40 g/1½ oz sultanas
½ onion, finely chopped
2 teaspoons finely chopped garlic
½ teaspoon curry powder
¼ teaspoon ground coriander
¼ teaspoon sea salt
⅓ teaspoon gro8und black pepper
4 tablespoons dry white wine
4 tablespoons panko breadcrumbs
25 g/1 oz flaked almonds, toasted

1 Mix the rub ingredients in a small bowl. Using a small, sharp knife, cut each pork chop almost all the way through, so that it opens like a book, with the fatty part as its spine. Lay them open on a work surface with the cut sides down. Lightly brush the outsides with oil and season evenly with the rub. Leave to stand at room temperature for 15–30 minutes before grilling.

2 Prepare the grill for direct and indirect cooking over medium heat (180–230°C/350–450°F). Meanwhile, combine the apricots and sultanas in a small bowl. Add enough boiling water to cover the fruit; set aside to soften for 5 minutes, then drain. Heat a large frying pan over a medium heat. When the pan is hot, add 1 tablespoon oil and the onion. Cook for about 5 minutes, stirring occasionally, until the onion begins to soften. Add the garlic, curry powder, coriander, salt, pepper and the drained fruit and cook for 2 minutes, stirring to combine. Add the wine, bring to a simmer and cook for 2–3 minutes, until the wine has evaporated. Remove from the heat and mix in the breadcrumbs and almonds.

3 Turn the chops over so the insides face up. Spoon some of the stuffing on to each chop. Gently press the chop together to close. Brush the cooking grates clean. Grill the chops over *direct medium heat* for 8–10 minutes, with the lid closed as much as possible and turning once or twice, until nicely seared on both sides. Move the chops over *indirect medium heat* and continue to grill for 4–6 minutes until they are still slightly pink in the centre. Remove from the grill and let rest for 3–5 minutes. Serve warm.

ROAST CHICKEN WITH CURRIED GREEN BEANS AND TOMATOES

SERVES: 4
PREP TIME: 30 MINUTES
GRILLING TIME: 35-47 MINUTES
SPECIAL EQUIPMENT: PERFORATED GRILL PAN

PASTE

2 tablespoons rapeseed oil
4 teaspoons curry powder
2 teaspoons finely chopped garlic
1 teaspoon mustard powder
1 teaspoon runny honey
1 teaspoon sea salt

4 chicken breast halves (with bone and skin), each
    300–375 g/10–12 oz

DRESSING

3 tablespoons rapeseed oil
1 tablespoon red wine vinegar
2 teaspoons finely chopped serrano chilli (with seeds)
½ teaspoon curry powder
¼ teaspoon sea salt
⅛ teaspoon ground black pepper

250 g/8 oz fine green beans, trimmed
500 g/1 lb cherry tomatoes

1 Mix the paste ingredients in a small bowl. Using your fingertips, carefully lift the skin from the chicken, leaving the skin closest to the breastbone attached. Rub 1 teaspoon of the paste under the skin all over the exposed meat of each breast. Lay the skin back in place and rub the remaining paste all over the chicken breasts.

2 Prepare the grill for direct and indirect cooking over medium heat (180–230°C/350–450°F) and preheat the grill pan. Whisk all the dressing ingredients in a small bowl. Combine the green beans and tomatoes in a large bowl, and use about half the dressing to coat them lightly. Spread in a single layer on the grill pan. Grill over ***direct medium heat***, with the lid closed as much as possible and turning occasionally, until the green beans are crisp-tender and the tomatoes are beginning to collapse. The beans will take 5–7 minutes and the tomatoes will take 2–3 minutes. Transfer the vegetables back into the large bowl to cool as they are done. Remove the grill pan from the grill.

3 Brush the cooking grates clean. Grill the chicken breasts, skin side up, over ***indirect medium heat*** for 30–40 minutes, with the lid closed as much as possible, until the meat is opaque all the way to the bone. If liked, to crisp the skin, grill the chicken over ***direct medium heat*** during the last 5–10 minutes of grilling time, turning once. Transfer to a dish and let rest for 3–5 minutes. Serve immediately with the grilled vegetables and the remaining dressing.

MEDITERRANEAN STUFFED CHICKEN BREASTS

SERVES: 4
PREP TIME: 20 MINUTES
GRILLING TIME: 10–14 MINUTES

STUFFING
40 g/1½ oz pitted kalamata olives, rinsed
4 tablespoons sun-dried tomatoes packed in oil, drained
2 tablespoons small capers, rinsed
Grated zest of 1 lemon
75 g/3 oz feta cheese, crumbled

4 thick boneless, skinless chicken breast halves, each about
   250 g/8 oz
Extra-virgin olive oil
¾ teaspoon sea salt
½ teaspoon ground black pepper

1 Pulse the olives, sun-dried tomatoes, capers and lemon zest in a food processor until finely chopped, but not puréed. Transfer the mixture to a bowl, stir in the cheese, and set aside.

2 Prepare the grill for direct cooking over medium heat (180–230°C/350–450°F).

3 Place the chicken breasts on a chopping board, smooth (skin) side down. Cut them in half horizontally, keeping the longer side intact, so that they open like books (see page 18). Rub the outside of each breast with oil and season evenly with the salt and pepper. Open up each breast and spread 2–3 tablespoons of the filling (depending upon the size of the chicken breast) on one side of each breast, leaving a small border. Do not overstuff the chicken. Fold the other side of the breast over, gently pressing round the edges to seal in the filling.

4 Brush the cooking grates clean. Grill the chicken, smooth (skin) side down first, over **direct medium heat** for 10–14 minutes, with the lid closed as much as possible and turning once (it's easiest to turn the chicken over on the uncut edge of the breast so the filling doesn't fall out), until the meat is firm to the touch and opaque but still moist. Remove from the grill and let rest for 3–5 minutes. Serve warm.

CHICKEN THIGHS AND OLIVE-FENNEL SALAD WITH GRILLED LEMON SLICES

SERVES: 4
PREP TIME: 20 MINUTES
MARINATING TIME: 1 HOUR OR MORE
GRILLING TIME: 8–10 MINUTES

1 lemon, cut crossways into 5-mm/¼-inch slices
1 teaspoon granulated sugar
Sea salt

SALAD
1 small fennel bulb
175-g/6-oz can pitted green olives, rinsed and drained if very
　　salty, each halved
Zest of 1 lemon, in long thin shreds
1 tablespoon fresh lemon juice
1 teaspoon finely chopped oregano
1 teaspoon finely chopped garlic
½ teaspoon finely chopped rosemary
Extra-virgin olive oil
Ground black pepper

6 boneless, skinless chicken thighs, each about 125 g/4 oz

1 Combine the lemon slices with the sugar and 1 tablespoon salt in a bowl. Mix well and let the slices marinate at room temperature for 1 hour or cover and refrigerate overnight.

2 Prepare the grill for direct cooking over medium heat (180–230°C/350–450°F).

3 Cut off the thick stalks and the root end from the fennel bulb and discard them. Cut the bulb lengthways into quarters and then cut away and remove the thick triangular-shaped core. Cut the fennel vertically into 2.5-mm/⅛-inch slices. Place in a bowl and add the remaining salad ingredients, including 1 tablespoon oil and ¼ teaspoon pepper. Set aside.

4 Drain (don't rinse) the lemon slices and brush them on both sides with oil. Then lightly brush the chicken on both sides with oil and season evenly with salt and pepper.

5 Brush the cooking grates clean. Grill the chicken thighs, smooth (skin) side down first, and the lemon slices over **direct medium heat** for 8–10 minutes, with the lid closed as much as possible and turning once or twice, until the meat is firm and the juices run clear and the lemon slices are nicely browned. Remove from the grill and let the chicken thighs rest for 3–5 minutes. Serve the chicken warm with the salad.

MOLE-RUBBED BUTTERFLIED CHICKEN WITH MEXICAN CREMA

SERVES: 4
PREP TIME: 20 MINUTES
MARINATING TIME: 24 HOURS
GRILLING TIME: ABOUT 40 MINUTES
SPECIAL EQUIPMENT: POULTRY SHEARS, INSTANT-READ MEAT THERMOMETER

MARINADE
Grated zest of 1 orange
125 ml/4 fl oz fresh orange juice
4 tablespoons extra-virgin olive oil
3 tablespoons finely chopped fresh coriander, leaves and tender stalks
1 tablespoon sea salt
1 teaspoon ground black pepper

1 chicken, about 2 kg/4 lb, giblets and any excess fat removed

RUB
2 tablespoons sea salt
2 tablespoons chilli powder
1 tablespoon cocoa powder
1 tablespoon ground black pepper
1 tablespoon granulated sugar
1 teaspoon paprika

125 ml/4 fl oz soured cream (thinned with milk, for drizzling)

1 Whisk the marinade ingredients in a 33 × 23 cm/13 × 9 inch glass baking dish.

2 Place the chicken, breast side down, on a chopping board. Using poultry shears, cut from the neck to the tail end, along either side of the backbone. Remove the backbone. Make a small slit in the cartilage at the bottom end of the breastbone. Then, placing both hands on the rib cage, crack the chicken open like a book. Run your fingers along either side of the cartilage in between the breast to loosen it from the flesh. Pull up on the bone to remove it along with the attached cartilage. The chicken should now lie flat (see page 18).

3 Place the chicken in the dish and turn to coat evenly with the marinade. Cover with clingfilm and refrigerate for 24 hours. Mix the rub ingredients in a small bowl. Prepare the grill for indirect cooking over medium heat (about 180°C/350°F).

4 Remove the chicken from the bowl and discard the marinade. Coat the chicken all over with the rub. The rub will get wet and become a paste.

5 Brush the cooking grates clean. Grill the chicken, bone side down, over ***indirect medium heat*** for about 40 minutes, with the lid closed, until the juices run clear and an instant-read meat thermometer inserted into the thickest part of the thigh (not touching the bone) registers 70–74°C/160–165°F. If liked, to crisp the skin, grill the chicken over ***direct medium heat*** during the last 5–10 minutes of grilling time, turning once. Remove from the grill and let rest for 5–10 minutes (the internal temperature will rise 5–10 degrees during this time). Cut the chicken into serving pieces. Serve warm with the thinned soured cream (crema).

LAMB KOFTA

SERVES: 4
PREP TIME: 15 MINUTES
GRILLING TIME: ABOUT 6 MINUTES
SPECIAL EQUIPMENT: 8 METAL OR BAMBOO SKEWERS (IF USING BAMBOO, SOAK IN WATER FOR AT LEAST 30 MINUTES)

YOGURT
175 ml/6 fl oz Greek yogurt
1 tablespoon finely chopped mint
1 tablespoon fresh lemon juice

KOFTA
625 g/1¼ lb minced lamb
1 onion, coarsely grated
2½ teaspoons ground cumin
1¼ teaspoons sea salt
3 large garlic cloves, finely chopped
¾ teaspoon ground black pepper

Vegetable oil
8 romaine lettuce leaves

1 Mix the yogurt, mint and lemon juice in a bowl.

2 Prepare the grill for direct cooking over medium-high heat ((200–260°C/400–500°F).

3 Using your hands, gently mix the the kofta ingredients in a large bowl. Shape into 24 meatballs (kofta), each about 2.5 cm/1 inch in diameter. Thread three kofta on to each skewer. Lightly brush with oil.

4 Brush the cooking grates clean. Grill the kofta over **direct medium-high heat** for about 6 minutes, with the lid closed as much as possible and turning once or twice, until they are nicely charred on the outside and the centres are still slightly pink. Remove from the grill.

5 Place two lettuce leaves on each of four plates. Slide three kofta on to each lettuce leaf. Serve warm with the mint yogurt.

SIRLOIN STEAKS WITH PROVENÇAL VEGETABLES

SERVES: 4
PREP TIME: 30 MINUTES
GRILLING TIME: 18–23 MINUTES
SPECIAL EQUIPMENT: LARGE DISPOSABLE ALUMINIUM
FOIL ROASTING TRAY

4 sirloin steaks, each 300–375 g/10–12 oz and about 2.5 cm/
1 inch thick, trimmed of excess fat
Extra-virgin olive oil
Sea salt
Ground black pepper

VEGETABLES
1 large courgette, cut into 1-cm/½-inch pieces
1 aubergine, cut into 1-cm/½-inch pieces
1 red pepper, cut into 1-cm/½-inch pieces
125 g/4 oz shallots, peeled and cut into 5-mm/¼-inch rings
4 tablespoons finely chopped oil-packed sun-dried tomatoes
2 tablespoons oil from the jar of sun-dried tomatoes
1 tablespoon finely chopped garlic
1 tablespoon extra-virgin olive oil
2 teaspoons finely chopped rosemary
1 teaspoon herbes de Provence

1 Prepare the grill for direct cooking over medium heat
(180–230°C/350–450°F).

2 Lightly brush the steaks on both sides with oil and season
evenly with salt and pepper. Allow the steaks to stand at room
temperature for 15–30 minutes before grilling.

3 Combine the vegetable ingredients in a large disposable foil
tray and mix thoroughly.

4 Brush the cooking grates clean. Grill the vegetables in the foil
tray over **direct medium heat** for 12–15 minutes, with the lid
closed as much as possible and stirring occasionally, until the
vegetables are tender. Wearing insulated barbecue mitts or oven
gloves, remove the tray from the grill. Increase the temperature
of the grill to high heat (230–290°C/450–550°F).

5 Grill the steaks over **direct high heat**, with the lid closed as
much as possible and turning once or twice (if flare-ups occur,
move the steaks temporarily over indirect heat), until cooked to
your desired doneness, 6–8 minutes for medium rare. Remove
from the grill and leave to rest for 3–5 minutes. Season the
vegetables with salt and pepper. Serve the steaks warm with
the vegetables.

POLLO AL MATTONE

SERVES: 4
PREP TIME: 30 MINUTES
MARINATING TIME: 30 MINUTES
GRILLING TIME: ABOUT 35 MINUTES
SPECIAL EQUIPMENT: POULTRY SHEARS, CAST-IRON
    FRYING PAN OR 2 FOIL-WRAPPED BRICKS, INSTANT-
    READ MEAT THERMOMETER

MARINADE
1 teaspoon grated lemon zest
1 tablespoon fresh lemon juice
1 tablespoon finely chopped garlic
1 tablespoon finely chopped oregano *or* basil
1 teaspoon crushed red chilli flakes
Extra-virgin olive oil
Sea salt
Ground black pepper

1 chicken, about 2 kg/4 lb, giblets and any excess fat removed

2 tablespoons red wine vinegar
1 tablespoon finely chopped shallot
2 oranges
125 g/4 oz red oak leaf lettuce, torn into bite-sized pieces
    (from ½ head)

1 Whisk the marinade ingredients in a bowl, including 4 tablespoons oil, 2 teaspoons salt and ½ teaspoon pepper.

2 Place the chicken, breast side down, on a chopping board. Using poultry shears, cut from the neck to the tail end, along either side of the backbone. Remove the backbone. Make a small slit in the cartilage at the bottom end of the breastbone. Then, placing both hands on the rib cage, crack the chicken

open like a book. Run your fingers along either side of the cartilage in between the breast to loosen it from the flesh. Pull up on the bone to remove it along with the attached cartilage. The chicken should now lie flat (see page 18).

3 Starting at the neck end of the chicken, carefully run your fingers over the breast meat and under the skin to loosen it. Rub a quarter of the marinade directly on the breast meat and the remaining marinade all over the outside of the chicken. Let the chicken marinate at room temperature for 30 minutes.

4 Prepare the grill for direct cooking over medium-low heat (about 180°C/350°F). Whisk the vinegar, shallot, 3 tablespoons oil, ¼ teaspoon salt and ⅛ teaspoon pepper in a bowl to make a dressing. Cut off all the peel and white pith from the oranges. Working over the bowl with the dressing, cut between the membranes to release the orange segments and let them fall into the bowl. Put the lettuce in a large salad bowl.

5 Brush the cooking grates clean. Place the chicken, breast side up, over **direct medium-low heat** and put a heavy cast-iron frying pan or two foil-wrapped bricks directly on top. Close the lid and cook for 15 minutes. Remove the bricks and carefully turn the chicken over. Replace the bricks, close the lid, and cook for about 20 minutes, adjusting the heat if needed to prevent burning, until the juices run clear and an instant-read meat thermometer inserted into the thickest part of the thigh (not touching the bone) registers 70–74°C/160–165°F. Remove from the grill and let rest for 5–10 minutes (the internal temperature will rise 5–10 degrees during this time). Cut into serving pieces.

6 Remove the orange segments from the dressing and whisk again. Lightly dress the lettuce and top with the orange segments. Serve the chicken warm with the salad.

ROSEMARY-BRINED ROTISSERIE CHICKEN

SERVES: 4
PREP TIME: 20 MINUTES
BRINING TIME: 6–12 HOURS
GRILLING TIME: 1¼–1½ HOURS
SPECIAL EQUIPMENT: KITCHEN STRING, ROTISSERIE, LARGE DISPOSABLE ALUMINIUM FOIL ROASTING TRAY, INSTANT-READ MEAT THERMOMETER

BRINE

4 litres/7 pints water
200 g/7 oz sea salt
125 g/4 oz granulated sugar
2 tablespoons dried rosemary
1 tablespoon caraway seeds
1 tablespoon garlic granules
2 teaspoons ground black pepper

1 chicken, about 2 kg/4 lb, giblets, wing tips and any excess fat removed

1 Combine the brine ingredients in a large saucepan or casserole. Stir well to dissolve the sugar and salt.

2 Submerge the chicken in the brine, breast side down, and refrigerate for 6–12 hours.

3 Prepare the grill for indirect cooking over medium heat (180–230°C/350–450°F).

4 Remove the chicken from the pot and discard the brine. Pat the chicken dry with kitchen paper. Truss the chicken with kitchen string (see page 19).

5 Following the grill's instructions, secure the chicken in the middle of a rotisserie spit, put the spit in place and turn on the motor. Place a large disposable foil tray underneath the chicken to catch the drippings. Cook the chicken over **indirect medium heat**, with the lid closed, for 1 hour.

6 If your grill has an infrared burner at the back of the grill, after 1 hour of cooking light the burner and set it to medium heat (leaving the regular outside burners on medium and the middle burners turned off). If your grill does not have an infrared burner, continue to cook the chicken as before. Either way, cook the chicken until the surface is deep golden brown and an instant-read meat thermometer inserted into the thickest part of the thigh (not touching the bone) registers 70–74°C/160–165°F. This should take 10–20 minutes with the infrared burner and 20–30 minutes without it. Watch carefully to ensure that the chicken skin does not burn.

7 When the chicken is fully cooked, turn off the rotisserie motor and remove the spit from the grill. Tilt the chicken upright over the foil tray so that the liquid that has accumulated in the chicken's cavity pours into the tray. Let rest for 10–15 minutes (the internal temperature will rise 5–10 degrees during this time). Transfer the chicken from the spit to a carving board. Cut into serving pieces. Serve warm.

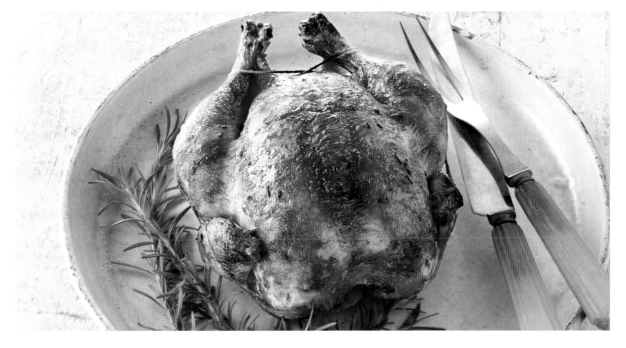

BRINED TURKEY BREAST WITH SWEETCORN AND PEPPER SALAD

SERVES: 4
PREP TIME: 30 MINUTES
BRINING TIME: 2 HOURS
GRILLING TIME: 10–12 MINUTES
SPECIAL EQUIPMENT: INSTANT-READ MEAT
    THERMOMETER

BRINE
125 ml/4 fl oz bourbon
4 tablespoons soft brown sugar
2 tablespoons sea salt
½ teaspoon crushed red chilli flakes
250 ml/8 fl oz ice cubes

2 turkey breast fillets, about 625 g/1¼ lb in total
Extra-virgin olive oil

SALAD
4 bacon rashers, finely chopped
2 red peppers, finely chopped
1 red onion, finely chopped
4 tablespoons sherry
1 kg/2 lb frozen sweetcorn kernels *or* fresh sweetcorn
    (from 4–5 cobs)
250 ml/8 fl oz whipping cream
½ teaspoon sea salt
¼ teaspoon ground cayenne pepper
4 tablespoons chopped flat-leaf parsley

1 Combine the bourbon, 125 ml/4 fl oz water, sugar, salt and chilli flakes in a saucepan over a medium heat. Stir until the sugar and salt dissolve. Remove from the heat and stir in the ice cubes to quickly cool the brine.

2 Place the turkey fillets in a large, resealable plastic bag and pour in the brine. Press the air out of the bag and seal tightly. Place the bag in a bowl or a rimmed dish and refrigerate for 2 hours, turning the bag every 30 minutes.

3 Remove the turkey fillets from the bag and discard the brine. Rinse the fillets under cold water and pat dry with kitchen paper. Lightly brush the turkey on both sides with oil.

4 Prepare the grill for direct cooking over medium heat (180–230°C/350–450°F).

5 Fry the bacon in a large frying pan over a medium-high heat for about 6 minutes, stirring occasionally, until crisp but not burnt. Place the bacon on some kitchen paper and pour off all but 1 tablespoon of the fat in the pan. Add the peppers and onion to the pan and sauté for 4–5 minutes until the onion is tender. Stir in the sherry, scraping any browned bits from the bottom of the pan, and cook for 2–3 minutes until the sherry evaporates. Add the sweetcorn and cream and simmer for about 5 minutes, stirring frequently, until the cream reduces and the mixture has the consistency of creamed sweetcorn. Season with the salt and cayenne, remove from the heat and cover to keep warm. Just before serving, add the bacon and parsley and stir to combine.

6 Brush the cooking grates clean. Grill the turkey fillets over **direct medium heat** for 10–12 minutes, with the lid closed as much as possible and turning once, until the meat is no longer pink in the centre and the internal temperature registers 70–74°C/160–165°F on an instant-read meat thermometer. Remove from the grill and let rest for 5–10 minutes (the internal temperature will rise 5–10 degrees during this time). Cut the breast fillets crossways into slices and serve on top of the salad.

BRINED TURKEY WITH HERBED PAN GRAVY

SERVES: 8–12

PREP TIME: 15 MINUTES, PLUS 2 HOURS FOR THE BRINE,
1 HOUR 10 MINUTES FOR THE STOCK, 30 MINUTES
FOR THE GRAVY AND TO CARVE

BRINING TIME: 12–14 HOURS

GRILLING TIME: ABOUT 2¾ HOURS

SPECIAL EQUIPMENT: LARGE STOCKPOT (CLEAN
BUCKET), STURDY PLASTIC BAG, LARGE COOL BOX,
KITCHEN STRING, 2 LARGE DISPOSABLE ALUMINIUM
FOIL ROASTING TRAYS, ROASTING RACK, INSTANT-
READ MEAT THERMOMETER, GRAVY SEPARATOR

BRINE

325 g/11 oz salt
250 g/8 oz soft light brown sugar
1 tablespoon whole black peppercorns
6 litres/10 pints iced water

1 turkey, 6–7 kg/12–14 lb, thawed if necessary
2 × 2.5-kg (5-lb) bags ice cubes (and/or thermal ice packs)

2 small onions, chopped
1 tablespoon vegetable oil
2 litres/3½ pints chicken stock
40 g/1½ oz unsalted butter, melted, if needed
50 g/2 oz plain flour
2 teaspoons chopped herbs, such as rosemary, thyme or sage,
or a combination
Sea salt
Ground black pepper

1 The night before grilling, brine the turkey. Combine the salt, brown sugar, peppercorns and 3 litres/5 pints water in a large non-reactive stockpot. Bring to the boil over a high heat, stirring to dissolve the salt. Remove the brine from the heat and cool it until tepid. Add the iced water. (If your stockpot is not large enough, pour the brine and the iced water into a clean bucket.) The brine should be very cold.

2 Remove the giblets, neck and lumps of fat from the tail area of the turkey. Place the giblets and neck in a bowl, cover with clingfilm and refrigerate. Discard the fat. Place the turkey inside a sturdy plastic bag. Arrange a thin layer of ice on the bottom of the cool box and set the turkey on top of it. Pour enough of the cold brine into the bag to cover the turkey as much as possible when the bag is closed and tightly tied. Discard any extra brine. Add ice and/or thermal ice packs to cover and surround the turkey, keeping it cold. Close the cool box and brine the turkey for 12–14 hours, no longer.

3 Remove the turkey from the bag and discard the brine. Pat the turkey dry inside and outside with kitchen paper. Tuck the wing tips behind the turkey's back. Add half the chopped onion to the body cavity. Tie the drumsticks together with kitchen string. Place one large disposable foil tray inside the other. Place the turkey on a roasting rack set inside the trays and allow to stand at room temperature for 1 hour before grilling.

4 Prepare the grill for indirect cooking over medium-low heat (about 180°C/350°F). Place the reserved lumps of fat in the roasting tray. Grill the turkey over *indirect medium-low heat* for about 2¾ hours, with the lid closed and keeping the grill's temperature as close to 180°C/350°F as possible, until an instant-read meat thermometer inserted in the thickest part of the thigh (not touching the bone) registers 70–74°C/160–165°F. Occasionally during grilling, tilt the bird so the juices run out of the cavity into the roasting tray. The juices will reduce and turn dark brown, adding colour and rich flavour for the gravy.

5 Meanwhile, heat the oil in a large saucepan on the hob, over a medium-high heat. Using a heavy knife or cleaver, chop the reserved neck into 5-cm/2-inch chunks. Add the neck and giblets to the saucepan and cook for 5–6 minutes, turning occasionally, until well browned. Add the remaining chopped onion and cook for about 3 minutes until softened. Add the stock and bring the mixture to a low boil. Reduce the heat to low and simmer gently for about 1 hour until reduced by half. Drain, discard the solids and set the stock aside.

6 When the turkey is done, transfer it to a platter and let it rest for 20–30 minutes (the internal temperature will rise 5–10 degrees during this time). While it is resting, strain the pan juices into a gravy separator. Let stand for 3 minutes so the fat rises to the top of the separator. Pour the pan juices into a 1-litre/1¾-pint measuring jug, reserving the fat. Add more of the giblet stock as needed to make 1 litre/1¾ pints.

7 Add the fat to a measuring jug. You should have 125 ml/ 4 fl oz. Add melted butter if needed to make up the quantity. Heat the fat (and butter) in a saucepan over a medium heat. Whisk in the flour and let bubble for 1 minute, stirring constantly. Whisk in the pan juice/stock mixture and bring the gravy to the boil. Reduce the heat to medium-low, simmer for 5 minutes and then pour the gravy into the roasting tray. Scrape up any browned bits with a rubber spatula, taking care not to pierce the foil. Return the gravy to the saucepan and add the fresh herbs. Simmer for 5 minutes to blend the flavours, whisking often. Taste and season carefully with salt and pepper (the brine may have seasoned the gravy enough).

8 Carve the turkey and serve with the gravy.

LOBSTERS AND SWEETCORN

SERVES: 4
PREP TIME: 15 MINUTES
GRILLING TIME: 10–15 MINUTES OR 20–30 MINUTES

250 g/8 oz unsalted butter
2 garlic cloves, finely chopped
Sea salt
Ground black pepper
4 live lobsters, each 750 g–1 kg/1½ –2 lb
4 fresh corn cobs, outer leaves and silk removed
2 tablespoons finely chopped flat-leaf parsley

1 Heat the butter with the garlic, ½ teaspoon salt and
¼ teaspoon pepper in a small saucepan over a low heat until
the butter is melted. Set aside.

2 Prepare the grill for direct and indirect cooking over medium
heat (180–230°C/350–450°F).

3 Place a lobster on a chopping board, shell side down. Insert
the tip of a large, sharp knife into the lobster's body just below
the head (no need to be shy about this process – it takes some
strength) and cut the lobster open down the centre, cutting
through the body but not through the back shell. (The shell will
hold the juices as it cooks.) Remove and discard the head sac
and intestines. Rinse the lobster under cold running water. To
help the lobster stay flat on the grill, insert a bamboo skewer
through the tail meat. Remove the rubber bands on the claws.
Brush the inside of the lobster with some of the garlic butter.
Repeat with the remaining lobsters.

4 Brush the cooking grates clean. Grill the lobsters, shell side
down, over **direct medium heat** for 10–15 minutes, with the
lid closed as much as possible and brushing occasionally with
more of the garlic butter, until the tail meat is firm and white.
(Soft-shell lobsters will cook more quickly than hard-shell
lobsters.) At the same time, if your grill is big enough, grill the
corn; otherwise, grill the corn after the lobsters. Brush the corn
with some of the garlic butter and grill over **direct medium heat**
for 10–15 minutes, with the lid closed as much as possible and
turning occasionally, until browned in spots and tender. Season
the corn with salt and pepper.

5 Transfer the lobsters and corn cobs to a large serving dish.
Heat the butter mixture over a medium heat until it comes to a
simmer. Add the parsley. Serve the lobsters with the corn and
the remaining butter mixture.

SEA BASS EN PAPILLOTE WITH PESTO AND VEGETABLES

SERVES: 4
PREP TIME: 35 MINUTES
GRILLING TIME: 20–25 MINUTES

PESTO
1 tablespoon plus 125 ml/4 fl oz extra-virgin olive oil
1 garlic clove
4 tablespoons pine nuts
75 g/3 oz basil leaves
50 g/2 oz Parmesan cheese, freshly grated
¼ teaspoon crushed red chilli flakes
Sea salt

4 waxy potatoes, cut into 2.5-mm/⅛-inch slices
4 skinless sea bass fillets, each about 175 g/6 oz and 1 cm/
    ½ inch thick
1 carrot, cut into very thin julienne strips
40 g/1½ oz sugar snap peas, cut into short thin strips
1 courgette, cut into very thin julienne strips
500 g/1 lb cherry tomatoes
Ground black pepper

1 Warm 1 tablespoon of the oil in a small frying pan over a medium heat. Add the garlic and sauté for about 2 minutes. Add the pine nuts and cook for 2–3 minutes until golden. Remove from the heat and let cool.

2 Combine the cooled garlic and pine nuts, the basil, cheese, chilli flakes and ½ teaspoon salt in a food processor. Pulse for about 30 seconds. With the motor running, slowly add the remaining oil and process until you have a pesto consistency.

3 Prepare the grill for indirect cooking over medium heat (180–230°C/350–450°F).

4 Cut four pieces of nonstick baking paper, each about 35 cm/ 15 inches square. On the lower half of each piece of paper, layer sliced potatoes from one whole potato, then top with one fish fillet and a quarter of the pesto, thinly cut vegetables and tomatoes. Season with salt and pepper. Fold the paper over and crimp the three open sides tightly.

5 Brush the cooking grates clean. Grill the packages over **indirect medium heat** for 20–25 minutes, with the lid closed, until the potatoes are cooked. To check for doneness, using tongs, carefully unfold one of the packages and remove a potato slice, taking care not to puncture the bottom of the paper. Gently pierce the potato with a knife to ensure doneness. When everything is cooked, remove the packages from the grill. Carefully open each package to let the steam escape and then arrange on serving plates. Serve immediately.

OYSTERS WITH SPINACH AND BACON BREADCRUMBS

SERVES: 4–6

PREP TIME: 30 MINUTES, PLUS ABOUT 15 MINUTES TO SHUCK THE OYSTERS

GRILLING TIME: 2–4 MINUTES

SPECIAL EQUIPMENT: OYSTER KNIFE

50 g/2 oz bacon, finely chopped
50 g/2 oz panko breadcrumbs
25 g/1 oz unsalted butter
1 shallot, finely chopped
2 teaspoons finely chopped garlic
¼ teaspoon sea salt
⅛ teaspoon ground black pepper
150 g/5 oz baby spinach, roughly chopped
1 teaspoon hot pepper sauce

12 large fresh oysters, each about 7 cm/3 inches long

25 g/1 oz Parmesan cheese, finely grated
2 tablespoons finely chopped fresh tarragon
Finely grated zest and juice of ½ lemon

1 Fry the bacon in a large frying pan over a medium heat for about 8 minutes until crisp, stirring occasionally. Stir the breadcrumbs into the pan, letting them soak up the bacon fat. Cook for about 2 minutes until they are golden and crispy. Set aside.

2 Melt the butter in a large frying pan over a medium heat. Add the shallot and cook for about 5 minutes until soft, stirring occasionally. Add the garlic, salt and pepper, and cook for 1 minute, stirring occasionally. Add the spinach and cook until completely wilted, folding the leaves over with tongs as you go, and then cook until all the liquid has evaporated, about 5 minutes. Add the hot pepper sauce, mix, and set aside.

3 Shuck the oysters: grip each oyster, flat side up, in a folded tea towel. Find the small opening between the shells near the hinge and prise it open with an oyster knife. Try not to spill the delicious juices in the bottom shell. Cut the oyster meat loose from the top shell then loosen the oyster from the bottom shell by running the oyster knife carefully under the body. Discard the top, flatter shell, keeping the oyster and juices in the bottom, deeper shell.

4 Prepare the grill for direct cooking over high heat (230–290°C/450–550°F).

5 Arrange the shucked oysters on a large roasting tray. Divide the spinach mixture between the oysters, spreading some over the flesh of each oyster. Top with the breadcrumb mixture, gently pressing it into the spinach to help it adhere. Evenly top each oyster with Parmesan cheese.

6 Brush the cooking grates clean. Grill the oysters, shell sides down, over **direct high heat** for 2–4 minutes, with the lid closed as much as possible, until the breadcrumbs have browned and the juices are bubbling. Using tongs, carefully remove the oysters from the grill. Evenly top each oyster with tarragon, lemon zest and lemon juice. Serve immediately.

GRILLED CLAM AND PRAWN CIOPPINO

SERVES: 6
PREP TIME: 20 MINUTES
GRILLING TIME: 45–48 MINUTES
SPECIAL EQUIPMENT: CAST-IRON LIDDED CASSEROLE

1.25 kg/2 lb 8 oz ripe plum tomatoes
1 large red pepper
500 g/1 lb large prawns, peeled and deveined, tails left on
Extra-virgin olive oil
Sea salt
Ground black pepper
75 g/3 oz pancetta, chopped
1 onion, finely chopped
2 celery sticks, finely chopped
2 garlic cloves, chopped
250 ml/8 fl oz dry white wine
1 tablespoon tomato purée
¼ teaspoon crushed red chilli flakes
48 clams, each about 5 cm/2 inches in diameter, scrubbed
    under cold running water

1 Prepare the grill for direct cooking over high heat
(230–290°C/450–550°F).

2 Brush the cooking grates clean. Grill the tomatoes and
pepper over **direct high heat**, with the lid closed as much as
possible, until the tomato skins are blackened and split and
the pepper skin is charred, 7–10 minutes for the tomatoes and
10–12 minutes for the pepper, turning occasionally to char all

sides. As the vegetables are ready, transfer them to a dish. Set
aside until they are cool enough to handle.

3 Lightly brush the prawns with oil and season evenly with
salt and pepper. Grill the prawns over **direct high heat** for 2–3
minutes, with the lid closed as much as possible and turning
once, until almost cooked through. Set aside.

4 Reduce the temperature of the grill to medium heat
(180–230°C/350–450°F). Peel, core and deseed the tomatoes,
working over a sieve set in a bowl to collect the juices. Discard
the solids remaining in the sieve. Chop the tomatoes, and add
any juices from the chopping board to the bowl. Peel, deseed
and chop the pepper.

5 Place a cast-iron casserole on the grill over **direct medium
heat**. Add the pancetta and 1 tablespoon oil. Cook for about
6 minutes, stirring occasionally, until the pancetta is lightly
browned. Add the onion, celery and garlic and cook for about
5 minutes until the onion is tender. Pour in the wine and cook
for 1 minute. Add the tomatoes with their juices, the pepper,
250 ml/8 fl oz water, tomato purée and chilli flakes. Simmer for
about 10 minutes until slightly reduced. Keep the lid closed as
much as possible during grilling.

6 Arrange the clams in the casserole and cover with the lid. Close
the grill lid and cook for about 10 minutes, stirring the clams
once, until the clams have opened. Discard any clams that don't
open. Add the prawns and cook for another minute. Carefully
remove the casserole from the grill. Serve warm in soup bowls.

BRUNCH QUESADILLAS

SERVES: 4–6

PREP TIME: 30 MINUTES

GRILLING TIME: 6–8 MINUTES FOR THE STEAKS AND 4 MINUTES PER BATCH FOR THE QUESADILLAS

2 sirloin steaks, each 300–375 g/10–12 oz and about 2.5 cm/ 1 inch thick, trimmed of excess fat
Extra-virgin olive oil
1 teaspoon ground cumin
Sea salt
Ground black pepper

6 large eggs
200 g/7 oz Cheddar cheese, grated
125-g/4-oz can diced green chillies, well drained
6 tablespoons finely chopped fresh coriander
6 flour tortillas (20–23 cm/8–9 inches)
Salsa
Soured cream
Lime wedges
Guacamole

1 Lightly brush the steaks on both sides with oil and season evenly with the cumin, salt and pepper. Allow the steaks to stand at room temperature for 15–30 minutes before grilling. Prepare the grill for direct cooking over high heat (230–290°C/450–550°F). Brush the cooking grates clean. Grill the steaks over **direct high heat**, with the lid closed as much as possible and turning once or twice, until cooked to your desired doneness, 6–8 minutes for medium rare (if flare-ups occur, move the steaks temporarily over indirect heat). Remove from the grill and then lower the temperature of the grill to medium heat (180–230°C/350–450°F). Let the steaks rest for 3–5 minutes. Cut the steaks into small cubes and then divide into six equal portions.

2 Crack each egg into a small bowl and whisk to blend. Divide the cheese into six equal portions. Set the steak, eggs, cheese, chillies and coriander on a large tray and place it near the grill.

3 When the grill temperature has reached medium, brush the cooking grates clean. Working in batches of two (or three at the most), arrange the tortillas on the grill and cook them over **direct medium heat** for 20–30 seconds, with the lid open, until grill marks appear. Flip the tortillas over. Working quickly, pour one beaten egg on to each tortilla and use a fork to spread the egg over as much of the surface as possible. Deflate the puffy spots of the tortillas to make spreading the egg easier. If the egg begins to spill off the side, bend the edges upwards with tongs. Don't worry if a little runs into the flame. Scatter the chillies over the egg on all the tortillas and top each with a portion of the steak cubes and grated cheese. Close the lid and cook for 3–4 minutes until the egg is set and the cheese is melted. The egg will look puffy and the tortilla may be quite brown. Transfer each tortilla to a plate, sprinkle with 1 tablespoon coriander, and fold it in half. Repeat with the remaining ingredients. Serve with salsa, soured cream, lime wedges and guacamole on the side.

EGGS PROVENÇALE

SERVES: 4
PREP TIME: 15 MINUTES
GRILLING TIME: 22–25 MINUTES
SPECIAL EQUIPMENT: 30-CM/12-INCH CAST-IRON
    FRYING PAN

2 x 425-g/14-oz cans chopped tomatoes
1 tablespoon extra-virgin olive oil
1 teaspoon finely chopped garlic
2 teaspoons finely chopped basil
2 teaspoons finely chopped thyme
1 teaspoon finely chopped rosemary
Sea salt
Ground black pepper
8 large eggs
4 thick slices toasted bread
50 g/2 oz goats' cheese, crumbled

1 Prepare the grill for direct cooking over medium heat (180–230°C/350–450°F).

2 Combine the tomatoes, oil, garlic, all the herbs, ¼ teaspoon salt and ⅛ teaspoon pepper in a 30-cm/12-inch cast-iron frying pan.

3 Brush the cooking grates clean. Place the pan over **direct medium heat**, close the lid and cook the sauce for 15 minutes, stirring once or twice. Stir the sauce again, and then, using the back of a large spoon, make eight shallow wells in the mixture so the pan is barely visible through the sauce. The liquid from the sauce may begin to refill the indentations, but the wells should at least partially remain. Crack one egg into each indentation, close the lid, and cook over **direct medium heat** for 7–10 minutes, with the lid closed, until the egg yolks have just started to cloud over and the whites are set as liked.

4 Scoop the eggs and sauce on to thick slices of toast. Top with the cheese and season with salt and pepper. Serve hot.

ASPARAGUS AND POTATO NAPOLEONS WITH TARRAGON VINAIGRETTE

SERVES: 6
PREP TIME: 20 MINUTES
GRILLING TIME: 6–8 MINUTES

VINAIGRETTE
3 tablespoons fresh lemon juice
2 tablespoons finely chopped tarragon
1 teaspoon Dijon mustard
Sea salt
Ground black pepper
Extra-virgin olive oil

500 g/1 lb asparagus
4 large King Edward potatoes, peeled
75 g/3 oz goats' cheese, crumbled
1 tablespoon small capers, rinsed

1 Prepare the grill for direct cooking over medium heat (180–230°C/350–450°F).

2 Whisk the lemon juice, tarragon, mustard, ¼ teaspoon salt and ⅛ teaspoon pepper in a bowl. While whisking, gradually add 125 ml/4 fl oz oil to make a smooth emulsion.

3 Remove and discard the tough bottom of each asparagus spear by grasping the end and bending it gently until it snaps at its natural point of tenderness, usually about two-thirds of the way down the spear.

4 Bring a saucepan of salted water to the boil over a high heat. Trim the bottom off one end of each potato so it can stand vertically on the chopping board without rolling. Cut the potatoes lengthways into 5-mm/¼-inch slices. Reserve the twelve largest slices and discard the remainder or save for another use. Add the potato slices to the water and reduce the heat to medium. Simmer for about 3 minutes until almost tender (do not overcook). Drain carefully, rinse the potato slices under cold water and pat dry with kitchen paper. Drizzle 2 tablespoons of oil on a roasting tray. Add the potatoes and asparagus to the tray and turn to coat them with the oil; season with salt.

5 Brush the cooking grates clean. Grill the potatoes and asparagus over *direct medium heat* for 6–8 minutes, with the lid closed as much as possible and turning once after about 4 minutes, until the asparagus is browned in spots but not charred and the potatoes are golden brown and tender. Remove the vegetables from the grill as they are done. Cut the asparagus into bite-sized pieces.

6 Place one potato slice on each of six dinner plates and build the Napoleons evenly with half the asparagus, another potato slice, the remaining asparagus, cheese and capers. Whisk the vinaigrette again and drizzle about 1½ tablespoons on and around each Napoleon. Serve warm.

SOBA NOODLES WITH GRILLED TOFU AND PEANUTS

SERVES: 4–6
PREP TIME: 30 MINUTES
GRILLING TIME: 6–8 MINUTES

300 g/10 oz soba noodles *or* 375–400 g/12–13 oz wholewheat spaghetti
150 g/5 oz roasted, unsalted peanuts
50 g/2 oz carrots, grated
175 g/6 oz sugar snap peas, cut diagonally into 5-mm/¼-inch pieces
3 spring onions (white and light green parts only), thinly sliced

1 tablespoon toasted sesame oil
1 tablespoon soy sauce
¼ teaspoon garlic powder
425 g/14 oz extra-firm tofu, drained and halved horizontally

SAUCE
175 g/6 oz creamy peanut butter
175 ml/6 fl oz boiling water
4 tablespoons chopped fresh coriander
3 tablespoons fresh lime juice
3 tablespoons soy sauce
2 tablespoons toasted sesame oil
1 tablespoon peeled, finely chopped fresh ginger
1 teaspoon hot chilli-garlic sauce

1 Bring a large saucepan of water to the boil for the noodles.

2 Prepare the grill for direct cooking over high heat (230–290°C/450–550°F).

3 Cook the noodles according to the packet instructions, rinsing well with cold water when they're done. Transfer the noodles to a large bowl and add the peanuts, carrots, sugar snap peas and spring onions.

4 Whisk the sesame oil, soy sauce and garlic powder in a small bowl. Brush the mixture on both sides of the tofu.

5 Brush the cooking grates clean. Lay a large sheet of heavy-duty aluminium foil, about 30 × 40 cm/12 × 16 inches, directly on the cooking grates and arrange the tofu on the foil. Grill over ***direct high heat*** for 6–8 minutes, with the lid closed as much as possible and turning once, until lightly browned.

6 While the tofu is grilling, combine the sauce ingredients in a food processor or blender and process until smooth. Add the sauce to the noodles and vegetables and mix gently with tongs until all the noodles are coated. Remove the tofu from the grill and cut into 2.5-cm/1-inch cubes. Add the tofu to the noodles and serve immediately.

SUMMER BERRY CLAFOUTIS

SERVES: 6–8
PREP TIME: 15 MINUTES
GRILLING TIME: 35–45 MINUTES
SPECIAL EQUIPMENT: 25-CM/10-INCH SPRINGFORM TIN

1 lemon
125 g/4 oz fresh blueberries
125 g/4 oz fresh raspberries
2 tablespoons orange liqueur, such as Grand Marnier

65 g/2½ oz unsalted butter
125 g/4 oz plus 1 tablespoon granulated sugar
¼ teaspoon ground cardamom
2 large eggs
2 large egg whites
125 g/4 oz plain flour

2 tablespoons icing sugar (optional)

1 Prepare the grill for indirect cooking over medium heat (about 190°C/375°F). Generously grease the inside of a 25-cm/10-inch springform tin.

2 Finely grate the zest from the lemon and set aside. Squeeze 2 teaspoons juice from the lemon and add to a bowl with the berries and liqueur. Stir gently to combine. Set aside.

3 Using a handheld electric mixer, cream the butter, 125 g/ 4 oz granulated sugar, the lemon zest and cardamom in a large bowl, beating for about 3 minutes. Beat in the eggs and egg whites for about 1 minute until well incorporated. Scrape down the sides of the bowl and add the flour, mixing well for about 30 seconds.

4 Spread the mixture into the prepared tin. Using a slotted spoon, remove the berries from the liquid and place on top of the mixture. Mix the remaining 1 tablespoon of granulated sugar with the liquid and drizzle over the berries.

5 Brush the cooking grates clean. Bake the cake over **indirect medium heat** for 35–45 minutes, with the lid closed, until light golden (check the cake after 30 minutes). Keep the grill's temperature as close to 190°C/375°F as possible. Wearing insulated barbecue mitts or oven gloves, carefully remove the cake from the grill and allow to cool for 10 minutes. Sprinkle with icing sugar before serving, if liked.

PLUMS WITH LEMON POLENTA CAKE

SERVES: 6–8
PREP TIME: 30 MINUTES
BAKING TIME: 1 HOUR–1 HOUR 10 MINUTES
GRILLING TIME: ABOUT 6 MINUTES
SPECIAL EQUIPMENT: 23 × 12 CM/9 × 5 INCH LOAF TIN

150 g/5 oz plain flour
1½ teaspoons baking powder
½ teaspoon sea salt
125 g/4 oz polenta
250 g/8 oz granulated sugar
250 g/8 oz unsalted butter, softened
1 tablespoon finely grated lemon zest
1 tablespoon fresh lemon juice
2 teaspoons vanilla extract
4 large eggs
125 ml/4 fl oz Greek yogurt

750 g/1½ lb large, firm but ripe plums, halved
Vegetable oil or rapeseed oil
2 tablespoons runny honey
¼ teaspoon ground cardamom

250 ml/8 fl oz chilled whipping cream
2–3 tablespoons granulated sugar

1 Preheat the oven to 180°C/350°F/Gas mark 4. Grease a 23 × 12 cm/9 × 5 inch loaf tin. Dust the tin with flour; tap out the excess.

2 Whisk the flour, baking powder, salt and polenta in a bowl. Beat the sugar, butter, lemon zest and juice and vanilla for 2–3 minutes in the bowl of an electric mixer until fluffy. Add the eggs, one at a time, and beat after each addition until well blended. Add the flour mixture in three additions alternately with the yogurt, beginning and ending with the flour mixture. Transfer the mixture to the prepared loaf tin and smooth the top.

3 Bake in the centre of the oven for 1 hour–1 hour 10 minutes, until the cake is deep golden and a skewer inserted into the centre of the cake comes out clean. Transfer the cake to a rack and leave to cool in the tin for 15 minutes, then turn the cake out on to the rack and cool completely. While the cake is cooling, prepare the plums and the whipped cream.

4 Prepare the grill for direct cooking over medium heat (180–230°C/350–450°F).

5 Lightly brush the cut side of each plum half with oil. Brush the cooking grates clean. Grill the plum halves, cut side down first, over *direct medium heat* for about 6 minutes, with the lid open and turning once after about 3 minutes, until slightly charred and grill marks appear. Transfer the plums to a board. Cool slightly, then cut each plum half into four wedges. Place the plums in a bowl. Add the honey and cardamom. Gently stir to combine. Beat the whipping cream in a bowl with 2–3 tablespoons sugar until soft peaks form. Cut the cake into 1-cm/½-inch slices. Spoon some of the plum mixture over each slice and top with dollops of whipped cream.

PEACH TART TATIN WITH CARDAMOM

SERVES: 8–10
PREP TIME: 30 MINUTES
GRILLING TIME: 1–1¼ HOURS
SPECIAL EQUIPMENT: 30-CM/12-INCH CAST-IRON
FRYING PAN

BASE
150 g/5 oz toasted almonds
175 g/6 oz plain flour
125 g/4 oz granulated sugar
½ teaspoon ground cardamom
½ teaspoon sea salt
125 g/4 oz unsalted butter, cold, cut into pieces
1 large egg

FILLING
4 tablespoons plain flour
125 g/4 oz soft brown sugar
1 teaspoon ground cardamom
1 kg/2 lb large, firm but ripe peaches, thinly sliced

1 Finely grind the almonds in the bowl of a food processor. Add the flour, sugar, cardamom and salt and blend. Add the butter and pulse until the mixture resembles fine breadcrumbs. With the machine running, add the egg and let it whirl until the dough pulls away from the sides of the bowl.

2 Spoon the dough into a 30-cm/12-inch cast-iron frying pan. With lightly floured fingers, press the dough to cover the bottom of the pan and 3.5 cm/1½ inches up the sides.

3 Prepare the grill for indirect cooking over medium heat (180–230°C/350–450°F).

4 Combine the flour, brown sugar and cardamom in a large mixing bowl. Set aside 4 tablespoons of the mixture. Add the sliced peaches to the remaining mixture in the bowl and toss to coat.

5 Sprinkle the dough with the reserved sugar mixture. Pour the sliced peaches over the dough and spread them out evenly.

6 Brush the cooking grates clean. Place the pan over **_indirect medium heat_**, close the lid, and cook for 1–1¼ hours until the crust is golden and the filling thickens. Wearing insulated barbecue mitts, remove the pan from the grill and allow to cool for at least 30 minutes before cutting into slices to serve.

CHOCOLATE CAKE WITH ORANGE GLAZE

SERVES: 8
PREP TIME: 30 MINUTES
GRILLING TIME: 40–50 MINUTES
SPECIAL EQUIPMENT: 23-CM/9-INCH ROUND CAKE TIN

CAKE
300 g/10 oz granulated sugar
50 g/2 oz cocoa powder
200 g/7 oz plain flour
1 teaspoon bicarbonate of soda
1 teaspoon baking powder
¼ teaspoon sea salt
3 large eggs
250 ml/8 fl oz buttermilk
250 ml/8 fl oz soured cream
75 g/3 oz unsalted butter, melted and cooled slightly

GLAZE
1 orange
125 g icing sugar

1 Prepare the grill for indirect cooking over medium heat (about 190°C/375°F).

2 Grease a 23-cm/9-inch round cake tin and line the bottom with nonstick baking paper.

3 Sift the granulated sugar, cocoa, flour, bicarbonate of soda, baking powder and salt into a bowl. Set aside.

4 Beat the eggs in the bowl of an electric mixer fitted with the paddle attachment for about 1 minute on medium speed, until frothy. Beat in the buttermilk and soured cream until well combined. Slowly beat in the sugar mixture. Remove the bowl from the mixer and fold in the melted butter by hand, working slowly so that it is completely incorporated.

5 Pour the mixture into the greased cake tin. Place the tin on the grill over *indirect medium heat*, close the lid, and bake for 40–50 minutes, until the edges pull slightly away from the sides and a skewer inserted in the centre comes out clean. Keep the grill's temperature as close to 190°C/375°F as possible. Wearing insulated barbecue mitts or oven gloves, remove the cake from the grill and cool completely. Once cool, invert the cake on to a platter and make the glaze.

6 Finely grate the zest from the orange and set aside. Squeeze 3 tablespoons juice from the orange. Combine 2 tablespoons of the juice with the icing sugar in a bowl. Mix, and add another tablespoon of juice, if necessary, until you have a spreadable consistency. Stir in the orange zest.

7 Glaze the top of the cake and refrigerate until ready to eat.

RESOURCES

RED MEAT GRILLING GUIDE

The cuts, thicknesses, weights and grilling times are meant to be guidelines rather than hard and fast rules. Cooking times are affected by such factors as altitude, wind, outside temperature and desired doneness. Two rules of thumb: Grill steaks and kebabs using the direct method for the time given on the chart or to your desired doneness, turning once. Grill roasts and thicker cuts using the indirect method for the time given on the chart or until an instant-read thermometer reaches the desired internal temperature. Let roasts, larger cuts of meat and thick steaks rest for 5–10 minutes before carving. The internal temperature of the meat will rise 5–10 degrees during this time.

CUT	THICKNESS/WEIGHT	APPROXIMATE GRILLING TIME
Steak: fillet, porterhouse, rib-eye, rump, sirloin and T-bone,	1.5 cm/¾ inch thick	**4–6 minutes** direct high heat
	2.5 cm/1 inch thick	**6–8 minutes** direct high heat
	3 cm/1¼ inches thick	**8–10 minutes** direct high heat
	3.5 cm/1½ inches thick	**10–14 minutes:** sear 6–8 minutes direct high heat, grill 4–6 minutes indirect high heat
	5 cm/2 inches thick	**14–18 minutes:** sear 6–8 minutes direct high heat, grill 8–10 minutes indirect high heat
Beef, minced	1.5 cm/¾ inch thick	**8–10 minutes** direct high heat
Fillet, whole	1.75–2 kg/3½–4 lb	**35–45 minutes:** sear 15 minutes direct medium heat, grill 20–30 minutes indirect medium heat
Flank steak	750 g–1 kg/1½–2 lb, 1.5 cm/¾ inch thick	**8–10 minutes** direct medium heat
Kebab	2.5-cm/1-inch cubes	**4–6 minutes** direct high heat
	3.5-cm/1½-inch cubes	**6–7 minutes** direct high heat
Rib roast, boneless	2.5–3 kg/5–6 lb	**1¼–1¾ hours** indirect medium heat
Rib roast, with bone	4 kg/8 lb	**2½–3 hours:** sear 10 minutes direct medium heat, grill 2⅓–3 hours indirect low heat
Rump joint	1–1.25 kg/2–2½ lb	**30–40 minutes:** sear 10 minutes direct medium heat, grill 20–30 minutes indirect medium heat
Skirt steak	5 mm–1 cm/¼–½ inch thick	**4–6 minutes** direct high heat
Veal loin chop	2.5 cm/1 inch thick	**6–8 minutes** direct high heat

RED MEAT DONENESS

DONENESS	CHEF STANDARDS	OFFICIAL GUIDELINES
Rare	49°–52°C/120°–125°F	n/a
Medium rare	52°–58°C/125°–135°F	63°C/145°F
Medium	58°–63°C/135°–145°F	70°C/160°F
Medium well	63°–68°C/145°–155°F	n/a
Well done	68°C +/155°F +	77°C/170°F

LAMB GRILLING GUIDE

CUT	THICKNESS/WEIGHT	APPROXIMATE GRILLING TIME
Chop: chump, cutlet, loin or shoulder	1.5–3.5 cm/¾–1½ inches thick	**8–12 minutes** direct medium heat
Lamb, ground	1.5 cm/¾ inch thick	**8–10 minutes** direct medium heat
Leg of lamb, boneless, rolled	1.25–1.5 cm/2½–3 lb	**30–45 minutes:** sear 10–15 minutes direct medium heat, grill 20–30 minutes indirect medium heat
Leg of lamb, butterflied	1.5–1.75 cm/3–3½ lb	**30–45 minutes:** sear 10–15 minutes direct medium heat, grill 20–30 minutes indirect medium heat
Rack of lamb	500–750 g/1–1½ lb	**15–20 minutes:** sear 5 minutes direct medium heat, grill 10–15 minutes indirect medium heat
Rib crown roast	1.5–2 kg/3–4 lb	**1–1¼ hours** indirect medium heat

Note: All cooking times are for medium-rare doneness, except minced lamb (medium).

TYPES OF RED MEAT FOR THE GRILL

Tender Cuts for Grilling
Beef fillet steak
Beef porterhouse steak
Beef rib steak/rib-eye steak
Beef sirloin steak
Beef T-bone steak
Lamb loin chop
Veal loin chop

Moderately Tender Cuts for Grilling
Beef flank steak
Beef rump steak
Beef skirt steak
Lamb shoulder chop
Veal shoulder chop

Bigger Cuts for Searing and Grill-roasting
Beef whole fillet
Beef rib roast
Beef rump roast
Leg of lamb
Rack of lamb
Rack of veal

Tougher Cuts for Barbecuing
Beef ribs
Brisket

PORK GRILLING GUIDE

The cuts, thicknesses, weights and grilling times are meant to be guidelines rather than hard and fast rules. Cooking times are affected by such factors as altitude, wind, outside temperature and desired doneness. Two rules of thumb: Grill chops and sausages using the direct method for the time given on the chart or to your desired doneness, turning once. Grill roasts and thicker cuts using the indirect method for the time given on the chart or until an instant-read thermometer reaches the desired internal temperature. The official recommendation that pork is cooked to 70°C/160°F, but most chefs today cook it to about 65°C/150°F, when it still has some pink in the centre and all the juices haven't been driven out. Of course, the doneness you choose is entirely up to you. Let roasts, larger cuts of meat and thick chops rest for 5–10 minutes before carving. The internal temperature of the meat will rise 5–10 degrees during this time.

TYPES OF PORK FOR THE GRILL

Tender Cuts for Grilling
Centre-cut chop
Fillet (whole or in medallions)
Loin chop

Moderately Tender Cuts for Grilling
Gammon steak
Shoulder steak

Bigger Cuts for Searing and Grill-roasting
Cured ham
Fore loin roast
Hind loin roast
Loin roast
Rib roast

Tougher Cuts for Barbecuing
Baby back ribs
Shoulder
Spareribs

CUT	THICKNESS/ WEIGHT	APPROXIMATE GRILLING TIME
Sausage, fresh	75 g/3 oz sausage	**20–25 minutes** direct medium heat
Chop, boneless or bone-in	1.5 cm/¾ inch thick	**6–8 minutes** direct high heat
	2.5 cm/1 inch thick	**8–10 minutes** direct medium heat
	3–3.5 cm/1¼–1½ inches thick	**10–12 minutes:** sear 6 minutes direct high heat, grill 4–6 minutes indirect high heat
Fillet	500 g/1 lb	**15–20 minutes** direct medium heat
Loin roast, boneless	1.25 kg/2½ lb	**40–50 minutes** direct medium heat
Loin roast, bone-in	1.5–2.5 kg/3–5 lb	**1¼–1¾ hours** indirect medium heat
Pork shoulder, boneless	2.5–3 kg/5–6 lb	**5–7 hours** indirect low heat
Pork, minced	1 cm/½ inch thick	**8–10 minutes** direct medium heat
Ribs, baby back	750 g–1 kg/1½–2 lb	**3–4 hours** indirect low heat
Ribs, spareribs	1.25–1.75 kg/2½– 3½ lb	**3–4 hours** indirect low heat

POULTRY GRILLING GUIDE

The cuts, weights and grilling times are meant to be guidelines rather than hard and fast rules. Cooking times are affected by such factors as altitude, wind and outside temperature. Cooking times are for the recommendation of 74°C/165°F. Let whole poultry rest for 5–10 minutes before carving. The internal temperature of the meat will rise 5–10 degrees during this time.

CUT	WEIGHT	APPROXIMATE GRILLING TIME
Chicken breast, bone-in	300–375 g/10–12 oz	**23–35 minutes:** 3–5 minutes direct medium heat, 20–30 minutes indirect medium heat
Chicken breast, boneless, skinless	175–250 g/6–8 oz	**8–12 minutes** direct medium heat
Chicken drumstick	75–125 g/3–4 oz	**36–40 minutes:** 6–10 minutes direct medium heat, 30 minutes indirect medium heat
Chicken thigh, bone-in	150–175 g/5–6 oz	**36–40 minutes:** 6–10 minutes direct medium heat, 30 minutes indirect medium heat
Chicken thigh, boneless, skinless	125 g/4 oz	**8–10 minutes** direct medium heat
Chicken thigh meat, ground	1.5 cm/¾ inch thick	**12–14 minutes** direct medium heat
Chicken, whole	2–2.5 kg/4–5 lb	**1–1¼ hours** indirect medium heat
Chicken, whole leg	300–375 g/10–12 oz	**48 minutes–1 hour:** 8–10 minutes direct medium heat, 40–50 minutes indirect medium heat
Chicken wing	50–75 g/2–3 oz	**35–43 minutes:** 5–8 minutes direct medium heat, 30–35 minutes indirect medium heat
Duck breast, boneless	300–375 g/10–12 oz	**9–12 minutes:** grill 3–4 minutes direct low heat, grill 6–8 minutes indirect high heat
Duck, whole	2.75–3 kg/5½–6 lb	**40 minutes** indirect high heat
Turkey breast, boneless	1.25 kg/2½ lb	**1–1¼ hours** indirect medium heat
Turkey, whole, not stuffed	5–6 kg/10–12 lb	**2½–3½ hours** indirect low heat

SEAFOOD GRILLING GUIDE

The types, thicknesses, weights and grilling times are meant to be guidelines rather than hard and fast rules. Cooking times are affected by such factors as altitude, wind, outside temperature and desired doneness. The general rule of thumb for grilling fish: 4–5 minutes per 1-cm/½-inch thickness; 8–10 minutes per 2.5-cm/1-inch thickness.

TYPE	THICKNESS/WEIGHT	APPROXIMATE GRILLING TIME
Fish, fillet or steak Includes halibut, red snapper, salmon, sea bass, swordfish and tuna	5 mm–1 cm/¼–½ inch thick	**3–5 minutes** direct high heat
	1–2.5 cm/½–1 inch thick	**5–10 minutes** direct high heat
	2.5–3 cm/1–1¼ inches thick	**10–12 minutes** direct high heat
Fish, whole	500 g/1 lb	**15–20 minutes** indirect medium heat
	1–1.25 kg/2–2½ lb	**20–30 minutes** indirect medium heat
	1.5 kg/3 lb	**30–45 minutes** indirect medium heat
Clam (discard any that do not open)	50–75 g/2–3 oz	**6–8 minutes** direct high heat
Lobster tail	175 g/6 oz tail	**7–11 minutes** direct medium heat
Mussel (discard any that do not open)	25–50 g/1–2 oz	**5–6 minutes** direct high heat
Oyster	75–125 g/3–4 oz	**2–4 minutes** direct high heat
Prawn	40 g/1½ oz	**2–4 minutes** direct high heat
Scallop	40 g/1½ oz	**4–6 minutes** direct high heat

TYPES OF SEAFOOD FOR THE GRILL

Firm Fillets and Steaks
Salmon
Squid
Swordfish
Tuna

Medium-firm Fillets and Steaks
Angler fish
Halibut
Mackerel
Mahi-mahi
Red snapper
Sea bass

Tender Fillets
Trout

Whole Fish
Mackerel
Red snapper
Sea bass
Trout

Shellfish
Clams
Lobster
Mussels
Oysters
Prawns
Scallops

VEGETABLE AND FRUIT GRILLING GUIDE

Just about everything from apples to tomatoes tends to cook best over direct medium heat. The temperature on the grill's thermometer should be somewhere between 180 and 230°C/350 and 450°F.

TYPE	THICKNESS/SIZE	APPROXIMATE GRILLING TIME
Apple	whole	**35–40 minutes** indirect medium heat
	1-cm/½-inch slices	**4–6 minutes** direct medium heat
Apricot	halved	**6–8 minutes** direct medium heat
Artichoke hearts	whole	**14–18 minutes:** boil 10–12 minutes; cut in half and grill 4–6 minutes direct medium heat
Asparagus	1-cm/½-inch diameter	**6–8 minutes** direct medium heat
Aubergine	1-cm/½-inch slices	**8–10 minutes** direct medium heat
Banana	halved lengthways	**6–8 minutes** direct medium heat
Carrot	1-inch diameter	**7–11 minutes:** boil 4–6 minutes, grill 3–5 minutes direct high heat
Corn, outer leaves removed		**10–15 minutes** direct medium heat
Corn, outer leaves intact		**25–30 minutes** direct medium heat
Courgette	1-cm/½-inch slices	**3–5 minutes** direct medium heat
Garlic	whole	**45 minutes–1 hour** indirect medium heat
Mushroom, button or shiitake		**8–10 minutes** direct medium heat
Mushroom, portobello		**10–15 minutes** direct medium heat
Onion	halved	**35–40 minutes** indirect medium heat
	1-cm/½-inch slices	**8–12 minutes** direct medium heat
Peach/Nectarine	halved lengthways	**8–10 minutes** direct medium heat
Pear	halved lengthways	**10–12 minutes** direct medium heat
Pepper	whole	**10–15 minutes** direct medium heat
Pineapple	1-cm/½-inch slices or 2.5-cm/1-inch wedges	**4–8 minutes** direct medium heat
Potato, new	halved	**15–20 minutes** direct medium heat
	whole	**45 minutes–1 hour** indirect medium heat
Potato, King Edward	1-cm/½-inch slices	**9–11 minutes;** simmer 3 minutes, grill 6–8 minutes direct medium heat
Spring onion	whole	**3–4 minutes** direct medium heat
Squash (750 g/1½ lb)	halved	**40 minutes–1 hour** indirect medium heat
Tomato, garden or plum	whole	**8–10 minutes** direct medium heat
	halved	**6–8 minutes** direct medium heat

GRILL MAINTENANCE

A little TLC is all it takes to ensure that you get years of use from your grill. Maintenance is the key. Each time you use the grill, remember to clean the cooking grates. With the grill on high (either right before cooking or right after) brush the cooking grates with a long-handled, stainless steel brush. Be sure to get in between the grates with your brush, too.

Monthly Maintenance Plan for Gas Grills

1. When your grill is warm, but not hot, use a wet, soapy sponge or dishcloth to wipe the inside of the lid. This will help keep natural carbon build-up from accumulating inside the lid.

2. Remove the grates and brush the metal bars that shield the burners. A good brush, like the one you use to brush the cooking grates, will work well. This will help to eliminate flare-ups. (If you grill often, you may need to do this a little more frequently than once a month.)

3. Gently clean the burner tubes with a steel brush. Brush side-to-side along the burner tubes and take care not to damage the openings themselves by brushing too hard.

4. Use a plastic putty knife or spatula to scrape the grease from the bottom of the grill. If your grill has a collection tray, scrape the bits into it. Then dispose of the contents of the collection tray.

5. Wash the inside of the grill with warm, soapy water. Take care not to get water in the burner tubes.

6. Reassemble, wait a month and repeat.

Monthly Maintenance Plan for Charcoal Grills

1. When the grill is cold, remove the ash from the bowl. Because the ash naturally contains a small amount of moisture, it is important to get the ash out of the bowl each time you use it and before storing your grill. If your grill has an ash catcher, empty after each use.

2. Wipe the inside of the bowl with a warm, wet sponge. This will help keep natural carbon build-up from accumulating inside the lid.

Monthly Maintenance Plan for Electric Grills

1. When your grill is warm, but not hot, use a wet, soapy sponge or dishcloth to wipe the inside of the lid. This will help keep natural carbon build-up from accumulating inside the lid.

2. Remove the grates. Use a plastic putty knife or spatula to scrape the grease from the bottom of the grill. If your grill has a collection tray, scrape the bits into the collection tray. Then dispose of the contents of the collection tray.

3. Wipe the inside of the grill with a warm, damp sponge, being very careful not to get the heating element wet.

SAFETY

Please read your owner's guide and familiarize yourself with and follow all 'dangers', 'warnings' and 'cautions'. Also follow the grilling procedures and maintenance requirements contained in your owner's guide. If you cannot locate the owner's guide for your grill model, please contact the manufacturer prior to use.

If you have any questions concerning the 'dangers', 'warnings' and 'cautions" contained in your Weber® gas or charcoal owner's guide, or if you do not have an owner's guide for your specific grill model, please contact Weber-Stephen Products LLC Customer Service, before using your grill. You can also access your owner's guide online at www.weber.com.

General Notes
1. Gas and charcoal grills are designed for outdoor use only. If used indoors, toxic fumes will accumulate and cause serious bodily injury or death.

2. Grills radiate a lot of heat, so always keep the grill at least 1.5 metres/5 feet away from any combustible materials, including the house, garage, fence rails, etc. Combustible materials include, but are not limited to, wood or treated wood decks, wood patios and wood porches. Never use a grill indoors or under a covered patio.

3. Keep the grill in a level position at all times.

4. Use proper barbecuing tools with long, heat-resistant handles.

5. Don't wear loose or highly flammable clothing when grilling.

6. Do not leave infants, children or pets unattended near a hot grill.

7. Use insulated barbecue mitts or oven gloves to protect hands while cooking or using the grill or adjusting the vents.

Gas Grill Safety
1. Always check the bottom tray and grease tray before cooking. They should be clean and free of debris. It prevents dangerous grease fires and deters visits from unwanted wild life.

2. If a flare-up should occur, make sure the lid is closed. Then, if necessary, move the food over indirect heat until the flare-up subsides. Never use water to extinguish flames on a gas grill.

3. Do not line the funnel-shaped bottom tray with foil. This could prevent grease from flowing into the grease catch pan. Grease is also likely to catch in the tiny creases of the foil and start a fire.

4. Never store propane tanks or spares indoors (that means the garage, too).

5. For the first few uses, the temperature of a new gas grill may run hotter than normal. Once your grill is seasoned and the inside of the cooking box is less reflective, the temperature will return to normal.

Charcoal Grill Safety
1. Do not add charcoal starter fluid or charcoal impregnated with charcoal starter fluid to hot or warm charcoal.

2. Do not use petrol, alcohol or other highly volatile fluids to ignite charcoal. If using charcoal starter fluid, remove any fluid that may have drained through the bottom vents before lighting the charcoal.

3. Do not use a grill unless all parts are in place. Make sure the ash catcher is properly attached to the legs underneath the bowl of the grill.

4. Remove the lid from the grill while lighting and getting the charcoal started.

5. Always put charcoal on top of the charcoal grate, not into the bottom of the bowl.

6. Do not place a chimney starter on or near any combustible surface.

7. If a flare-up should occur, place the lid on the grill and close the top vent about halfway. If the flames are still threatening, open the lid and move the food over indirect heat. Do not use water to extinguish the flames.

8. Never touch the cooking or charcoal grate or the grill to see if it is hot.

9. Use the hook on the inside of the lid to hang the lid on the side of the bowl of the grill. Avoid placing a hot lid on carpet or grass. Do not hang the lid on the bowl handle.

10. Keep electrical flexes away from the hot surfaces of the grill.

11. To extinguish the coals, place the lid on the bowl and close all of the vents (dampers). Make sure that the vents on the lid and the bowl are completely closed. Do not use water, as it will damage the porcelain finish.

INDEX

INDEX

SOURCES

'Propane'. How Products are Made. Ed. Stacey L. Blachford. Gale Cengage, 2002. eNotes.com. 2006.
http://www.enotes.com/how-products-encyclopedia/propane (accessed January 19, 2011).

'Propane'. need.org.
http://www.need.org/needpdf/infobook_activities/SecInfo/PropaneS.pdf (accessed January 19, 2011).

'Smoke in Your Eyes'. CampFish.net.
http://campfish.net/campfire-smoke.php (accessed January 19, 2011).

'Smoke Follows Beauty'. 'bodhi'. newsgroups.derkeiler.com. 2005.
http://newsgroups.derkeiler.com/Archive/Alt/alt.gathering.rainbow/2005-11/msg00669.html (accessed January 19, 2011).

dictionary.com.
http://dictionary.reference.com/browse/vapor (accessed January 14, 2011).

merriam-webster.com.
http://www.merriam-webster.com/dictionary/vapor (accessed January 14, 2011).

'Fire'. wikipedia.org.
http://en.wikipedia.org/wiki/Fire (accessed January 19, 2011).

'Fire Physics'. mb-soft.com.
http://mb-soft.com/juca/print/317.html (accessed January 19, 2011).

'Chapter 1–Chemistry and Physics of Fire'.
maiif.org. http://www.maiif.org/pdf/fire_chapter1.pdf (accessed January 19, 2011).

'Charcoal'. wikipedia.org.
http://en.wikipedia.org/wiki/Charcoal (accessed January 19, 2011).

'What Is Charcoal?' Tiffany Maleshefski. 2007. chow.com.
http://www.chow.com/food-news/53975/what-is-charcoal (accessed January 19, 2011).

'All About Charcoal'. virtualweberbullet.com.
http://www.virtualweberbullet.com/charcoal.html (accessed January 19, 2011).

'Charcoal, The original source of the cookout'. Derrick Riches. about.com.
http://bbq.about.com/od/charcoal/a/aa071997.htm (accessed January 19, 2011).

TOP TEN TIPS FOR SAVING TIME

1 **SHARPEN YOUR KNIVES.**
Much of the time required to make a recipe is spent slicing and dicing. Dull knives will slow you down and sharp knives will speed you up.

2 **STOCK YOUR STORE CUPBOARD WITH INGREDIENTS THAT YOU CAN QUICKLY TURN INTO SAUCES AND SIDE DISHES.**
Get to know convenient items like peeled garlic cloves in jars and shop-bought pizza dough.

3 **SHOP FOR MORE THAN JUST TODAY.**
To cut down on trips to the supermarket, pick up ingredients for tomorrow and the next day too.

4 **READ THE WHOLE RECIPE BEFORE YOU GRILL.**
Be prepared for any times required for marinating meats or letting charcoal burn down to low temperatures. Plan to use those times for other steps.

5 **PREP THE FOOD WHILE PREHEATING YOUR GRILL.**
You can get a lot done in those 15 minutes. Just don't forget to light the grill first.

6 **BEFORE YOU GRILL, ASSEMBLE ALL YOUR INGREDIENTS AND TOOLS NEARBY.**
Running back into the kitchen might waste time, and it can be risky to leave your food unattended.

7 **PREPARE YOUR GRILL WITH MORE THAN JUST ONE HEAT ZONE.**
Two or three areas of various heat levels mean you can grill two or three things simultaneously.

8 **BRUSH THE COOKING GRATES CLEAN WHILE THEY'RE HOT.**
It's much faster and easier to brush a hot grate than a cold one, so do this after you preheat the grill or when you have just finished grilling.

9 **GRILL WITH THE LID CLOSED AS MUCH AS POSSIBLE.**
The heat reflecting off the lid helps to cook food from both sides, which shortens the grilling time.

10 **DON'T OVERCROWD YOUR GRILL.**
You should always leave about one-third of the grill free for manoeuvring your food from place to place. Otherwise, you might need to take food off the grill and slow down the cooking.